THE CREATIVE
COPYWRITER'S
COMPANION

**One of America's most award-winning copywriters
explains how to write great creative copy**

Covers all traditional and digital media

TOM ATTEA

RHB
Really Helpful Books

Library of Congress Control Number: 2018956537

ISBN: 978-0-9821218-3-2 (hardback)
        978-0-9821218-4-9 (paperback)

Printed in the Unites States of America.

Really Helpful Books
www.ReallyHelpfulBooks.com

DEDICATION

This book is dedicated to great copywriters and is a tribute to their unique achievement – the consistent creation of copy that is strategically right and creatively bright.

All you have to do is look at the amateurish advertising that even most leading advertisers have to know how rare and refreshing their achievement is.

I'd also like to acknowledge the exceptionally gifted designers and account executives I've had the privilege of working with and the many clients who've demonstrated that they appreciate the right, bright branding and advertising. I often say the orchestra is only as good as the audience. It doesn't matter how great your performance is without an audience who can hear the welcome difference.

OTHER BOOKS BY THE AUTHOR

The Secrets of Successful Creative Advertising

"What creative wouldn't want to get his hands on this book? ... What you need to know about creative ... Just go get the book!"

- BRAD FORSYTHE AND RAY SCHILENS,
HOSTS OF THE ADVERTISING SHOW, SPONSORED BY *ADVERTISING AGE MAGAZINE*

"Extremely well-written and chock full of great ideas and concepts ... It's a great book! Bravo!"

- JAMIE TURNER, CHIEF CONTENT OFFICER,
THE 60SECONDMARKETER.COM

"Tom's book rocks! It tells you how to create advertising that succeeds - reliably! - and wins creative awards, too. Tom Attea is a genius - and I don't say that lightly. Read, study, and apply The Secrets of Successful Creative Advertising if you want to create or buy the kind of advertising that gets noticed and makes more money!"

- DOUG HALL,
AUTHOR OF THE BEST-SELLING MARKETING BOOK
JUMP START YOUR BRAIN AND FOUNDER OF THE EUREKA!
RANCH INTERNATIONAL FOR TRAINING IN INNOVATIVE MARKETING

"I love this book! It will help a lot of people."

- MARC RUBIN,
AWARD-WINNING NEW YORK CREATIVE DIRECTOR & ART DIRECTOR

"The Secrets of Successful Creative Advertising should equip downtown marketers to grasp the creative process in an optimally productive way and select work that is most likely to achieve success. Author Tom Attea is a razor-sharp, thorough thinker and an excellent writer to invest time with and learn from."

– PAUL FELT,
EDITOR, *DOWNTOWN PROMOTION REPORTER*

How to Write Websites that Convert

"Once in a while, someone will come out with a new book that really lives up to its name. How to Write Websites that Convert by Tom Attea is probably the best book I have ever read on the subject of what it takes to make a website effective ... If you want to learn how to convert visitors to your website into real buying customers, this has got to be the best book you will ever read on the subject."

– BRUCE BLECHMAN,
BEST-SELLING CO-AUTHOR OF GUERRILLA FINANCING

"Tom Attea's 'How to Write Websites that Convert' is an illuminating work of instructional brilliance from a master copywriter ... it's just as reliable a guide for current or would-be copywriters who want to improve their copywriting skills in general ... The bottom line? "How to Write Websites that Convert" is an important book that I will re-read many times. I recommend it to both new and experienced copywriters alike who want to fulfill their obligation to clients, and just as importantly, experience the heights, benefits and rewards of what being a truly exceptional web copywriting professional is all about."

– READER REVIEW,
AMAZON.COM

TABLE OF CONTENTS

PREFACE

This book will teach you everything you need to know to be a great copy-writer. While no one can make you more creative, insightful or sensitive, I will give you the techniques and insights that will enable you to achieve your potential for greatness.

Along the way, I'll reveal the first clear explanation of the advertising creative process. Understanding it, instead of considering it a mystery, is the first step to putting it to work for consistent success.

When you learn what is in this book, you will be one of the most powerful people in mass communications. What you create will persuade millions of attentive and trusting people to do what you ask them to do. Since most of the world receives its primary messages through media, you will also be, when granted an outlet by a major advertiser, political candidate, or charitable cause, one of the most powerful people in the mass culture.

The ability invites responsible use, and I urge you to live by it.

PART 1

General Guidelines for Great Copywriting

CHAPTER 1

THE BASIC GUIDELINES

Great copywriting is rare, because only a few copywriters understand how to create it. The difficulty begins with advertising creativity in general, because it's still generally considered a mystery. Once I describe what it is, you'll see all advertising with new insight and be able to use the understanding in your own copywriting.

Advertising Creativity, Explained

Creativity in advertising consists of imagining an appropriate verbal and visual magnification of the selling proposition, or brand promise. Magnification is the key. Now, when you watch a TV commercial or visit a website, you have an exact way to judge it. Simply ask, is it an appropriate verbal and visual magnification of the selling proposition? You'll find that precious few are.

How is the magnification achieved? In great copywriting and design, we use the complete resources of verbal and visual art.

Some consider hard-sell advertising more effective, but it is structurally incapable of competing with creative advertising when it is done correctly. Why? The usual hard-sell advertising relies on less dramatic and inviting means of magnification, such as shouting, excessive repetition, typographical stunting, and commonplace visuals.

This structural superiority is why creative copywriting and design can maximize the advertising opportunity.

What is the critical difference? Great advertising uses the resources of language and visuals to emphasize – in inviting, dramatic ways – why the customer should buy the product. Commonplace advertising may or may not emphasize the selling proposition and, in fact, may subordinate it. Clever visuals that distract from the selling proposition are sometimes referred to as vampire video. There is also such a thing as vampire verbiage. Even the improper use of type sizes can subordinate why people should buy something, especially on billboards and on homepages above the fold.

Strategically right and creatively bright advertising nearly always produces remarkable sales results. I call such advertising transparent. It allows the audience to see right through it to the product or service in its most appealing light. So the advertising actually measures the appeal of what is being advertised, instead of the advertising being measured as just another way to present the product or service.

An especially captivating distraction is a "great" creative idea that may not be strategically right. How do we free our minds from its grip, so we can continue to explore the creative potential of the brand? By keeping our goal in mind, which is to go beyond the usual concept of "good" or even "great" advertising to advertising that is not only strategically right but also creatively bright.

I've developed a unique way to develop such advertising and branding consistently. I call it The Creative Exploratory. I'll explain what it is and how you can use it in a later chapter.

The Three Basic Questions: What to Say, How to Say It, and Where to Say It

Great copywriting and all consistently successful advertising is based on the answer to three basic questions.

1. What is the right thing to say?

2. What is the right way to say it?

3. What are the right places to say it?

When these questions have been answered correctly, all that's left is implementation.

The answer to the first question is arrived at through the development of an incisive strategy. The answer to the second is achieved through the creation of appropriately innovative copy and design. And the third is based on expert media planning and buying. Since a great copywriter must understand all three, I'll cover the essentials as we go along.

When you know how to create copy and design in this way, and the client knows to buy it, you can all put your heads on your pillows at night, knowing that advertising is doing everything it can to sell the product or service.

Can you make a reality check? The pragmatic way is to track the sales. On the Internet, we get almost instant feedback and detailed analytics.

But before traditional or digital advertising is launched, you can ask yourself a variation of the three fundamental questions. Can I or anyone else involved with the brand think of something better to say about it? Can any of us think of a better way to say it? And can we think of better places to say it? If your answer to any of these questions is yes or maybe, you still don't have the strategically right and creatively bright advertising.

Once it locks in, the experience is like the tumblers in a combination lock falling into place. Suddenly, everything fits together just right. In fact, you can sense the pieces falling into place. Why? The advertising is the simultaneous answer to all the sensible demands that have been placed on it. As a result, it's the key that opens the door to the largest marketing opportunity. If you have the key, you can unlock the door and walk right into the room where optimal success awaits. If you don't, you can bang on the door until you've exhausted every resource, but you can't get in. It might as well be made of steel.

Make the Most Appealing Brand Promise and Prove It with Every Credible Support Point

When we wish to develop great copy, the first thing we should do is discover and express the core brand promise. Once we have it, our job is to prove it with every credible support point we have.

If you're working in an agency, you'll be provided with the strategy. Then you job is to express it optimally. When you're on your own, as a freelancer or creative consultant, you'll often have to develop the strategy yourself.

For a copywriter with a strategy, branding consists of developing the right, bright expression of the brand promise, not as marketing speak, but as a market-ready slogan. During the early days of the campaign, it can serve as the substance of the headline. After the branding has been established, it can simply appear under the brand name. It should also be printed on the company's stationery and business cards.

I'll explain an innovative way to explore the likely options for the brand promise and arrive at a recommended promise in the chapter on The Creative Exploratory. As you'll discover, the Exploratory enables clients, for the first time in advertising, to choose their brand promise, not just from a recommendation, but also with a knowledge of the likely options.

You've already seen insights – or, if you'll excuse the expression, some of Attea's Ideas – and learned principles that you're unlikely to find in any other book on copywriting or advertising. Now, let's move on to other insights and guidelines.

CHAPTER 2

HOW TO POSITION AND BUILD BRANDS

Positioning a brand properly is the first step to building it on a solid foundation, so let's cover positioning first.

Positioning a Brand

While developing the position, which is the essence of the brand strategy, is usually done by the account team, implementing the expression of it to the target market is up to the copywriter and designer. This step can be seen as taking the brand position and overall strategy to the front lines. There are challenges there that account people never experience. It's up to you to discover them and solve them.

Let's begin by explaining what a brand position is. It's a statement that places the product or service in its category so that it can sell on a unique benefit or benefits.

Specifically, it defines the category the product competes in and the benefit or benefits that differentiate it, or create brand preference.

The Frame of Reference and the Point of Difference

Structurally, a brand position consists of two parts: the frame of reference and the point of difference. The frame of reference denotes the category we decide the product can do the biggest business in and the point of difference is the product attribute or attributes that, communicated as a benefit or benefits, will allow it to claim its maximum share of the business in the category.

Let's take a simple positioning statement and explain it. It's one that has been used by a major brand. "The coffee that's naturally decaffeinated." The frame of reference is coffee. We didn't say "The decaffeinated coffee that's naturally decaffeinated." We would select our market more exactly as people who drink decaffeinated coffee, but we would also limit the market we're talking to. If we can appeal to all coffee drinkers, we might have a bigger business. We suspect there may be drinkers of regular coffee who might choose a decaffeinated coffee if they knew it wasn't a chemical feast, especially if we talk about how good it tastes because of natural decaffeination.

Generally, we want to pick the largest business we can credibly be in, so we want to pick the largest frame of reference the product attributes can justify. The bigger the frame of reference, the more people we're appealing to.

The lesson is that we want to think in market-expansive terms, not market-limiting ones.

On the other hand, if we make the frame of reference too big for the product to justify, it won't be doing business where it should. Our position will be inexact, so the consumer won't know exactly how to think of the product.

The frame of reference is not only a marketing tool. It gives the consumer a recognizable way to place the product. She knows to think of it in terms of the category.

Now, we come to the point of difference. It should consist of the main reason the consumer should prefer the brand. We highlight the most significant attribute. It's naturally decaffeinated. If the appropriate position were more complex, we would have a secondary point of difference and perhaps a tertiary one.

What if we realize that we are not the first coffee that is naturally decaffeinated? We need to add a differentiator. Let's opt for what most people want: great taste.

In this case, we add "great taste," not only to offer people what they usually want, but also to defend ourselves against the possible objection that if it's decaffeinated in any way it doesn't taste good.

Now, our position becomes "The coffee that's naturally decaffeinated and great tasting." We might also have opted to make our frame of reference "great-tasting coffee." Then we would recast our position as "The great-tasting coffee that's naturally decaffeinated." Either way we state the position when we include "great taste," we now have a definite "what to say" to develop creatively.

Is there any easy way to think about positioning? Here's an original way I developed to help my copywriter trainees at Young & Rubicam understand the subject. Think of the two aspects of the positioning statement as the hands of a clock that you adjust manually. Move one hand around until it points at what you believe is just the right frame of reference, and then move the other one around until it points at what you think is the right point of difference. You can move either hand first, since you may know the point of difference before you decide on the frame of reference.

Let's apply the technique to other products. I'm sure you can see the frame of reference and the point of difference. Benecol® claims to be "The delicious spread that helps lower cholesterol." Here's the position for a Drupal agency I wrote the website copy for: "The digital agency that specializes in Drupal websites."

Now, let move on to brand building.

Building A Brand

The essence of brand building becomes clear if we think of it as owning intellectual real estate in the mass consciousness, which is made up of the general content of most minds in the marketing area – whether a town, the nation, or the globe. The goal of brand building is to own an over-increasing share of it, in terms of the brand promise we wish to be known for, not only verbally, but visually, too.

I provided a simile for a book on advertising when the author called to ask for a quote she could use in it. My answer appears in her book, *Advertising Without An Agency Made Easy* by Kathy J. Kobliski (Entrepreneur Press.)

You'll recognize a summary of the core principles we've discussed. The punctuation is as the quote appeared: "Figure out the one best thing about your product or service. This is the foundation of your message. Decide on words and pictures that say it the best. This is the first floor of the building you will erect over time called your brand image. Then say it in the places that reach your target market to the extent that your budget allows. If you keep building on the same foundation, over the years you may have one of the highest buildings in your category; that is, your product will be more top of mind.

"When you say the right thing, the right way in the right places, advertising will do as much for you as it can. So you can put your head on your pillow at night knowing that the business you're doing is the business you *can* do in terms of how your advertising can help. You can spend your time taking care of the other aspects of your business. Advertising done this way is not a guessing game. It's a very skillful and powerful business tool."

Let me elaborate on the quote. We can view the mass consciousness as a cityscape. Each block can be seen as a category, with buildings of different heights. The leading product or service in the category owns the tallest building. That's a metaphorical way to account for why we say the leading brand in a category has "top-of-mind awareness." Mention toothpaste, and most people will think of Crest. Say soft drink, and most will think of Coca-Cola. The building usually takes a long time to erect, and new advertising primarily functions to maintain and enhance it.

If we wish to be the leader in the category, we have to make our building taller than the market leader. So an advertiser should see himself or herself as buying intellectual real estate. To begin our building process, the first thing we must do is lay in a solid foundation. If the brand doesn't already have the right, bright position, or core brand promise, we must create it and initiate a campaign that communicates it properly. Then stories can be added to the "brand building" year after year.

Adopting a new strategy, unless the brand changes significantly, or launching a new campaign that doesn't feature it is like starting to put up a building and then deciding to tear it down and start to put up another one. The approach takes the wrecking ball to the goal of building, over time, the tallest building.

With proper brand positioning, we can put in the right foundation. Then over the years, we can build a higher and higher building on the block. Given enough marketing acumen and creative talent, along with good faith on the part of the client, one day the brand can dominate the skyline.

CHAPTER 3

HOW TO CREATE GREAT SLOGANS

Creating just the right, bright slogan is like minting a bar of gold. Once you create it, it sits there, aglow with the intelligence, talent and skill that went into it. Such a slogan has immediately apparent, unique value, and, unless the content of the message changes, it should last for years. So you can enjoy the rewards of, not only seeing it continue in its original use, but the uses multiply, such as appearing on the client's stationery, the package, the delivery trucks, and even hearing consumers quote it.

In the early days of the slogan, it can be the core content of the headline. Using it this way signs in the core brand promise. The headline can also enlarge on the promise. Later, the slogan can simply appear under the logo.

The Brand Promise Exploratory

How do we create such slogans? I have a unique approach, which I call The Brand Promise Exploratory.

I assume your account team or client has provided a completed Creative Brief. (You'll find a copy of the one I use in the Appendix. It based on the briefs at a number of New York's leading ad agencies, along with my own input.)

After I study the creative brief, I think about the content for a while. Then I launch The Brand Promise Exploratory.

How? I begin to ideate, expressing each way of looking at the product or service as a market-ready slogan. As I proceed, I can push into new areas. At a certain point, I start to see where the most appealing area is. I also begin to sense that I've covered the likely options. I know I'm closing in on the expression of the brand promise that I'll recommend. I continue to ideate until I finally mint what I think is just the right, bright slogan. Then I stop. Now I create a presentation. It consists of a recommended brand promise, other favorites, usually about ten, and just more slogans I came up with on the way to the recommendation. Then I present it to the account team or send it to the client. The account people and the client usually buy the recommendation, but some may choose another one of them, because they see something in it that works especially well for the business. The important thing is the agency and the client can choose the slogan, or expression of the core brand promise, not just from a recommendation but also with a knowledge of the likely options.

The Slogan We're Looking For

We must first isolate the unique attribute or benefit of the brand. It serves as the content or core brand promise. We find it in the creative brief. Then we must express the content in a compact, deftly appropriate way.

As a way of working, it helps to remember Lewis Carroll's advice: "Take care of the matter, and the manner will take care of itself."

When the product is compellingly unique, the uniqueness of the right slogan becomes readily apparent. Yet each product or service is in some way unique, even if only in its heritage. So the right claim, said the right way, produces a slogan that is unique – perfectly matched to the brand and brightly original. The key test: it usually can't be torn off the brand it was created for and stuck on another one. Think of how many major marketers have slogans that can be applied to many products or services.

Sometimes the uniqueness might be so slight that we work to create a slogan that makes it appear as uniquely appealing as we can make it.

Perhaps there's an appealing but still untold truth in the category that we can preempt. In such a case, it's especially important to mint the slogan so that it goes well with the brand name euphonically and/or visually.

The content should present, or effectively imply, the brand benefit that we hope will irresistibly invite the largest number of intended consumers to buy it.

The slogan should appear to be alive, instead of just lie there. How do we achieve such a vibrant result? The meaning is usually not just one-dimensional. It has a main meaning, along with one or more secondary ones. When we first hear or see it, we get the main meaning. But we also detect a second possible meaning. And maybe even a third one. These subsidiary meanings may be very apparent or subtle. A statement that has just one meaning is like window glass. Flat. But a statement that has two or three meanings has various facets, like a diamond. It sparkles.

Optimally, the main meaning and the secondary meaning or meanings should be positive. One may, for example, infer a secondary benefit. Another might comment on the wisdom of the people who buy the product.

All the meanings need not and probably will not relate to the product. One or more may relate to the culture and thereby help relate the product to the target audience.

Yet, even with all of the demands placed on the right slogan, the final expression of it must seem as natural as an off-handed comment.

Since we know exactly what constitutes such a slogan, we should survey the category we're working in and measure the skill of the marketing communications in it. The survey should be done early, as part of our estimation of how much further we can take the communications.

Surprisingly, you'll discover that most categories are still essentially wide open for the minting of a slogan that owns the intellectual high ground. Why? The random nature of the usual advertising creative process.

Tactics For Memorability

There are many usual tactics for making a slogan especially memorable. Succinct appropriateness is one. Euphony is a frequent source, including rhyme, alliteration, and consonance. Structure can also be a source, such as parallel and contrasting phrases.

Here's another one – relating the name and the claim. The most effective way is to create a slogan that actually contains the brand name. It can still be quite clever. The advantage is obvious: the consumer only has to remember the slogan to know, not only why to buy something, but what to buy.

Here are examples from my own work:

First, let's take a slogan I minted The Village Voice, a publication that is known for airing the gripes of veteran New Yorkers. The slogan I minted for it is, "In this city, you need a Voice." The agency I freelanced the job for won the account, and the campaign ran for many years.

On a tamer note, when I was at Young & Rubicam, I created a slogan for Jell-O. The campaign – a correctly gauged, recipe-driven one – saved the account, turned the brand around, and ran for eight years. The slogan was simply, "Start with Jell-O." It was executed in color spreads and TV commercials. The headline for the kickoff ad was simply, "To make tonight's dessert special, start with Jell-O." One of the recipe ads was, "To make a cool summer salad, start with Jell-O."

Notice how tightly the brand unity is maintained.

The advertising, basic as it was, worked so well that Y & R took out a full-page ad in *Advertising Age* to promote the agency. Headline: "To make television and print advertising work together, start with Young & Rubicam."

Here's a slogan that I crafted for Drake's Bakeries that's a straightforward instance of the principle: "If it's Drake's, it's delicious." It simply highlights the one thing people need to know about the snack cakes in a way that ties it to the brand name. It helped make the company successful enough for the conglomerate that owns Hostess to buy it.

The second level of this type of aided recall is to allude to the brand name in the slogan.

Here's one such slogan I wrote for A & P Supermarkets. At the time, the chain needed to win back customers who had been lost due to store conditions and service that were less than optimal. I was hired as a creative consultant by the new CEO, James Wood, who had been brought in to turn the business around.

I knew the slogan would have to contain, or at least imply, an apology for the past and a pledge that things were better now and would remain that way. I also wanted the slogan to be one that A & P could own.

I went to work, exploring the creative possibilities, and recommended "We watch our P's & Q's".

The "P" stood for prices and the "Q" for quality, while the expression contained an implied apology and a vow to do better.

For aided recall, the "P & Q" is a parallel structure to "A & P." The look and sound are similar. So the two structures complement each other visually and resonate verbally. The structure also makes the slogan proprietary. It belongs to A & P. So it passes the acid test of ownership.

The slogan also gains memorability because of another frequently employed advertising technique: taking a saying from elsewhere and applying it in a new way. When the consumer realizes the tie in, the slogan achieves added resonance. It's a minor form of what the literary critic Edmund Wilson called "the shock of recognition." The apparent offhandedness also helps make it inviting.

To achieve brand unity, I created stickers and signs with green "P's" on them to indicate items that were on sale. The ad introduced the symbol for the specials with the headline: "Introducing Green P's. A fresh new way to save at the new A & P." When the customer went to the store, he or she saw the Green P labels, shaped by my designer like the company's oval sign, stuck on the weekly specials, along with shelf tags pointing to them, with the line "Pick this Green P and save!"

I told the quality story with the headline, "The new A & P would like to Q you in."

Notice how everything ties together to unify the campaign.

The advertising served as the turnaround campaign for the chain and ran for four years. During that time, I also created a store brand called brand, called "The P & Q Brand." At one point, it accounted for 6% of sales.

Of course, there can be great slogans that have no linguistic relationship to the brand name. If such a slogan is stylish and impactful enough, it will be remembered by consumers, valued by clients, and maybe help the advertising win creative awards.

The problem is, the consumer has to remember two things to know what to do – the claim and the name. The efficiency of the recall, while probably not cut in half, is certainly reduced. These kinds of slogans have another shortcoming. They can apply to a host of different products.

So I often wonder if the same thoughts might have been expressed in witty but more appropriate ways in terms of aided recall.

Yet I've had the pleasure, and the subliminal guilt, of writing such slogans myself. For instance, I created one for Futuro supports, "The science of support." The client liked it so much he put it on all the packages and, yes, on the company stationery. It had many merits. It preempted a scientific approach in the category. The initial "s's" on the two main words alliterated. It was also visually memorable because the two main words were two syllables each and both of the smaller words were one syllable.

Let's look at a couple of well-known but rootless slogan I didn't write:

"Fedex. The world on time."

"Servpro. Like it never even happened."

Despite their merits and longevity, can you think of other uses for them? For example, could they apply to competitors or products in other categories?

So, while ideating in an open playing field does invite innovation, it's generally more effective, and challenging, to create a slogan that the client can own and invest in, as his or her own property, for years to come.

The right slogan, which is a form of summary, can dawn on us at any time, especially after we launch The Creative Exploratory Or it might come in a flash even as we're being briefed on the assignment. Then the Exploratory will simply confirm its correctness.

There's just no telling when the higher faculties of our minds might synthesize the right slogan and drop it into our conscious minds, like a gift. So it's a good idea to carry a notebook or use your smartphone to jot down or dictate inspirations. It's also smart to keep either one or both on the night table for when inspiration comes in the wee hours. Some people prefer index cards, which provide the freedom to file or toss the work as it's created, instead of carrying around a notebook until it's filled.

To conclude our section on minting great slogans, remember that most women like to shop at brick and mortar stores and on the Internet. A slogan gives her something to shop for in a way she can remember. The better job it does, the more likely the advertiser will be to continue talking to her the same way. The admirable results are that the brand keeps succeeding, the agency keeps the account, or at least is more likely to, and the creative person gets to enjoy seeing his handiwork find a somewhat lasting place in the ever-changing mass consciousness and enhance his or her creative reputation.

CHAPTER 4

HOW TO CREATE A GREAT CAMPAIGN OR HOMEPAGE

While many more innovations for great copywriting lie ahead, we now know enough to consider how to create a great campaign or a homepage.

First, Get the Poster Right

When we create a campaign or a homepage, the first goal is to get the poster right, which is t. Every other tactic will consist of adapting and elaborating it appropriately to each communication channel.

Creative development is concentrated on the foundational verbal and the visual content.

We ask ourselves, if the campaign or homepage can be seen as just one headline and one visual, what would they be? The headline would be the slogan, or core brand promise, and the picture would be the main visual that is the magnification of the promise. The first commercial, print ad, or homepage launches the core development of the poster. Its function to sign in the campaign. So the commercial and/or print campaign should run with more media weight than the work that

17

develops the campaign, and the homepage should stay in place for an extended period.

Second, Address Immediate Opportunities and Questions

How do we decide what the subsequent commercials, print ads, and digital communications should be? They should all be presentations, variations, and elaborations of the poster. In an overall sense, they create appropriate variety within the unity. To borrow a musical phrase, they are variations on a theme.

Specifically, how do we decide what the second commercial, print ad, or digital tactic should be, as well as the third or fourth one? We can proceed in the usual way and just think up a variety of other great verbal and visual executions that magnify the same selling proposition, with the same core content, and then select the ones that seem to develop the message most effectively.

Here are more precise ways.

We consider if there are aspects of the strategy that we should reinforce or were not able to feature adequately in the launch commercial, print ad the homepage – primarily the claims and proofs. We also turn to our realization that every campaign launch creates opportunities and provokes questions.

So we ask what opportunities the campaign opens up for further tactics. For instance, if we're selling a suntan lotion, and our first commercial or print ad talks about the great protection it gives, we've opened an immediate opportunity to reinforce our proof. So the next commercial could be set at a beach where the sun is known to be particularly intense but, thanks to our lotion, everybody's skin is doing just fine. In fact, maybe the campaign will consist of a series of commercials shot at different famous tropical beaches.

We also ask what immediate questions the sign-in commercial or ad has provoked. Will the audience be asking such things as, "How do I know if it works as well as the advertising says it does?" "If it gives such great protection, will I still get a great tan?" We decide the most important question to be answered is the first one. So the second commercial or print ad will ask why it's so effective and feature a demonstration, probably an ingredient story. The third commercial might reverse the emphasis and subordination to feature "wow" tans and great protection. As you can see, the most important opportunity or question becomes the basis of the second commercial or ad in the campaign. The next most important one becomes the basis of the third.

When we proceed in this orderly manner, we can develop the campaign in the way that is most likely to make it optimally successful.

PART 2

How to Write Great Copy for Traditional Media

CHAPTER 5

TELEVISION COMMERCIALS

As the first traditional medium we'll consider, let's cover how to create great TV commercials. Some of the examples will be pretty basic, but the same principals will enable you to create commercials that are appropriately innovative.

A Commercial in Dramatic Terms

The first thing we must understand is what a TV spot is in dramatic terms.

A commercial is a compact dramatic event that makes a selling point or points. When well crafted, it is the perfectly appropriate visual-verbal magnification of the selling proposition.

The one apparent exception is corporate-image advertising, where the intent is to characterize the company in a favorable way, to the public and, often even more, to potential investors. Yet the goal is really to sell the company or, in the words of W. S. Gilbert, to "polish up the handle on the big front door."

Overall Guidelines

1. Concentrate the Material

We must concentrate the content to present the core message with maximum effect. Every unessential shot or word – even extra syllable – should be excised. It's better to find a clever way to repeat the most important content than to allow unnecessary material to dilute it and, worse, to consume precious seconds. As a metaphor, consider yourself a chef who's reducing a sauce to concentrate the taste.

2. Shape the Material Vertically

We must shape the material vertically. Rather than telling a horizontal tale, we want to make our primary point and then line up the proof. Although the comparison is a bit heavy handed, consider each element that proves the point the tap of a hammer on the head of a nail. Hammering to the side does not help drive the point home. The tap of the hammer can be done seriously or humorously.

3. Present Important News

To be arresting, a commercial should present important news, or, at least, the appearance of it. Media were originally invented to communicate news, and it's still the ingredient it welcomes most.

The purest form of news is the announcement of a new product; next, a product improvement; and, most usual of all, a new way to look at an existing product or at its core message.

4. Give the Spot "Moment"

Every spot should be staged with "moment"; that is, it should appear to have immediate relevance to the current psychological state at which it addresses the intended consumer. It should also appear to be timely in a cultural or overall sense. Taking care of the first kind of moment usually accomplishes the second.

5. Make the Opening Captivating

When the spot begins, whether seriously or humorously, it should start in a captivating manner, like the 4-note motive that begins Beethoven's Fifth Symphony. The intent is to make the audience sit up and take notice. It's also an effort to disarm the audience from surfing away with the remote. George Bernard Shaw made the point in his typically outrageousness manner, saying that the way to begin a play is to fire off a gun.

As you may know, I'm also a frequently produced playwright. When I was in the Playwrights Unit of The Actors Studio, I had a great mentor I collaborated on a show over a 10-year period. He used to say, "When the curtain goes up, the question is, where's the fire?" He meant the emergency, which is actually what precipitates dramatic conflict. In a commercial, it can be a person with a headache who needs relief.

6. Stage the News or Conflict Immediately

A correct beginning stages the news or character conflict immediately. We want to arrest attention with the subject of the commercial, not with ancillary material.

The cleverness, seriousness, or other tone should be made up of the core material, not an attempt to set it up or, worse, irrelevant content.

7. A Note about Conflict

The usual books on dramatic art tell us that conflict is the foundational element that makes a drama work. So beginning writers often create characters who are always screaming at one another. But some of the greatest conflicts are silent. The root of the problem is, conflict is an effect, and you can't work with effects. You have to work with causes. In workable terms, you create an emergency, without a ready escape for the characters. So the emergency precipitates a conflict, or problem, which may complicate, but which leads to a resolution of it, or a solution, with, in advertising, the entrance of the product as the hero who solves the problem. Whether a commercial is serious or humorous, ask yourself, as my mentor suggested, "Where's the fire?" Then stage it.

Strive for a tone that appears natural and inviting, that is, aim for, in the usual dramatic term, "a sense of truth." If people don't believe what's happening, they won't readily be convinced by what you're staging. As we say in advertising, "If superman flies, he needs a cape." Yes, even he needs a reason for the audience to believe he can fly.

Prototypical Example

Here's a prototypical example. Admittedly, it's not creative. But the same basic principles would apply if the commercial was humorous, serious, or inspiringly creative in another tone.

The Emergency, or Problem

Let's stay with a headache. It could just as well be a character's inability to find a natural soft drink that tastes good.

A male character, our antagonist, has a headache and needs relief, now. The dramatic emergency is driven by the villain, which is his continuing pain, but the sub-textual villain is the cause of it, which is the character's usual inadequately effective pain reliever.

The Conflict Is Joined

The protagonist, who is the character driving the scene and providing the solution, enters, as the man's sympathetic and knowing wife, who is the champion of the product-as-hero.

The Conflict Intensifies

He's skeptical, which invites us to stage a brief contest of wills.

Enter the Solution

She confronts his skepticism, and sub-textually the audience's skepticism, by providing proof that our heroic pain reliever can solve his problem. At this point, we may also introduce a reinforcing character, in the person of an announcer, who may have at this disposal a visual/verbal demo to help overcome the character's resistance.

The Resolution

The reverse, or resolution, begins when our skeptical actor agrees to try our pain reliever. To compress the passage of time, we do a dissolve (soft move from one scene to the next, as opposed to a cut) to reveal the antagonist, experiencing the joy of relief. He provides, as an emotional reward for his wife, a sign of appreciation, which also serves as an indirect message to wives everywhere that their husbands will love them if they go out and buy our pain reliever.

Conclusion or Button

We conclude the spot with a compact recapitulation of our argument, in the form of the brand name and the slogan, with the brand name often introduced with a call to action, as in "Try (brand name)."

And our compact dramatic event completes.

Notice that it has, in Aristotelian terms, a beginning (problem), middle (introduction of the answer and support for it), and an end (antagonist relents and enables the solution).

Corresponding to this three-part analysis, the timeframe of a usual commercial can be seen in roughly three segments – a 30-second commercial in three 10-second units and a 15-second commercial in three 5-second ones.

Specific Guidelines

1. A Commercial Should Have a Star

Many people in advertising think the star of the commercial is the product. It is if it is the only "character" in the commercial. In commercials with people in them, we need to create with a knowledge of who the star is, or, in some instances, who the co-stars are.

While the advice to have a central character or a star seems like basic piece of wisdom, a great many commercials lack one. The dialogue is sprinkled among the characters as indiscriminatingly as salt and pepper. So the audience doesn't know who to look to for the big lines, or the main points. These lines should be given to the star, and the other actors should only ask questions or make comments that bring out or highlight the main lines, along with the actions, of the star. Otherwise, the consumer has to go from character to character for snatches of dialogue, in an effort to put the message together. The central character also gives the consumer a fellow human being to identify with, or the spot will lack human contact, as crowd scenes inevitably do.

How do you decide who the star is? He or she is the actor who tells most of the story and drives the mini-drama, that is, the protagonist.

In commercials that don't have an extensive message about the product, the star can be seen as the character with the most interesting story. For instance, let's say a teenage son comes home late one night and his father confronts him about where he has been. Who, we ask, has the interesting story? The son. So the father should let us enjoy what happened by just asking his son a question or two and making little comments, even if his goal is to tell the son that his late night out has given him a headache. If he does most of the talking, while his son pretty much just sits there, we're listening to the story of the character we're not nearly as curious about.

Even when a commercial is composed of bi-play, that is, dialogue between two people, their conversation should not be all tangled up in overdone efforts at steady wit. One of the characters should ask questions and make brief comments and let the other character, our star, answer them. The questions act as a setup, and the answers deliver the product "punch" lines. To grasp how bi-play works, listen to some of the classic radio comics, especially George Burns and Gracie Allen. Did George ever crack a joke? Maybe he made an occasional humorous aside. But his primary role was to ask Gracie a straightforward question, to which she would provide a whacky answer. The same goes for Abbott and Costello. Bud asks a logical question and Lou provides a zany answer.

The by-play format is also an effective way to create a commercial for two actors when the tone of the commercial is serious. The audience knows to focus on the star to hear the key points of the message.

Even in a dramatic situation with two characters who have essentially equal roles, as co-stars, you still must decide who is the antagonist and who is the protagonist – the person with the problem and the person with the answer. You also have to determine who is driving the scene. This format is the commercial version of a film with a leading man and leading lady. Any other members of the cast are the supporting characters.

2. The Star Should Have a Goal that Proves the Point of the Commercial

This aspect of our compact drama is called, in the language of stagecraft, the spine of character. What does he or she want? Due to the brevity of the commercial form, the star's goal also functions as the spine of the story.

3. Support the Main Point or Points with Physical Actions

As the star or co-stars proceed to make their point or points, they should function as more than mouthpieces. Along with words, they should be given concrete physical tasks that help make the point or points, as well as make them more at home and credible in their environment. It's one thing for a man to say he got a closer shave and another to have him say it while a woman touches his face on sighs about how smooth it is.

When I used to attend the Directors Unit at The Actors Studio, Elia Kazan used to make the point, often by slamming his hand on a table, to exclaim, "Concretize! Concretize!"

4. The Star and Secondary Characters Should Usually Be Attractive

For many years, it has been stylish to cast actors who have the look of everyday people or a look that's highly unusual. A variety of talent agencies satisfy the demand. One was called Funny Face. Such character actors do have a place in advertising, because a lot of consumers find it easy to relate to them and because their looks can be memorable. When they're appropriate to the message, they can be the stars.

But the fact remains that most people pay more attention to attractive people. They like to look at them, imagine what their lives might be like, and what it might be like to be them. Who do you look at most when you walk down the street? And what does the history of Hollywood tell us? There's usually more box-office appeal in a handsome leading man and lovely leading lady, while more usual looking actors perform supporting roles and, in the process, make the stars look, by comparison, even more attractive.

We are not recommending the regular use of actors and actors who are so gorgeous many consumers would have difficulty relating to them, although they do serve well in commercials that present ideals of beauty for emulation.

As a rule, few things make a commercial more inviting than a handsome leading man and/or a lovely leading lady. As Chekhov said about the craft of playwriting, "The basic weight is two – a man and woman."

As a practical note, it's easier to "dress down" an attractive person to perform in the role of an engaging everyday human being than it is to make an average-looking person appear engaging. For instance, a beautiful woman "dressed down" in a uniform with her hair back is an effective way to present an inviting spokeswoman/server for a fast-food chain.

5. A Commercial Must Have Unity, because Unity Is a Key Aspect of Impact

Most events that have impact have unity, for instance, the fall of a rock. When I ran the copy training program at Young & Rubicam, I developed ways to magnify the techniques of great copywriting.

To reminisce, each spring and fall my office would fill up with portfolios, which had been dropped off by recent graduates of communications and journalism courses, along with a few would-be copywriters with unusual backgrounds. I would leaf through the portfolios, looking for bright thinking, and call any candidate in whose work I spotted it. If I had an opening, I'd invite him or her in for an interview and, if it went well, I'd offer a job. If I didn't have an opening, I'd offer encouragement and the promise to call when one arose. At any time, I had, in cubicles and small offices near me, about a dozen copy trainees. I'd give them assignments and do my best to make helpful suggestions while nourishing their usually shaky confidence.

To explain to them the principle of unity, I would offer the following metaphor, which is, to borrow a title from Swift, admittedly from a story that applies to a far more consequential matter, "A Contemplation Upon A Broomstick." If you take a broom and hit someone over the head with the end that is made up of all the straws, what happens? Not much. But, if you turn the broom around and whack the person with the handle, it hurts. Why? Of course, the handle is stiffer. But there's another reason. The handle is made up of one thing, and the force is concentrated in it. So, if a commercial or an ad is unified to achieve a goal, instead of made up of loosely connected fragments, it will have much more impact.

I also used to tell them to imagine a boxing match in which the boxers aren't wearing gloves but, instead, are swinging at each other with their hands open. There's a lot of slapping going on, but obviously nobody is going to score a knockout. Same reason. Five separate fingers and an open palm do not form a unity. Result: less impact. What do gloves do? They may cushion the impact of a bare fist but, more to the point, they help unify the impact of hand.

6. Balance the Use of the Words and Pictures

What is more important, the copy or the visuals? Many copywriters insist that the words are, and art directors usually maintain that the visuals are. As a copywriter, I sometimes refer to ads and commercials as verbal-visual events, instead of the more usual visual-verbal nomenclature. The truth is that the relative importance of each of the two ingredients varies from commercial to commercial and from ad to ad.

I could remind the art director, "In the beginning was the word..." and fancy illumination, as well as music, came later.

He might remind me that a picture is often worth a thousand words, to which I would reply that most of us think and communicate primarily in words.

Obviously, in slogans, we're primarily persuaded by words.

Language can also help guide the selection and presentation of the visual. Yet the visual can guide the selection of the words.

Truth to tell, most people look more than they read or hear. For instance, when they walk out of a movie, they usually don't talk about what they heard (unless they're musicians, who many prefer to talk about the soundtrack). Most people talk about what they saw, as in "Did you see what happened when she kissed him?"

When it comes to balancing the two ingredients correctly, here are guidelines.

With a straightforward announcer, the words are usually more important (unless there's something special about the look of the announcer).

In a dialogue commercial, the words and the visual are generally about equally important. But the smaller the action or the visualization is, the more important the words become, and the bigger the action or visualization is, the more supportive the words become.

When the commercial contains exactly the right main visual or visuals, as well as, if required, the right secondary, or support visual or visuals, and they're attention-getting on their own, the words, important as they are, should just help the visuals along, like a hand tapping a colorful balloon through the air. If the words become too assertive, the effect is as if they grab the balloon and push it back down to the earth. The visual magic is subordinated.

Fortunately, we can all imagine pictures, and the ability to imagine ones that are related to a message becomes part of a mind that can think of visual examples that magnify meaning. A great copywriter can think, not only in words, but also in word pictures and pure visuals. All of us can think in language, too. So a great art director thinks, not only visually, but also verbally. True, many art directors see type more than they actually read it, but many others read it and think well verbally. Their verbal skill may not go much further than the ability to coin bright headlines, slogans, and snatches of copy. But, since most key verbal thoughts in advertising are brief and colloquial, art directors can be quite adept at copy. The copywriter can supply any editorial niceties required to complete the art director's suggestions. The brightest art directors also know how to make incisive editorial suggestions to the copywriter.

7. The Aristotelian Unities Apply

In the *Rhetoric* and *Poetics,* Aristotle provided many principles that apply to creative advertising. Among them, we find the classic dramatic unities of time, place, and action. One major event, happening in a single location, or in locations that hold together, within at least the illusion of real time, create impact.

Advertising often adheres to these unities but, at times, it departs from them, sometimes disastrously, but at times, with great effect. The usual successful departure is what is called a vignette commercial, which is made up of a number of separate shots, hopefully unified with a theme. For example, imagine once again a commercial for a suntan lotion that shows quick cuts of lots of energetic people at the beach, enjoying the sun without concern. In these cases, unity is often enhanced by a design motif, lively music, or a distinctive voice-over announcer.

When a commercial must show diverse elements, it's especially important to unify the commercial in creative ways, including tone, lighting, design, or music.

8. Don't Use Too Many, or Too Few, Words

The number of words in a commercial should be based on what will most effectively maximize the communications power of the commercial. The basic values to consider are how to make the spot clear, convincing, and likeably memorable.

The product story should be told at a pace that allows the actors and/or announcer to make the most of each word and for the consumer to grasp the message as if he or she is listening to it at what appears to be a normal pace. When actors or announcers are forced to rush, the audience has a hard time keeping track of all the words and, even more damaging, the credibility of the actors and the announcer is undermined, because the consumer is reminded that they are not speaking for themselves but are just tools of the advertiser. It's far more effective to give the performers space to perform convincingly and retain their dignity, so that the consumer can listen to the words as carefully as you hope and become involved with the actors and announcers as human beings and, best of all, believe what they're saying.

My rule of thumb is that a 30-second spot should have no more than 65 to 70 words.

How few words can a commercial have? When appropriate, very few. For example, I once wrote some 10-second spots for a maker of audio equipment. The usual form of the words was a sentence of copy, followed by a one-word slogan: "Listen."

Once in a while, a spot can be made up of only visuals, with whatever words it contains superimposed on the pictures as type, that is "supered," or "titled," in which the type appears on a white, black, or color background. The type generally communicates the slogan and/or the brand name. Such commercials are the dream of art directors, especially visually gifted ones who may be uncomfortable with the importance of words.

9.   *The Argument Should Be Vertical, Not Horizontal*

Longer persuasive pieces can move horizontally from subject to subject and then become vertical for each subject, such as a properly structured political speech. But a short argument intended to persuade is unified to communicate one subject and should be arranged vertically – that is, the main point should be made and then the reasons to believe it should be piled one on top of the other, starting with the most important reason and ending with the least important one. This approach applies to the visuals, too. We're not a roving tour guide; we're standing before one attraction, telling the audience about its merits.

When artfully employed, working this way enables every big and little part of the communication to go toward communicating the selling proposition convincingly.

The same sort of structure also applies to print advertising.

The copy in a commercial or a print ad usually begins with the topic sentence or overall idea of the argument. There should also be a main or "topic visual."

Occasionally in a commercial, the main argument can be introduced a few seconds after the commercial begins; prior material may include a dramatization of the problem the product solves or another particularly arresting verbal or visual event.

After the topic idea is introduced, we present the main reason to believe the claim and then the second most important reason to believe it. The visual evidence should mount in step with the words. The end, or button, is, in rhetorical terms, the peroration.

Let's consider an example of a vertical argument. As we often do, we'll exaggerate for clarity.

Say we're writing a commercial for a new deodorant soap with a natural herbal fragrance, called "That's Fresh." First, we focus on the core word we must communicate: "fresh." We want our communication to seem offhanded, knowing the informality makes it easier for consumers to relate to it and like it. We also want them to remember the brand name.

Since we know how concise the brevity of a commercial allows us to be, we realize that the brand name can also function as a compact slogan. So the spot might open with a lovely lady standing under a pristine waterfall with our soap in hand, lathering up, as she exclaims, "That's

Fresh!" Then we cut to a guy, surfing on the curl of a wave and holding out the soap. He performs his own version of "That's Fresh!"

What are we doing? We've stated our claim with the brand name and the slogan, united in one efficient mass-communications entity; reinforced the content with a second instance piled right on top of the first, and done so in a colloquially credible way.

Now we cut to an extreme close shot of a person in a shower, lathering up, as our jingle enters with the claim and the name:

What's fresh
Like never before?
New That's Fresh!
It's made just for
A clean that's fresh!

Now, we cut to a demo of liquid cleansers and fresh herbs transforming themselves into a bar of our soap, as the voiceover announcer says, "What makes That's Fresh so remarkably fresh? A refreshingly different combination of natural herbs and gentle cleansers."

As a final visual reinforcement, we can cut to another shot of a person enjoying the soap, say, on a waterslide, or, to save money on talent payments, we can reprise one or both of the shots of our first two actors.

Our jingle provides the verbal button: "Fresh, Fresh, Fresh – That's Fresh!" As we hear it, our bar drops down from above, now in its wrapper, so the consumer can see what it looks like on the shelf, and nevertheless splashes into water at the bottom of the screen. Our announcer might add a call to action, such as "Get fresh, fresh like never before, today."

Out of consideration for the consumer, we refrain from duplicating the name with a super that says, "That's Fresh!" It's already plainly visible on the wrapper.

Although we overdid the exercise, repetition with stylish variation can function like advertising's version of the musical form of a theme and variations. When done gracefully, it need not annoy and can actually intrigue and delight the audience.

You might also consider how many times a song – from a classic aria to a pop tune – repeats its refrain or "hook" but with nuanced variety. For instance, In *The Barber of Seville*, Rossini has Figaro repeat his name over and over but at different pitches, dynamics, and tempos.

To magnify our point with contrast, let's consider what happens when an argument is laid out horizontally, even in a well-structured way, for example, as a sort of history lesson.

Let's say we're introducing the OTC version of the pain reliever naproxen sodium, which is Aleve. The strategy says the U. S. P. is that it works for eight hours, while all other pain relievers on the market only work for four. In our execution, we put down the leading brands in succession, as our voiceover announcer tells us, "The quest to alleviate pain. First, came aspirin; then acetaminophen; next, ibuprophen. What did they have in common? Four hours of relief. Introducing relief that lasts twice as long. New Aleve. It provides 8-hours of pain relief. That's right. Eight hours of relief with just two tablets." Now, we elaborate on eight hours of relief, tying together the sound of Aleve and relief as often as possible. Then we recap the unique benefit and provide a call to action. The result, while perhaps effective, is what you'd expect from a linear argument. It delays the main news and entrance of the product. And it requires the consumer to sit there and follow the unfolding.

If there is no way to avoid a linear argument, unify it as best you can. But even the above argument could have been accomplished vertically. How? We announce the advent of the first pain reliever that provides eight hours of relief in a single dose, including the visual and verbal entrance of the product. Then we tuck behind the announcement the comparisons in a more vertical manner; for example, "That's right. Eight hours of relief. Aspirin only provides four. Not eight, like Aleve. Acetaminophen only gives you four, too. But Aleve gives you eight. And ibuprofen? The same four hours." Now we tuck in any demo for proof of the claim, such as how doctors recommend the same ingredient for eight hours of relief, if we feel we need the reinforcement; then we continue to the summation/call to action), "So get relief that lasts twice as long. Get new Aleve."

10. *The KISS Principle Still Applies: Keep It Simple, Stupid*

This traditional and flagrantly insulting mnemonic is based on the early discovery that effective mass communication should be as simple as a dimple. Simplicity is important, not because the average consumer is dumb, but because consumers don't pay rapt attention to advertising. Additionally, the goal of advertising is to persuade as many prospects as possible – the most and least attentive. Even the simplest message is bound to go right past many people. This inevitability is one reason media planning includes, not only how many people the advertising ought to reach, but also how frequently it ought to reach them. Our ideal should be to communicate with elegant simplicity and captivate everyone who hearkens to our message.

What can you do when a brand story seems too complex to simplify? Find a way to feature the main message and subordinate the details.

Keep in mind that a good commercial is like the flight of a rocket. The details may be rocket science, but the movement we see from the launch to the goal is simple and direct. If the rocket begins to wobble, as if to cover a detail of the flight here and there, we become concerned. Will it make it to its destination? In fact, how did it even get off the launching pad?

11. *Aim for a Sense of Truth*

Does advertising represent real life? Does entertainment? Neither do, but most of us are willing to suspend our disbelief, or participate in verisimilitude – providing the creators don't violate it. As soon as we detect anything false, we sit back, scoff at the work, and dismiss it. The awareness of this principle presents the insightful creative person with an opportunity, especially in television, where verisimilitude is violated almost as standard operating procedure. In fact, it happens so pervasively that I call television a pretend medium. The actors in the commercials and the shows hardly ever deliver performances based on the skillful actor's ideal of "a sense of truth." Encouraged by equally frivolous directors, they pretend to be characters the roles call for them to be, instead of aiming to be convincing. There are exceptions, which often become classics. Did Ralph or Alice pretend to be who they were in "The Honeymooners?" No, they went for a sense of truth.

Nothing grips and persuades more than an event that appears to be true – real people, with real dialogue, in what appears to be a real setting, in a story that seems to be occurring in real time. A commercial that works to be real stands out. These basic esthetic principles hold, regardless of whether the tone of the advertising is serious, humorous, or even tongue in cheek. Real people live in all of these tones. So should advertising.

Most troubling of all, if consumers don't believe what's happening in the commercial, how can they be expected to be convinced by its message?

To achieve great advertising with maximum persuasive power, I also suggest that you limit the use of special effects, which are often lumped together under the moniker of "the magic of television." Visual trickery, even the kind that seems germane to the medium, when used in excess, can undermine the credibility of a commercial, just as, when you see a magician at work, you're not sure what to believe. Do you trust a thing he says or does?

12. Make Every Word and Picture Count

For the sake of simplicity, let's say that a 30-second commercial costs $300,000 to run. This figure means the client is paying $10,000 a second. Meanwhile, we've got a certain amount we have to say and show while we make sure the commercial doesn't appear rushed. The answer is to make every word and picture count. We don't want to devote precious seconds to extra conjunctions, prepositions, adjectives, adverbs, phrases or even syllables. Nor do we want any gratuitous visuals. Every syllable and every picture has to pay its way. Yet everything has to unfold with disarming naturalness. So we want to concentrate, everything. When we do, we make every moment richer.

13. Understand the Five Basic Levels of Emphasis

There are five basic levels of emphasis in television advertising. They are, from weakest to strongest, as follows:

1. The message as just a voiceover announcer, while various marginally related pictures clip along. The result is largely just words in the air, flying by, while the audience attempts to grab some of them.

2. A voiceover with a concrete on-camera demonstration of what is being said – or words in the air, along with one or more visual ideas to help us grasp them.

3. An announcer or other actor speaks the words on camera, so we can watch him while we listen – a talking head.

4. An on-camera announcer who has concrete tasks that help make the point or points – a taking head with illustrative materials.

5. An actor or actors who say and act out the point or points in a situation that appears to be real. This choice provides the power of drama itself. It's usually referred to as a "slice of life" commercial. Since many of them are quite plain, the connotation is that the commercial is boring. But the fact is, the format, used with its artful power, is the same one with which drama proceeds: "character in action." It's potential for serious or funny dramatic metaphors to make the point of the commercial is generally highly underutilized. It's an area that's always ready to support award-winning spots.

Appropriate Uses of Level One

Level one – a voiceover announcer over marginally related visuals – can be appropriate when the visual excitement is the core of the selling proposition, as in a vacation destination. In fact, anytime we have a dramatic core visual and few or no words are called for, this form can work with great effect. For example, there's a famous award-winning commercial for "Keep America Beautiful" that ran way back in the last century that showed various scenes of pollution and then introduced a symbol from an idyllic America, before such ravages had blighted it – an Indian paddling his canoe though the awfulness, while the camera provides a close-up of his face with a tear flowing down his cheek. Sometimes, silence is golden.

The level is also the occasion of one of the most unskillful approaches to the medium: actors apparently having a conversation, while all we see are their lips moving, as the announcer explains what these silenced actors are supposed to be helping him or her explain. When I see such a commercial, I wonder if the creators ever attended a play or saw a movie.

Appropriate Uses of Level Two

Some of the most effective commercials have been created with level two – a voiceover with a core on-camera demonstration. One value this form enables is for the announcer to adopt the pose of being unusually intelligent, as he comments on whatever is unfolding visually; in fact, he can almost play God with the visual scene occurring within his all-seeing purview, as in a spot that compares two brands.

The technique often leads to commercials that win awards, partly, no doubt, because it enables the ad people who are voting to feel intelligent.

The technique also has a basic use in presenting reason-to-believe demos in the middle of commercials. What makes the moment electrifying is just the right deft visual; for example, a feather dropping in slow motion while an announcer talks about something downy soft. This visual was, in fact, used for an award-winning commercial way back when, too. Occasionally, the visual may consist only of a title or a "crawl" of important-looking type that selects from or replicates what the voice-over is saying.

Today, we often see this technique in video sales letters, or VSL's, done with Camtasia or in PowerPoint. The words appear on the screen as the voiceover announcer reads them.

Appropriate Uses of Level Three

The third level of emphasis, an announcer or other actor speaking directly to the camera, works especially well in presenting brand news of such consequence that a simple production is all that is required. This level of emphasis is also the usual form of a testimonial. When the advertiser pays for a star to appear, there is a logical justification for featuring him or her. Getting close also enhances the person-to-person potential of the form. Visual interest and credibility can be enhanced by placing the announcer or the testifiers, famous or not, in interesting backgrounds, appropriate to the subject of the spot or to their lives. The tone is often sincere but it can also be amusing, as in the well-known classic commercial where the on-camera madam screeches, "Where's the beef?"

Sometimes this level is staged with the person appearing to speak off to the side a bit. The denial of the camera's presence seems false and annoying, especially since the spot is usually intended to be very personal, which includes, at its most credible, eye-to-eye contact.

Appropriate Uses of Level Four

The fourth level of interest is often used for show-and-tell comparisons. The announcer talks to you, head on, while he compares two products or a variety of them. Such a staging can be very persuasive. It can also include another actor or actors who reinforce the message. Yet, done with a heavy hand, the form can become what we sometimes refer to as "logic-ing them to death."

Appropriate Uses of Level Five

From *The Bible* and Plato's *Dialogues* down to your favorite sit-com or action-adventure flick, the most powerful communications vehicle is character in action. Why? We're all people, our favorite subject is people, and our usual way of experiencing life is through our own character in action, with or without the interaction with others. Unfortunately, this form can conjure up visions of "laundry room" commercials, such as the ones that lend their dullness to daytime television. We all know the usual example. One woman convinces another one that her detergent gets clothes whiter.

Yet every film, play, novel or other work of fiction is based on this form. While it's used well from time to time in advertising, its resources have hardly been plumbed. Many of the humorous Dr Pepper commercials I wrote were based on it. They grew out of spoofing old movies, along with well-known scenes from plays and operas, and playing them for real. I recommend that you use the form when it's appropriate. There's always room to pop a demo in the middle. Yet when the message is complex, a more straightforward presentation is logistically more manageable.

The basic guide is to fit the form to the message, not the message to the form. As state-of-the-art SEO specialists say today, content should come before design. Thankfully, the days of the wireframe first, which straitjackets the copywriter, seem to be finally fading into the past.

14. Capture Specific Visual Excitement

It's one thing to put someone or something on camera and entirely different to capture the specific visual excitement or action, or we might say the explicit benefit. Knowing the difference can make all the difference.

For example, if a guy wears a cologne or a girl a perfume, what does the guy or girl really want the effect to be? The action can portray romance, with soft shots and soaring string music, but at some point the scent-to-be-sold ought to propel them to dramatize the hoped-for benefit. They should be irresistibly drawn into each other's arms and the camera might move in for a big close-up of the guy or girl kissing the person who used the product right where we saw the scent being applied.

Since the communication to children is primarily visual, this principle is especially relevant in toy advertising. Children, especially younger ones, see something and decide they want it much more readily than they can be convinced by a verbal argument.

Staying with kids for the moment, if the product is, for instance, a racing set, you may think, at least when first considering the matter, that the action consists of the cars going around the track and in and out of the loops. Wrong. The real action is the appearance of speed.

I learned this lesson the hard way. An art director and I once did a commercial for a racing set that followed all the guidelines of The National Association of Broadcasters for children's advertising. It opened with a wide establishing shot and did not portray any kind of exaggeration. Another advertiser was not so inclined. The company elected to buy regional advertising widely and thereby skip the requirements of the NAB. The spot exploded onto the screen, packed with blurred close-ups of what appeared to be cars flashing by at incredible speeds, accompanied by high-powered music and an excited voiceover. Guess which racing track kids began to race to the stores for with their parents? The product grabbed such a big share of the market it almost put our racing track and the other entries in the category out of business.

Meanwhile, back at the agency, no one could believe the commercial had gotten past the network watchdogs. As soon as possible, our injured client, along with representatives of one of the largest toy makers, took the offending advertiser to court. They succeeded in getting the commercial taken off the air, but there was no way to repair the damage. Kids just couldn't be talked out of the images of those speeding cars. It's one of the few incidents of blatantly misleading advertising I've seen.

It's somewhat of a consolation to be able to use the experience to communicate the importance of capturing the right visual action.

15. How to Work with Tension

In a commercial, just as in any other form that attempts to involve people in its wholeness, interest depends on establishing and then retaining tension from the opening to the resolution. In advertising, maintaining the tension is easier than it is in larger forms, because there is no need to develop the idea extensively. The verbal and visual development required to cover the basic content can fill up the time. And the impetus of a dramatic beginning, with the addition of the imperative content, can carry a commercial from the start to the finish excitingly.

Yet we can create commercials more effectively when we know how to work with tension. The line of tension must be based on a wholeness that develops and only completes at the end. It must begin with the first word and visual, which can cast a long line, intimating material that must come to complete what it sets up. Then it must continue through every verbal revelation and visual surprise, through the middle, or proof, if there is one, and relax only at the final moment of the reassuringly satisfying conclusion. If the tension relaxes at any point along the way, that is, if the story of the commercial wanders off track, breaks up, or the story appears to have been told entirely before the spot is over, a loosening or loss of tension will occur. The wholeness, or unity, of the spot will be lost, so the impact will decrease, and the viewer's attention will likely wander.

We see the merits of tension in films. As a simplistic example, will the gangster be caught by the hero or will he escape? Although we know the inevitable answer, we never learn for certain until the story reaches its climactic moment, or denouement. We are interested, not so much in the "what" of the ending, but the "how."

I used to tell my copy trainees that all advertising is involuntary watching and reading. So you don't want to feed it to viewers or readers like macaroni, so they can stop eating whenever they want to. You want to feed it to them like a strand of spaghetti. Once they get the tip into their mouths, you must continue to feed it to them as a unit. Then they're likely to eat the whole thing.

16. The Problem-Solution

The usual form for presenting an advertising argument is called the "problem-solution." Advertising refers to the form in a proprietary way, but it is, in fact, the form of every story.

The message begins with the problem; in our frequent example, with a headache. Then a solution is introduced: relief in the form of the product.

As pointed out earlier, there is an exception. When our job is to introduce compelling news, such as an important improvement in an existing product or a new product with a breathlessly exciting benefit, we may elect to announce the solution first, as a breakthrough. Then we transition to the problem and return to more about the amazing new solution, including the proof of the claim. The merit of this reverse is that it relieves you from subordinating the unique solution to a more usual problem.

I told you we would cover original material. I assume the chapter on the usual topic of television commercials has demonstrated what I mean.

CHAPTER 6

RADIO COMMERCIALS AND JINGLES

Radio Commercials

When a radio commercial invites your participation, what's going on? The argument or situation may be interesting just as a voice or voices. But many creative radio commercials, like many good lyrics, are made up of more than just sound. The basic secret is, the writing and sound effects transform the medium into sound with mental pictures. You not only hear the spot; you also see it. In fact, we may say that radio is a special instance of what creative writing classes advise students to do: "Show, don't tell."

When a radio spot has been created to be seen, instead of just heard, a very effective event occurs: the listener recreates the commercial in his or her mind visually. It no longer unfolds as something outside the listener, but in the ideal place the advertiser would like to get the message.

The second secret of effective radio advertising recognizes that the medium is auditory. As a result, an unusual and hopefully tasteful statement or sound effect at the start of the commercial can attract attention.

Of course, a dramatic beginning applies to all works that intend to engage an audience.

A jingle, when appropriate, can also help make a radio or TV spot involving, as well as memorable. It can communicate the main point while it provides a unique sound. The music track can also help unify the spot.

Our final secret is the little-recognized advantage that radio is the only medium in which the use of the stars is usually free. The stars are the personalities who work at the station. Disc jockeys and other announcers are, after all, the people the audience tunes in to hear. So the audience is more likely to pay attention to what they say and consider any other announcer you can hire a distraction. Best of all, radio stations often offer the services of their personalities to advertisers free or for a modest fee. The stars will either read the spot on the air, variously enhancing it or detracting from it with their asides, or they'll prerecord it. Sometimes, the station will also agree to mix the announcer's voice with a music track that you supply. The latter offering is especially helpful when quick or regular changes in the spot are required, for instance, to include weekly specials at a retail store. All you have to do is fax the station a revised script.

Of course, if you prefer absolute control over what is said, it's better to prerecord the spot.

Jingles

The basic secret of writing a successful jingle is to realize how audiences have been conditioned to listen to songs. The lyrics often dwell primarily on the refrain or "hook," while the development is often less enthralling and, in contemporary songs, generally undistinguished. So a great many people are conditioned to hear pretty much only the refrain. I call this condition being lyric deaf. Yet dwelling primarily on the "hook" is as ancient as song itself and occurs in all styles of music, from pre-Bach through opera to rock.

Since our job is to reach as many people as possible, clearly and persuasively, it's best to sing only the slogan and let an announcer or another actor speak the rest, perhaps with the instrumental music continuing under him or her. The commercial will score better, especially in terms of how many details the audience recalls.

The slogan can be repeated in whole or in part, just as refrains are sung repeatedly with interesting variations. The compositional term for singing or playing only parts of an idea as part of the development is called fragmentation.

Occasionally, a slogan can be effectively combined with one rhyming line or a brief couplet. At most, you might create a brief quatrain. Any further development leads to low recall of any details that are sung.

Since most slogans are short, they can usually be set to music and sung, even when not originally intended to be.

If you're writing a slogan that you intend to be sung, it's helpful to know a few of the basics of lyric writing.

The best way to get the words to line up into a singable slogan is to sing them yourself or imagine them being sung. Most songs are composed this way and then written down. The usual composer's advice is to "find the truth in the words."

The result should obviously have a poetic cadence to it, a recognizable regularity and grace of unaccented and accented syllables. Write the lines with naturally flowing metrics, as if they were living creatures, instead of with heavily accented metrics that tick along like a rattling skeleton.

The slogan will be more singable if the final syllable ends with a vowel or, at least, a soft consonant (such as *l, m, or n*). Skillful singers can make a line that ends with hard consonant (like *k* or *t*) sound mellifluous by extending the vowel that comes right before it and then just using the final consonant as a momentary bridge to the next line or to the end. However, a final *r* encourages a roar, an *s* or sibilant a hiss, and a *p* a pop.

The mellifluous singers know to emphasize the vowels and use the consonants pretty much as brief bridges between them. Yet consonants are critical for understanding. The best singers know to lean on and pronounce the vowels while they also enunciate the consonants.

It's best not to end-stop every line, that is, to end it with a period. Wrap the lines naturally. Try to "pearl" the stanza into a smooth and expressive whole. The lines can be of uneven length, and the rhymes can be very tight or light. As always, it's better to be freely creative before you're corrective.

If you're stuck with a slogan that has a verbal clinker or two in it, relax. You can only do what you can do. And the short form will usually come to your rescue. Most jingle pros can set just about anything to music and do.

CHAPTER 7

PRINT ADVERTISING

What makes a print advertisement successful? Of course, it must say the right thing in the right way. But saying it in the right way means the ad must have impact.

How do we achieve impact in print? The communication of important news, a catchy headline, or a dramatic visual will achieve it.

But how can we maximize impact and do it consistently? Here is a little-understood secret.

The Setup and Release

A powerful print ad that has a headline and a visual derives its power from a setup and a release. The form, whether the subject is serious or humorous, is actually the same one that makes a joke work. The headline sets up the visual or the visual sets up the headline. Neither is complete in itself. Readers see one and then the other. Then they put the two elements together. When they do, the thought completes itself in their minds. The completion is the momentary event that maximizes the impact.

When a headline is complete in itself, the visual adds nothing new, and vice versa. One merely repeats or illustrates the other. Since there is not a setup and release, there is less impact, regardless of the content, unless, of course, the content is an astounding piece of news in itself. These are the workable principles of gaining attention, which is an effect, and you can't work with effects. You must work with causes. In fact, the entire usual AIDA principle – attention, interested, desire, action – is based on asking for effects. No wonder new copywriters struggle to implement the components.

Maintaining Interest

Once we achieve impact, how do we maintain interest? It's another effect. So we must ask, what is the cause or what are the causes?

Print advertising is like a good story. It works best when tension is maintained from start to finish. The story begins with the headline and visual, which achieve impact, or gain attention, and launch the tension by provoking unanswered questions. The story is told so the questions are answered in order of importance and the last one is only answered toward the end. This unfolding is the basic way we maintain interest.

To help unify the content, the headline should be seen as the topic sentence of a paragraph that includes, in its development, all of the other elements. The parts of the story, with or without subheads, should all be organized to accomplish specific goals, which should only be completed by the final word.

Let me provide an example of a how an advertisement achieves impact through a setup and release. Take a classic print ad for Mobil, created in the pre-Omnicom days at Doyle Dane Bernbach. The campaign was based on the relatively altruistic theme, "We want you to live."

One of the art directors who worked on it at Doyle Dane was Lenny Sirowitz, a frequent creative teammate of mine when I was a senior vice president and creative management supervisor at the agency he founded with another creative star out of Doyle Dane, the copywriter, Ron Rosenfeld. Their agency has gone the way of many former hot shops, but the year Len and Ron hired me away from Young & Rubicam with many attractive inducements, it had been named The Agency of the Year by *Advertising Age*.

I'm not sure the Mobil campaign sold any gasoline. It has the same weakness of much advertising that heralded and then undermined the creative revolution: it was "creative" without using the unique power of creative advertising to magnify a salable attribute of the product and sell it better than hard-sell advertising. But sales effectiveness is not the subject before us.

The ad we'll look at, which was one of the most impactful ones in the campaign, featured the headline "Fresh-killed chicken." Seen alone, what could it mean? Yet one look at the visual and the meaning became complete. The photograph depicted a teenager, lying on the highway, covered with a white sheet. If the reader had seen the visual first, the meaning would have been incomplete, too, until he or she read the headline.

When we put the two elements together, we realize that the teenager had been killed in a car accident while playing "chicken," a term, in case you don't know, that describes two drivers who head their cars toward each other, and the first one who veers away is called a chicken.

The impact is achieved from a setup and release, or, to put it another way, out of a dramatic question prompted by one element and an answer provided by the addition of the other one.

All-Type Advertisements

What about an advertisement that consists of only type? It can achieve its impact through the content and style of the language, as well as from the layout. What about the infrequent ad that is primarily made up of a visual, with only a wisp of copy? It achieves impact primarily through the content and style of the main photograph or illustration and the layout.

One frequently employed technique to add impact to an all-type ad is to print the headline in reverse, that is, as white type against a black background; the body copy can be in reverse type, too, but it's harder to read, so the more effective way to present it is to make the part of the ad that contains the copy regular black type against a light background, especially when the copy is long.

Headlines should have copy drive

When you read a headline, it should have copy drive; that is, it should provoke questions or present opportunities that drive the reader to want to know more.

How do we create headlines that have copy drive? Basically, we want to present news in the headline of maximum self-interest to the target market in a compact, compelling way. It must intimate more relevant information, rewards, and, if witty, amusement to come. In a phrase, a headline with copy drive features concentrated news of urgent self-interest to the consumer. David Ogilvy's boast applies: that he could write a headline and fill an entire newspaper page with copy, and you would read every word. The headline, as you remember, was, "This ad is about you."

The content of a headline is usually, or should be, simple enough to allow for flexible expression, so we can poise it to achieve copy drive. A visual that presents self-interest for the reader and provokes questions or promises rewards and/or amusement can also achieve copy drive.

Achieving Interest Despite Cumbersome Headline Content

What do we do when the content we must communicate in the headline is cumbersome? The problem usually occurs when we are obliged to make a straightforward announcement. First, state the content or make the announcement as directly as possible. This tactic achieves the primary goal of the ad. Now, think of a brief comment you can make on it – a word, a phrase, or even a short sentence. Our goal is to intensify the self-interest with wit or another tone. Think of adding sugar to the medicine.

Let's say we're introducing a new car that has a brand name with a reputation for reliability. We'll invent the model. Here's the headline: "Introducing the Lexus LS 1000. It's really not that different from the LS 999."

We've announced the new model, which was our primary job. Then we've made an unexpected and interesting comment on it. The reader is used to a lot of hype about how different a new car is. We've said the opposite. The unusual statement provokes curiosity. Now, having invited the reader to continue, we admit that it does have some great new features and enumerate them. But then we might say something like, "Amazingly different? Other carmakers might say so. But why would we make amazing improvements in a car that's always been amazingly well engineered?"

Principles of Writing Body Copy

When we write body copy, we want to answer questions and present opportunities in descending order of importance. We don't save the big news until the end, because some readers won't get there, and we want to communicate the most important information to as many readers as possible.

As you write the copy, remember to bind all of the elements together as a whole. Keep it appropriately inviting by using all of the germane devices without overdoing them; for instance, subheads, short sentences, point-counterpoint words and phrases, even single words as entire para-graphs. The structure makes long copy easy to read; in fact, the goal is to make it seem shorter than it might be.

If you develop it with the attributes and benefits of the product or service in terms of the target market, you'll create desire.

Remember to include a call to action at or near the end to tell the reader exactly what you'd like him or her to do.

An inviting way to open the copy and to close it is with an appropriate play on the idea in the headline. At the beginning, the reference serves as a transition from the headline to the copy. At the end, it serves as a uni-fying and reinforcing recapitulation of the main content of the headline.

CHAPTER 8

SHORT SPOTS, SMALL-SPACE ADVERTISEMENTS AND LABELS

Here's an appropriately brief chapter on especially small forms of advertising.

All advertising – broadcast, print, or digital – begins, as we noted earlier, as just the right poster: One perfectly appropriate line that expresses the main benefit and one visual that helps magnify the main meaning. This is the trunk of the tree; everything else in the campaign is a branch, a leaf, a bud, or a seed. You might also consider the poster the whole note of a note tree, which descends to half notes, quarter notes, eighth notes, sixteenth notes, etc.

Smallness actually has some benefits. It helps us concentrate our thinking. We know we must attract attention, so smallness may invite us to be more outrageous than we can usually justify. We can appear in media we might not otherwise be able to afford. We can also appear with more frequency.

To attract attention, we must make a provocative statement verbally and/or visually. Daring content or wit can help.

To achieve an effect, we must make one point well. So we concentrate the message by selecting only the words and pictures that most effectively communicate the core selling proposition.

We must also utilize all the applicable techniques for larger formats. For instance, no matter how short the form, it should have a beginning, a middle, and an end, even a 10-second spot or a 1-column-inch ad.

Given a choice, we don't usually want to skimp on production. In fact, if we can, we'll be lavish. Then the piece will look great, like a small gem. Such an appearance will help attract attention and give the impression of quality.

The Gray Poupon Success

Let me share a successful example from my own work. When I was a creative consultant to one of the Interpublic agencies, I was asked to create a print campaign for Gray Poupon mustard. This was early in the mass-marketing of the brand. The client wanted full-page magazine ads and, for budgetary reasons, the ads would have to be black and white, instead of color.

The art director who was assigned to work with me and I began to ideate. We wanted to do something extraordinary and knew the brand had to exude taste appeal and quality. I wrote four headlines which I felt highlighted, or magnified, the unique selling proposition of the brand, which was, as you probably know by now, that it contains white wine. One of the headlines I wrote is "Every year is a good year." My art director provided a visual of a pair of hands, holding the bottle as if it were a fine bottle of wine. White cuffs and black sleeves indicated that it was being presented by a sommelier in a tuxedo. Another headline was "Maybe we should seal our mustard with a cork." The visual was the bottle of mustard, amid appetizing cheeses and deli meats, with a wood-handled corkscrew lying beside it. The other two ads also presented the mustard as if it were a gourmet's delight. The agency and the client loved the work.

Now to our point. We suggested that, instead of full-page black-and-white ads, the campaign be produced as small but gorgeous color ads. The client agreed. The ads would be only 1/6 of a page but we produced them with values that would usually be lavished only on a full-page color food ad. The campaign successfully launched the product as a well-known national brand, so successfully that lately it has been presented in preposterous, price-justifying TV commercials that might contain, not only one, but two Rolls-Royces.

When confronted with an assignment to create a small form, you might remember Leopold Mozart's advice to Wolfgang, who was apparently listening. He advised his precocious son to do something simple but to do it beautifully.

The Secret of a Good Label

Let's conclude this chapter with a very small venue: the label. It has a variety of functions, but an important one is that it can be a poster that allows you to present the name and the claim at the point-of-purchase – and to do it without paying for media. The clear communication of the brand promise in the label is not only helpful when the shopper sees the product on her own but when cross-promotions with related products send new consumers to look it over.

This principle was reinforced for me when I was walking through a supermarket with the chairman of a beverage company. He had retained me to create advertising for the brand. As we stood before the shelf with his product on display, he pointed to them, and said, "I think of every label as a free ad."

CHAPTER 9

MORE ABOUT HOW TO BEGIN, DEVELOP, AND CONCLUDE COMMERCIALS AND PRINT ADS

I'd like to add some details about these subject, which will, inevitability, include a bit of repetition.

How to Begin Commercials

In a word, dramatically. You must first gain attention, a goal that is relatively easy to achieve. If there's a challenge, it's to gain attention tastefully. Then the advertising will not only be remembered. It will be remembered fondly.

Specifically, we want to make sure that something arresting is right at the start of a commercial or in the headline and/or visual of a print ad. The dramatic event will usually be made up of words and pictures working together, but one aspect will generally be more dominant. Otherwise, they will compete with each other, instead of working synergistically.

A dramatic beginning also has a secondary function that many people are not aware of. It applies to commercials, print ads, and even website homepages. It must select the target audience. This necessity alerts us to the need to achieve the arresting beginning through content that is immediately relevant to the audience.

In a commercial, it's best to come in high, instead of at a low level of energy, and build from there. The high-energy start helps gain attention, but, more importantly, the form is too short to begin at a low-level and build from there gracefully. Commercials that only arrive at a larger event or a clever twist at the end usually don't do as well; not enough people are captivated at the start and even fewer are attentive by the time the major event or twist arrives. This guideline does not eliminate the possibility that a commercial that achieves its dramatic effect through an especially low-level of energy cannot arrest attention and make a point.

If the commercial starts off with only a voiceover announcement, without a major visual, the art director may choose to reinforce the words with a "title" of some or all of the words in white type against a black background.

How to Begin Print Ads

A print ad requires a headline that contains important news, or the appearance of it, presented in the clearest and most inviting way for the target audience. It also requires a dramatic, relevant visual or visuals.

A compact headline or visual that achieves its impact through the power of its content can command attention. A clever headline or visual can invite it. Either or both can make the ad stand out, amid the usual commonplaces of media content. The two ingredients should be presented with a balance that best communicates the selling proposition.

The ad will also stand out and look more appealing if it has white space. The type should be simple, appropriate, and direct. The visuals should be focused.

Recent advertising has, with a new hipness, made more use of odd type and visual effects. These stylizations have been enabled by the capabilities of digital design. It's fine to have fun. But the overall goal must be to capture the attention of the target audience with, we trust, good taste.

How to Develop The Story

Once you've got people's attention, it's time to tell the story of the product or service. We must do it in a way that maintains the interest of the audience. The basic rule is to keep the news that's important to the consumer coming in a concentrated, winning way.

It's time to reveal more of and/or prove your claim. The words, strong or lithe as they may be, have a basic job to do. A deftly appropriate visual or visuals that help reveal or prove the claim or claims can be invaluable.

It may, or may not, be appropriate to include a comparison to the competition.

How to Develop Commercials

Let's begin with how to get people to stay tuned to a commercial.

We assume an arresting beginning, often compelled by the demand of many clients that the commercials they choose to invest in will have achieved a high recall score in a test with consumers, even if a visual stunt was required.

But how can you get the consumer to stay tuned for the entire commercial, instead of surfing away?

The first technique is, as mentioned above, to keep providing news, packed with self-interest for the consumer, with the words and pictures working in complimentary ways.

The second is to unify the commercial into one compact, dramatic event. If there is ever a break in the perceived and arresting unity, it creates the occasion for the generally involuntary viewer to lose interest.

A dramatic proof, unfolding in an involving way, will make a commercial score higher and succeed better.

The script, with or without dialogue, should be shaped as one tight paragraph, with a compelling and inviting topic sentence, at or near the beginning; a coherent development of the argument in the topic sentence, in the most effective order and with the most logical emphasis and subordination; and then a concluding sentence that reinforces, in a memorable way, the main selling proposition, usually as presented in the topic sentence, with or without a call to action and/or an offer. It's also smart to include an emotional reward at the end for viewers who have stayed with you, usually as an entertaining quip or visual event; then, when they see the spot again or another spot for the same product, they have an additional incentive to stay tuned again.

The visuals should have a similar form; that is, they should begin with an arresting visual and proceed in a coherent, impactful form. In fact, the first image can be seen as the "topic visual," or the one that sets up the commercial; then come the visuals that will develop the "paragraph," in their most logical order and with their most fitting emphasis and subordination; finally comes the visual that will reinforce or clinch the argument. Aim for the efficient use of highly communicative visuals. Naturally, any supers or titles should be placed for maximum efficacy while remaining visually inviting.

Aim for exactly the right production values, which are usually the highest the client can afford but not always. For instance, if we're selling a quality product, quality production is essential. On the other hand, if we're selling a bargain item, quality production may contradict the message.

The same essential principles apply to radio commercials. The words themselves, verbal pictures, and special auditory effects can all work together to retain the listener from arresting start though the revelatory development to the persuasive wrap-up.

How to Develop Print Ads

In a print ad, interest is maintained in much the same way – by continuing to unfold the news in a way that is steadily interesting for the appropriate consumer. The proof is often presented as a visual insert or inserts with a caption or captions.

If an advertisement looks interesting, a great many people will pause to note the headline. The challenge is, of course, to get them to read the copy.

The headline must have what I've called copy drive. It must capture the interest of consumers in a way that makes them want to know more.

How? The headline must contain news that, at least, appears to be of great consequence to readers; specifically, it must communicate compelling self-interest. And it must forthrightly state or arrestingly imply that there is more the readers must know for their own benefit. Technically, it provokes a dramatic question or questions that the consumer wants the answer or answers to.

Once consumers start to read the copy, how do we get them to keep on reading? There is a basic form for the body copy that seems to work best.

The first sentence or short paragraph does two things. It provides an inviting and involving bridge from the headline to the copy by repeating or restating with variation the news in the headline while it provides the promise of exciting news to come. It might also cast a unifying line through the rest of the copy by stating something that applies to the entire content, such as, "There are three important things you should know."

The next sentence, or short paragraph, launches the middle of the copy and elaborates on the news in the headline by presenting the most important thing that must be communicated in detail. This is usually the entire or partial answer to the primary dramatic question provoked by the headline.

The second task of the middle part of the copy is to present the next most important fact or answer the primary dramatic question in more detail or answer the next most compelling question. And so on.

Along with or after the claims, the proofs, or support points, should be presented. These proofs can also be presented as each claim is introduced. You might experiment with trying to make a claim in a way that implies or contains the proof. The tactic makes the claim self-evidently true.

Any details that must be included are added as we approach the end.

At the end, it's time to reinforce the main message of the advertisement, often by referring back to the headline in an insightful or witty way that also reinforces the selling proposition. When this recapitulation of the headline is done in a winning way, the copy ends with a neat button that brings it to a satisfying close.

The end often gains its feeling of satisfaction as the result of providing the reader with an intellectual or emotional reward for having stayed with the copy. For instance, a satisfying conclusion might state or imply how much smarter the readers are or how much better they are able to deal with the aspect of life the ad pertains to.

It's usually better to include the call to action and/or offer or offers right before the button. So you leave the consumer with a generous sentiment, instead of one that expresses your own self-interest.

Such an intellectually or emotionally winning end can be done with the affirmation of sincere fellow feeling or a flash of good-natured wit, whatever is appropriate to the overall tone of the ad.

When long copy is required, the basic technique is to make it seem, as much as possible, like short copy. The goal is achieved as follows:

Break the copy up into short paragraphs.

Use crisp, reader-involving subheads that tell the main aspects of the story.

Utilize the forms of linguistic dexterity that are characteristic of good advertising copy, which we'll discuss in a later section. For now we'll mention that you ought to use short sentences and, when appropriate, the anathema of English teachers, the sentence fragment. The brevity of the parts helps move the reader along with transparent clarity and as little mental effort as possible.

Tie the paragraphs, including the subheads, the sentences, fragments, and words together in surprising and witty ways that also help make the points. The parallels and contrasts, usually among the phrases, can be inviting and provide reinforcement.

The proximate repetition of the same word, particularly when the meaning changes, is also an often-used technique.

If you would like to know more about the resources available for verbal enchantment, although in a more formal sense, and see plenty of examples, I suggest you look into the classic book *English Prose Style* by Herbert Read.

How to Conclude Effectively

At the end of a commercial or print ad, the goal is to seal the deal. We must tell or ask, as well as show, the consumer exactly what you want him or her to do. It's time for a single-minded call to action, that is, to ask for the sale.

Yet we must still maintain interest. In fact, we want to end in a way that is satisfying for the consumer. Despite the very specific goal of closing the sale, you can still make room to be seriously compelling or wittily charming.

The most usual approach is to tie together the end with the beginning in a literal reinforcement or with a bright variation of it. Also, aim for a memorable visual that recapitulates the problem, reinforces the solution, or demonstrates the action of the sale.

When any form begins to repeat, the recurrence can signal a movement toward the conclusion. Experience tells us that the tide comes in, the tide goes out, and when the tide comes in again, we've seen a complete event. This cycle is also a sound reason to avoid repeats early in the telling of the story.

The appropriate completion leads to a feeling of satisfaction.

Now, let's move on to digital media.

PART 3

How to Write Great Copy for Digital Media

CHAPERT 10

INTRODUCTION

The internet changed my copywriting career. I've basically gone from primarily writing TV and radio commercials to primarily writing websites and Google Ads.

I was fortunate to get into digital media very early. I met Steve Case when he was a product manager at Pizza Hut. I had been retained by the vice president of advertising to create new pizzas. As you know, Steve was the founder of AOL.

He left from a job neither the VP nor I understood. A few months later he called me and said he needed advertising for the company he had joined and asked me to come to Vienna, VA, to discuss it with him.

We had lunch, and he told me he had joined a company called Gameline. It delivered video games over the phone line, so children could play them for a fee and parents didn't have to buy them, only to see their child tire of them.

I created all the advertising he needed: a TV spot, print advertising, window banners, and a brochure. During the process, I may have become the first person to write the words "get online." The slogan I developed was, "Get online with Gameline."

The campaign was successful, and two or three years later, Steve renamed the company Quantum. A couple of years after that, he renamed it American Online.

How the Internet Has Evolved and Changed Our Lives

Since its inception, the internet has evolved from a medium based primarily on technological wizardry to one based primarily on advertising wizardry. For instance, while the wonders of Google Search and social media like Facebook are based on computing power, the companies make the majority of their revenue as advertising mediums.

Of course, the internet has changed our lives through vastly improved communication. It has also empowered the individual, including small businesses. Among the small businesses we find an unprecedented number of freelance copywriters and designers, who find their work by freelancing at agencies, running search advertising to attract clients, or creating a profile at one of the main freelance sites, like Upwork, and pitching the jobs that are posted there by prospective clients.

Today, digital copywriters are often kept busy by writing websites and landing pages. A website has become the centerpiece of contemporary marketing, and landing pages attempt to feature and sell one product or service. Digital advertising is often used to drive traffic to landing pages.

CHAPTER 11

WEBSITES AND LANDING PAGES

When a copywriter begins to work on a website, he must consider that the average visit to a website these days is about seven seconds. So the writer knows that most people who arrive at the site will make the decision about whether or not to remain based on what they see "above the fold," or on the screen without scrolling or clicking anywhere. What is that space?

Simple stated, it can be seen as a slightly more robust poster. When we see it this way, we can proceed as we always should with a campaign in any medium – by getting the poster right first. It must have a main verbal idea and a main visual idea that select the target audience and communicate a compelling brand promise to it. Unlike a billboard, it can also contain a sentence or, more often, a few sentences of copy to relate to the audience, show we understand their pain points, and promise that they've arrived at the solution to them. Then it can be following by a list of bullet points that are the core proofs of the promise in the headline.

A few sites, and landing pages in particular, will also place its first call to action, or CTA, so it appears above the fold. A landing page is likely to contain a prominent response form.

There are basically two types of websites: one used to sell, called a transactional or e-commerce website, and one used to communicate content, known as an informational website.

If you're in a digital agency, you'll be given the marketing strategy for the website. Your job will be to express the strategy, or core brand promise, in the headline and write the copy to prove it.

The designer, as well as other members of the team, will work on the structure of the wireframe, or the sections into which each of the pages are divided.

Today, most SEO people recommend content before form, or the wireframes. Sometimes I'm still given a wireframe and write to it, but I feel it straitjackets my creativity. It seems more logical to me to develop the content optimally and then allow the designer to lay it out optimally.

The copy and design may result in a short homepage or a contemporary flat homepage, which enables the visitor to scroll down and get most of the company's core pitch, along with a testimonial or two at the end and social icons.

How to Proceed

You'll want to study the strategic brief or, if you have one, the creative brief to understand what you should be saying and to whom.

You'll also want to review what the competitor websites look like. You can refer to the list of competitors you've been provided with in the brief or you can enter a relevant core keyword or so in Google search and read the websites of the major competitors.

If you've also been provided with the keywords that are most relevant to the content of the website, you'll refer to them. If not, you'll go to a keyword tool, such as the Google Keyword Tool, enter a core keyword or more, and then click to get ideas about what the other keywords in the category are, their relative search volumes, and the average cost per click.

When you begin, the first thing we need to do is develop the ideal expression of the core brand promise. To do this, I suggest you use an adaptation of my Creative Exploratory. Take the Creative Brief and study it. Then begin to ideate in market-ready slogans, looking at the product from all the different angles you can, with the content of the Creative

Brief as a reference point. Since it will originally be the only content or main content of the headline, remember that the content of the brand promise will also select the audience. Obviously, it should be written to select the target market.

Once you see the likely possibilities and hit on the brand promise, expressed in the way that seems just right and bright, you might do as I do: arrange the work into a recommended brand promise, other favorites, and just more brand promises you came up with that you still think have value.

If you're in an agency, share your recommendation and maybe a few options with your designer, supervisor and account team. Once the team agrees on the slogan, use it as the headline. If you think the headline should express a bit more content, you can enlarge on the slogan when it appears as a headline, which is where it should be in the introductory period of the brand promise/brand position. It can also appear with the logo, but once is generally enough on a homepage. It can appear with the logo on the other pages to help unify the site. Later, when other content is required for the homepage headline, it can simply appear there with the logo.

Now your job is to write the copy to prove the brand promise. The best form, as summarized in the introduction, is usually a short introductory paragraph that identifies with the audience, often by noting a problem or two that the audience has, today often called a pain point. The first sentence is often expressed as a sentence, such as, "Do you have belly fat you just can't lose?" You might even ask up to three questions. Then you reassure the visitor that your product provides the answer he or she is looking for and then list the key support points or poofs as bullet points.

It's good to write this part of the copy so the viewer will see the promise and the core proof immediately on arriving at the website.

You follow this core content with the main subdivisions of the content, expressed as short subheads with a sentence or a few to develop each section. In flat homepage designs, the visitor can simply scroll down to read it.

Once you've proven you're promise, it's time to provide the call to action, or CTA. We often accompany it with an incentive offer or two, and sometimes more of them, to increase the conversion rate.

In hard-sell website pages, I often say you know it's going to convert when the incentives appear to be such a bargain that the viewer must be wondering how the company can possibly be making money.

These days, I usually prefer the format of the flat homepage, where the visitor can scroll down or click on the main navigation and be taken to the section of the page where the content is located.

A Website Is a Brand Unit, Not Separate Pages

While most people think a website is made up of separate pages, it's actually the unified presentation of the brand promise, divided appropriately into pages. To achieve the unity, theme each page to the brand promise. For example, the About page can talk about how the company is dedicated to achieving the brand promise.

As you theme the different pages to the promise, you'll be repeating and varying it, which will reinforce it. By proceeding in this way, you'll unify the copy of the entire website. The wholeness with which you involve the visitor and, of course, the compelling content are what give the site the proverbial accolade of being "sticky."

Website Slides

Instead of static bullet points, the core brand promise and the main support points can be presented on the homepage in slides, which begin to change shortly after the visitor arrives. I hesitate to use more than 5 of them. I may also repeat the content in the slides, or at least the headlines, in the copy.

A video can be an effective ingredient on the homepage. If you wish to present one, I suggest it be relatively short. I also suggest you allow the visitor to decide to watch it, rather than starting it automatically, which can startle and annoy your more sensitive or persnickety visitors, who may be your most valuable prospects.

I discourage you from using popups, such as a chat option, before the visitor has had time to read the core brand message, main support point, and secondary support points.

Sometimes, it's good to put a CTA right after the initial proof of the promise, so you capture conversions from people who are already sold on the product or service. Of course, you'll repeat it at the end of the homepage copy.

Tone

The tone of all the copy should be personal, whether the site is for consumers or a business-to-business site. Even copy for professional services should speak to the visitor like a thoughtful, responsive, helpful person.

Visuals

The main visual should magnify the brand promise or illustrate the lifestyle of the prospect, while subsidiary visuals should illustrate the various points. Icons are often used to accent the bullet points and short copy that presents the detailed information.

Search Engine Optimization

The copywriter's job is to get the copy correct for on-page SEO, basically by using the core keywords in the H1, H2, and H3 headlines, as well as in the copy, while avoiding "keyword stuffing," and getting demerits from Google because the crawlers detect the overuse. The copywriter can leave the other aspects of SEO up to specialists, such as optimizing the internal links and growing quality external links.

As Google tells us again and again, the most important way to earn a high rank in organic search is to provide original quality content.

If your job is also to write the metadata, make sure your title for the homepage contains the URL. The name of each page can come first if you're using the format of the name of the page, a hyphen, and then a short description, which should use the appropriate keywords. If you're using the format of vertical lines dividing the title, you can put the primary benefit, product, or service first, the secondary benefit second, and the URL last. The same applies to the titles in the other pages but, instead of the URL, you use the name of the specific pages, such as the About page.

The meta description should elaborate on the content of each page with keyword-rich copy.

Remember that you currently get up to 70 characters for the title and 170 characters for the description. I try to keep it at a maximum of 60 and 160. Some split the difference at 65 and 165.

When the website shows up in Google organic search, the homepage title is usually the blue headline at the top of the listing and the homepage description is usually the content in black type. Obviously, it's much better if the entire title and description appear, instead of cutoff by ellipsis marks.

What about putting keywords in the metadata? We've been told for a few years now that Google no longer pays attention to keywords and more recently we've been told the same from Bing and Yahoo. The search engines prefer that their crawlers can divine the content. Yet if you, for example, go to nytimes.com, right click the page, and scroll down to the first big paragraph, you'll see it's all made up of keywords, and the keywords are changed daily to reflect the content and what people are searching for. Since the entire future of the paper depends on its digital success, it spends a great deal on SEO.

I just checked Alexa.com, and of this writing, nytimes.com is ranked 29 in the United States and 116 globally. So including keywords is obviously not hurting its rank in organic search. Maybe the lesson is that content that changes daily or frequently can still benefit from the use of keywords in the metadata, perhaps because such sites can't wait for the crawlers to make their weekly visit or so.

Since robots can't read pictures, remember to fill out the alt tags that describe the images, including the logo.

The Visual and Verbal High Ground

When you know what's in this book, you'll realize that many companies, even major advertisers, do not have optimal brand promises. The fault carries over to their websites. Since companies large and small have a more equal footing on the internet than they do in traditional media, you have an especially good opportunity to discover the visual-verbal high ground in the category; that is, the words and pictures that most appropriately define, and thereby intellectually own, the category.

Landing Pages

When we drive traffic to achieve a specific conversion, it's always best to send it to a landing page, which is a bit like a website homepage, but it has a singular focus. The usual intent is to sell a product or service. If we send the traffic to the homepage or even to a page within the site, the visitor simply has too many ways to be distracted.

A great landing page consists of the right, bright brand promise in the headline, usually a sentence or short paragraph to relate to the visitor, bullet points to prove the promise, and a prominent contact form for the visitor to take the action the page is intended to elicit. The response or contact form should ask for only what is necessary. It should be, in the jargon, a "low friction" form. The line at the top of the form should direct the visitor to "fill out the simple form." It's usually better to include a submit button at the top and bottom of the form.

Most effective landing pages include an incentive or two or more to increase the conversion rate.

Many also contain upsells as part of the "sales funnel." For example, the person clicks to buy what is offered and then is offered something more. He or she clicks on it and is then offered even more, etc. While an upsell or two are fine, the risk is that when we seek to sell too much, we may end up selling much less. Not all prospects have as much time or patience to consider what we're selling as we would like them to.

There should be a testimonial or two at the bottom of the copy to act as "social proof."

Visually, there is generally at least a main image to attract attention, present a problem/solution, or display a product.

The only escape route should be the conversion. There should not be a link to the main website or even clickable social icons. Once we attract a visitor, we want to direct his or her focus solely on the argument for the conversion and the response form that invites the conversion.

Checklist: Sixteen Steps to Writing Websites That Convert

1. Create a Focused Brand Promise

When a visitor arrives at the website, the first thing the copy must do is present a brand promise that selects the target market.

The headline should present the brand slogan, as developed or extended with other critical content.

To the extent you can present the optimal brand promise, you can connect with and interest the appropriate visitors.

The product or service can have a secondary or tertiary business promise, but they must be presented with the subordination that reflects their relative importance.

2. Write a Few Sentences to Relate to the Audience

The headline should be followed by a short paragraph that shows we understand the need or needs of the audience. The usual way to do it is to express their problem or problems, often as a question or questions, and then assure them that the product or service is the ideal solution.

3. Add Support Points as Bullet Points

Now, we present the support points for the brand promise, or the reasons to believe it. The most effective way to communicate them is a list of bullet points.

4. Include a Short Testimonial or Two

After the bullet points, include a short testimonial or two to provide social proof of the promise and support points.

5. Include the First Call to Action

If we keep the copy concise enough, we can place the first call-to-action, or CTA, so it appears above the fold. In other words, we can present the core of our entire argument for conversion so it can be read without the visitor having to do any scrolling or navigation. If we like, we can include the usual incentive to convert in the first CTA, such as the opportunity to save or to schedule a free consultation.

6. Prefer a Contemporary Flat Homepage

Now, a small carat or arrow indicates that the visitor can simply scroll down to read more about why the product or service is just right for their needs. I believe these homepages provide an easier user experience than requiring them to navigate to different pages for aspects of the basic brand story.

7.   Unify the Copy and Pages with the Brand Promise

A website is not, as many people think, made up of separate pages. It's a unit that tells the brand story by theming it to the brand promise. The unity lends impact and helps make the site sticky.

How do you unify the copy? Theme the pages by repeating, paraphrasing, or otherwise playing off of parts of the brand promise.

For example, if I say my product is "the smart way" to do something, my copy would unfold, not as the "bright" way to do it, but as the "smart way." I would also look for ways to repeat and resonate with the branding slogan in the subheads, captions, names of models or services, and at any other place in the copy where you can naturally achieve it. For instance, you might refer to "smart design," "smart model 101," and "smart customer service," etc.

The correct branding slogan will generally feature the most important keyword or keywords in the category. So unifying the claim around the branding slogan will also improve the SEO of the site in a way that unfolds naturally.

In the above example, the keyword would probably be what "the smart way" refers to. Maybe it's how to do website design. So the keyword would be "website design." The development of the site might include headers like "Smart Website Design," "Smart Website Design: Templates," "Smart Website Design: Premium Services," etc.

In this case, the lively or hot word is "smart." You'll generally want a hot word in the slogan. It may or may not be an important keyword in the category. Hot words are often more general, like "discover," "revolutionary," "breakthrough," or "unique." But they give the branding slogan energy and power.

The categorical keywords are usually relatively factual. So the energy comes from how you present them. In fact, a good way to think about bringing a slogan to life is to think about hot words that might go with the keywords.

The branding slogan can appear on every page, usually designed as part of the logo, so it doesn't conflict with the headline for each page. If it is part of a design element, make sure it's presented verbally in the alt tag for the logo. As you know, the crawlers only read words, not pictures and other design elements.

8. *Include a Special Offer or Offers*

To increase the conversion rate, we should present a special offer that incentivizes the visitor to convert. Generally, it's some sort of discount on the main offering.

It should be as significant as possible. Consumers are very savvy about weighing the merits of special offers.

Think of the popularity of coupons. There is nothing more revealing than working on a supermarket account that drives traffic by featuring specials and seeing how many people show up at checkout with not much more in their carts than the items that are on special. It's not good for the retailer, but it's a good lesson for anyone in marketing.

We all know stores sell more when they have sales. A website that converts should always appear to have an irresistible sale going on.

9. *Make the Featured Offer or Offers Irresistible*

Nothing is more frustrating than driving traffic to Websites for clients who will not put an irresistible special offer or offers on the homepage or the other page where the PPC campaign and other marketing is driving the traffic.

They just can't bring themselves to give a generous discount. But anyone who spends a great deal of time in Internet marketing comes to understand that the more you give, the more you'll probably get. Generosity begets sales, as well as inspires customer loyalty.

Of course, clients have to protect their margins. We all want the sites to be profitable. The key is to structure offers that seem like an irresistible bargain while we protect our margins.

Don't stop until you look at the offers and wonder how anyone is his or her right mind wouldn't convert. At their best, offers make the shopper wonder how you could possibly still be making money.

If the usual or everyday price of a product or service is too low to allow for dramatic specials, then the regular price should be raised.

It's no great secret among retailers that when a sale is about to happen, the merchandise is often retagged to show a higher regular price and, due to the sale price, a steeper discount.

10. On Landing Pages, Include a Persuasive Bonus or Bonuses

Most landing pages that convert well offer a bonus or a whole series of bonuses to get the consumer to convert. They're usually presented in sequence as the story unfolds on the landing page and then recapitulated after the benefits of the product or service have been presented.

A bonus often allows the visitor to get a free download of an e-book or white paper. It might also allow the visitor to view one of a number of videos in a series.

11. Two Critical Things to Include in Bonuses

Every bonus or other offer should have a time fuse. The offer is only good for so long. It's pending expiration helps create the urgency for the consumer to convert now.

The product or service should also offer a money-back guarantee, with an easy return policy. It's always good to offer a 100% money-back guarantee for a reasonable period. It's a reassurance that makes the purchase seem risk-free and helps provide what is known as "permission to buy." As you know, such guarantees often wisely include the phrases "No obligation whatsoever," and "No questions asked."

Naturally, the site should explain how purchasers can get their money back.

12. Drive Traffic to a Dedicated Landing Page or to the Page Most Likely to Convert

Many marketers drive all traffic to the homepage of a site. Then the visitor has to click to get to the page with the content that prompted the visit.

The ad or other vehicle that drives the traffic should go hand in glove with the landing page or other page on the website.

If the site is well known, so the consumer is already sold on the company, the link can go straight to the product.

On the other hand, if the site is not well known, there will generally be a need to create credibility, which means the core promise of the site, the reasons to believe, and the offer with any incentives should be presented when the consumer arrives.

We must remember that a sale depends, not only on what is being bought, but on the company from whom it's being bought. Consumers take both things into consideration. We must write websites and landing pages so that we satisfy both.

13. *Make the Writing Generous in Terms of Reader Interest and Gracefully Inviting*

Many websites are written with the emphasis on what the company wants from the visitor. The self-interest is readily apparent, and the visitor will promptly detect it and decide, "Nothing much here for me."

A site should express just the opposite. It should be all about the best interests of the visitor.

We don't want to write about what we want them to do. We write about the benefits of doing what we'd like them to.

When a site primarily expresses self-interest, it becomes cold and uninviting. When the opposite is true, it becomes warm and inviting. The visitor thinks, "These people have my best interests at heart. I may stay and even buy something."

This aspect of the writing is generally easy to manage. Most of us know how to be generous.

Writing with grace is something that takes time to develop. Long, clumsy sentences that seem to plod on and on just won't convert optimally.

There are easy fixes for this, though. Thankfully, good internet style, as all good copywriting, depends on short sentences and paragraphs, often phrases as sentences, even a single word as a paragraph.

Good website style also includes frequent bullet points, rather than running prose.

So the easiest way to create at least the impression of graceful copy is to keep the sentences and paragraphs short and put a lot of the content in bullet points.

As a rule, put one thought in each sentence or, at most, two. Practice thinking a main, or independent, thought and then modifying it with a dependent thought. For instance, you might think, "You'll really like this product." Then you might add, "If you try it, you'll really like this product."

More polished writers will, of course, lend natural grace to the flow of the copy. It's a talent that creates a place for gifted copywriters in the division of labor. The copy proceeds with a combination of thought and thoughtfulness that is emblematic of great copywriting.

14. Make All of Your Claims Credible

It's astonishing how many sites are written with absolutely no evidence that the copywriter is aware of the critical importance of credibility.

It matters little to make a claim if it's not believable.

To make an entire landing page that is peppered with incredible claims creates overwhelming skepticism. The latter is one of the most grievous shortcomings on the internet. It's especially prevalent on e-commerce and affiliate sites that look, with their extravaganza of clunky red headlines, as if they were designed by an escapee from the publicity department of a circus. Simply put, no credibility, no conviction, no conversions.

Given the prevalence of such claims, there's a great competitive advantage to making credible ones. In fact, the more credible our claims are, the more consumers we'll be able to convert.

Credibility begins by estimating how much we can claim while our claim or claims remain convincing. I'd rather convince visitors of a benefit that's a bit more modest than have them dismiss one that's more extravagant.

How else can you make your claims credible? Always present the reason to believe in close proximity to the initial mention of the claim. The most immediate way to do it is to include the proof within the statement of the claim. For instance, if I tell you a supplement will improve your digestion, I might say, "The supplement contains lactobacillus, which has been shown to improve digestion." Notice I didn't just say it improves digestion.

For emphasis, I might present the initial claim with the truth embedded with it in the headline or a subhead.

There's a saying in advertising and filmmaking about the importance of credibility. If Superman flies, there has to be a reason. That's why he wears a cape.

15. Include the Most Popular Keywords in the Category

When a site contains the most popular keywords in a category, it's most likely to show up when and where the target audience is doing a search. So it's most likely to attract visitors who will purchase the product or service. We don't just want to attract traffic. We want traffic that is most likely to convert.

I'll use the most frequently searched keyword in the branding slogan and the other popular ones in the headlines and subhead, as well as I the copy as they flow naturally into the sales story.

If you take care of the content in a way that's highly relevant to the product or service, it's difficult to imagine doing it without using at least some of the keywords that are most relevant to the search.

Remember not to confuse cause and effect. The cause of the keywords is the terms people use to search a category. The effect is we want to include them in websites that are directed at people who search the category.

16. Do Your Part to Get the SEO Right

Getting the SEO right should not be completely up to a great copywriter; for instance, building links, writing blog articles, and posts on social media sites. There is so little great marketing copy on the internet that anyone who can create it should specialize in doing so.

But there are some services you may want to perform for clients in addition to using the right keywords in your copy.

You might agree to write the meta data, which includes the meta title, meta description, and, if you decide to include them, the meta keywords. It can also include the alt tags to describe the images.

Here are a few tips.

The title on the homepage will usually show up as the blue header when the entry appears in search. It's usually wise to include the name of the site but with spaces between the words. You can also put a hyphen after the name and add a short description, which is also likely to show up in the header. I recommend you do so. You can also separate the elements with vertical lines. Sometimes the main benefit can go first and the name of the site last.

The meta description is a direct, brief sentence that should provide the primary promise, or benefit, of the site. It's the second element that will show up in search, in black type right below the header.

Should you decide to ignore the protestations of Google and Bing/Yahoo that they now ignore the keywords? It depends. If a site specializes in content that changes every day, such as a newspaper, it's a good idea to include them, simply because the crawlers don't come by every day but people search every day.

The keywords should be listed with a comma between them but no spaces. Begin with the most relevant keyword and list them in descending order of relevance.

Today, some sites are so tightly focused on niche and micro-niche markets that the SEO consists of only one keyword, usually the most relevant one in the category. The right number of keywords is generally between ten and twenty-five. Anymore will have little influence on how the site shows up in search results. So-called long-tail keywords may be more affordable but they usually attract marginal traffic or, when it comes to people who are likely to convert, long shots.

When you do the alt tags, make the descriptions of the pictures are as relevant to the search as you can make them.

Remember that company names, logos, and slogans that are presented as images need alt tags, too.

Twelve Reasons Websites Don't Convert

Now that you know how to write websites that convert, here are twelve reasons they don't.

The internet presents us with abundant evidence that very few people know why they don't.

Here are twelve, which will sound a lot like the opposite of the previous section:

1. The site does not present a focused brand promise.

2. The promise is not presented in a compelling way.

3. The site fails to make immediate contact with the visitor.

4. The copy is not unified around the branding slogan for impact.

5. There is no special offer or offers.

6. The featured offer or offers are not irresistible.

7. There are no persuasive bonus offers.

8. Traffic is not being driven to the page most likely to convert.

9. The writing is too self-interested or clumsy to invite readership.

10. The claims are made without making them credible.

11. The site does not contain the most popular keywords in the category.

12. The SEO has not been optimized to reach the target audience.

Now, let's move on to ways to drive traffic to websites and landing pages.

CHAPTER 12

GOOGLE ADS, FACEBOOK ADS, AND OTHER DIGITAL ADS

I've been doing Google Ads since Adwords began. I remember when Google bought a technology called Urchin, so it would have a way to track ads. I actually edited a book on how to master Adwords way back in the late 1990s.

These days, I'm a Google Certified Partner in all aspects of advertising – search, display, mobile, video, and shopping. I'm also Google Certified in Analytics. I've developed my own way of working, some aspects of which you may or may not agree with. It probably depends on whether your special talent is copywriting or data.

Now, let's turn to creating successful Google Ads, as well as successful Facebook, LinkedIn and other social ads. The same copywriting principles apply to all the formats.

The great news for copywriters is that since Google has expanded text ads from one headline of 25 characters to two and then three headlines of 30 characters each and from two separate lines of description of 35 characters each to one description and then two descriptions of 80 characters each, the quality of the copy plays a more significant role than ever in the success of the advertising. Before the expansion, people who emphasized data more than copy could simply paste or type core content in the headline and descriptions. Now, they have to exert more effort to write copy. Since search advertising has traditionally been done by people who are more adept at data, I often find that the current reason many campaigns underperform is the quality of the copy.

The Importance of Relevance to the Search

All search engines have the same goal: to deliver the most relevant content to the searcher. So the way for your ads to show up where we want them to is to serve the goal by making your campaigns highly relevant to the search.

The more relevance to the search you bring to your campaigns, the more you'll serve Google or the other search engines. So the search engines will give our campaigns high "quality score," which Google now calls a "health score." As a result, your client will pay less per click and your ads will get better positions, even appearing at times above the ads of clients who are paying more per click. At least, that's what we're told by Google.

There are, of course, exceptions to such a sure solution. Some of the blame for a low health score is due to the historical performance of the campaigns or even the quality of the landing page the ads are driving traffic to. For example, if we have had a lower click-through ratio (CTR), it means Google or the others must show our ads more often to elicit clicks and make money, that is, they have to work harder. Some average costs-per-click are quite high. The cost is usually attributed to the competitive nature of the category, but some categories with a relatively low search volume have high rates, too. These may be attributed, at least partially, to the zeal of the search engines to make money.

Setting Up the Account

Unlike many providers, I usually encourage my clients to set up the account. Part of the setup requires a credit card to be entered that the cost of the advertising will be charged to. If the client enters the card, you don't have to worry about payments for the advertising. In addition, if the client ever wishes to try another service, he or she can simply remove you as an admin.

Start with a Keyword Search

Remember to use the Google Keyword Tool or another keyword service to find the optimal keywords to feature in the campaign and the ad groups. Select the ones with the highest traffic, while you also keep an eye on the average cost per click. If you make the campaigns as relevant as I suggest, you'll usually find the average cost per click to be much lower than what's listed. When you're setting up the ad groups and start to enter the keywords that are relevant to it, you'll see that Google will also start to suggest other keywords.

Selecting Your Audience

When you create a campaign, you'll have to complete the Settings page. It will determine the overall parameters of the campaign. Google primarily uses geographic targeting in the settings, but you can select your audience more exactly with your keywords and ads. You can also select them with the Audience tab, with offers such choices as Affinity Audiences, or people similar to the ones in your target market.

Facebook offers myriad demographic choices, based on its knowledge of its members. You can, for example, choose people by income, credit card use, luxury purchases, travel habits, and more. By simply checking a box, your campaign can also appear on Instagram, which, as you probably know, Facebook owns.

LinkedIn allows you to choose your target, as you might guess, by occupation, such as CEO, vice presidents, marketing executives, and business owners. .

When you become familiar with these methods of audience selection, you'll find it relatively easy to do on the other social sites.

Google Campaign Settings

Some of the choices in Settings are self-explanatory, such as the location or locations you'd like your ads to appear.

In Campaign Type, you'll generally want to prefer the Google Search Network over the Display Network. The search ads can reach your relevant market efficiently, while the Display Network includes many small sites where your budget may be clicked away by a greater proportion of curiosity seekers. I generally select All Features of the Search Network.

You'll also have a choice of including Google Search Partners, which includes sites like AOL. I suggest you select it if your budget is large enough. If not, I suggest you leave it unchecked.

In Devices, I usually select All. If one type of device, such as Mobile, is more important to you, you can adjust the bid for the device.

In the Bid Strategy section, you'll be able to choose between Manual and Enhanced Bidding. I suggest you choose Enhanced Bidding. Doing so will allow you to benefit more from Google's AI, especially in the early days of the campaign. Google will then adjust your bids to maximize conversions. I usually enter a Maximum Cost Per Click in the bidding section to prevent Google from getting carried away by how much it charges per click.

If the campaign becomes marked as Limited, the cause is usually the Maximum Cost Per Click you've set. Google wants you to raise it to show up in more searches. Be careful. You can end up paying more per click, which can expend the daily budget while you get fewer clicks than you were at the lower cost per click.

Ad Groups and Ads

To be relevant to the search, you'll also want to divide your campaigns into Ad Groups. Each group should feature a specific aspect of the brand, whether a benefit, attribute, or offer. I vary the headlines in each ad in an Ad Group, but I generally keep the descriptions the same in all the ads. By doing so I can see which headline appeals are working best without other variations influencing the results.

When you type out the ad, remember to put an initial capital on all the words in the headline. Such headlines are standard and get more clicks. Creating Ad Extensions and Sitelinks will expand the communication capacity of your ads and enlarge their presence on the page.

If you're creating Display Ads, you can have Google scan the landing page or website you're driving traffic to and deliver sample layouts for the campaign in different ad sizes. It's a convenient tool, especially if you don't have a designer you're working with in PPC advertising.

Keyword Match Types

There are different ways to enter each keyword or keyword phrase. Besides just listing the word or phrase, which is known as a broad match, we can put quotes around it or brackets. The first variation is called a "phrase match." The ad can appear in a search when the searcher enters the keyword or keyword phrase.

The third variation is known as an "exact match." You enclose each word or phrase with a bracket. This match type is the most selective, and I emphasize it. The keyword or phrase has to be entered by the searcher precisely as it appears.

There is also a keyword variation called modified broad match. Each word is preceded by a plus sign, with a space between each word and the next plus sign. This match type means the exact words have to appear in the search, but they can appear in any order.

Finally, there are negative keywords, which we enter and put a minus sign (hyphen) in front of. We use negative keywords to avoid showing up in searches that are irrelevant to what we're advertising; for instance, when we're selling homes, we can make "rental" a negative keyword. We don't want to show up in those searches and burn up our budget with clicks by searchers who are unlikely to buy what we're advertising.

Instead of using single keywords, which everybody in the category uses, we should look for keyword combinations and keyword phrases that are relevant but more unique. Google and Bing/Yahoo encourage these kinds of keywords because they can be more specific to the search. As a result, the words usually get a higher quality score, which means a lower cost per click. These are sometimes called long-tail keywords. The more extreme ones usually don't have a high search volume and Google will mark them as such when they appear in the ad group.

For relevance to the search, I use only exact match keywords and modified broad match.

The easiest way to change the match type from broad match is to save the ad group. Then click to check them all and click on Edit, Change Match Types, select from Broad Match to Exact Match and save. You can't do a bulk edit for modified Broad Match. The easiest way to create them is to copy and paste them all in the keyword panel again, remove the brackets, and add the plus signs, as in +this +is +a +modified +broad +match +keyword.

Optimizing Campaigns

You can optimize the campaign by deleting poorly performing ad groups, ads, and keywords to emphasize better performing ones. For example, a keyword that has gotten a lot of impressions but very few, if any clicks, or a keyword of marginal relevance that's getting clicks but the cost per click is burning up too much of the budget.

You'll find that most of the data you need to optimize the campaigns automatically shows up in Google Ads in the line above the campaigns, keywords, ads, and ad groups. You can add any result a client wants simply by, in the relatively new Google Ads format, the Columns icon.

I'm certified in Google Analytics, but I don't get into much more detail than how many impressions and clicks each ad group, ad, and keyword is getting, the click-through-rate, the cost per click, and the conversion rate. You can go into a lot more detail, but these key elements will give you a pretty good idea of what's working.

If a client wants a Dashboard, it's easy to create. You can select all the items you think the client will want to keep track of. Some clients want a great deal of data in Google Analytics. I don't find them ideal for copywriters. You're too valuable writing copy to spend your days gathering and analyzing data.

When I began, my first job was in DR for a New York publisher, selling encyclopedias and other books through print ads and snail-mail sales letters. The only result we got was the sales volume. If it was from a letter, we also got the percent of the letters that led to sales. We found even that basic data to be sufficient to decide if we had a winning campaign or needed to optimize it.

However we proceed, we watch which ads and keywords produce the best results. Some people will pick the best-performing ad group or ad and try to create a new ad group or ad that can beat it – a version of the proverbial A/B test. Somewhat like direct marketing, we learn as we spend. As usual, it's smart to spend less until we learn what works. One of my clients began as a mathematician who won a Ford scholarship in it when he was sixteen. Once he told me something only a mathematician would think of, but it makes infinite sense: "When my advertising is making money, my budget is infinite."

When our ad shows up on a page, chances are there will be other paid-search ads there. Do we want the top position? Not usually. Why? We'll attract a lot of clicks from curiosity seekers. It's better to be in the third to fifth position. The people who search that deeply are usually serious about what they're looking for and more likely to buy. It's especially important not to show up in the top position when you're advertising a product that creates a great deal of curiosity value, such as a headline for the Caribbean that might say "Vacation in Paradise." You know a lot of people would simply like to know where "paradise" is.

Google and the other providers do not share the algorithm by which the Health Score of a campaign is arrived at, so we're in a position similar to playing cards with someone who sees more of them than we do. But if you follow my suggestions for making your campaigns highly relevant to the search, you'll find the Health Score is usually in the high 90's, if not 100%. Sometimes, it will start lower, but you'll see it rise quickly.

"Opportunities" in Google Ads

When you're running a campaign in Google Ads, you'll start to see "Opportunities" from Google. I pay close attention to them during the first month of the campaign, because I know they're delivering results based on Google's AI learning. But I review any I accept carefully. Make sure everything about each one is highly relevant to the search. Pay special attention to the suggested keyword additions, making sure none are broad match or phrase match. Otherwise, you'll make it easier for Google to show your ads to a less-than-ideal target audience and burn up the client's daily budget.

After the first month, I see how the campaign is doing. My principal measure is the bottom line: is the client getting the sales volume he wants? If so, my job from then on is primarily to protect the campaign. I become very selective about the "Opportunities" I accept. In addition to diluting the relevance of the campaign, accepting too many opportunities for new ad groups, ads, and keywords and result in a campaign that's so big it becomes difficult to manage optimally.

"Learning" and "Limited" Notifications

When you launch a new campaign, Google will often note the campaign with (Learning). It's AI is tracking how your campaign is doing and doing all it can to optimize it. You must wait at least a week or two before you make changes, so you have a solid foundation of learning to base them on. Otherwise, you'll begin to create variables based on incomplete learning and find yourself limited by imprecision.

The "Limited" notifications is usually related to the Maximum Cost Per Click you have the option to set when you create the campaign. Google is usually attempting to get you to raise it, by indicating that some clicks you could be getting are higher, so you're not getting them. Before you raise it, check the position of the ad. As noted above, the ideal position is in the 3rd to 5th from the top. If that's where the average position is, don't raise the bid.

Bidding

When you do the Settings for a campaign, you can choose Manual Bidding or Enhanced Bidding. Manual bidding is just as it says it is. You set your bids yourself and adjust them as you see fit.

I prefer to use Enhanced Bidding, which allows me to take advantage of Google's AI and saves me from having to patrol the account with unnecessary regularity. When you select it, you have the choice of entering a Maximum Cost Per Click. I recommend that you do so. It helps control how surprisingly high Google's AI can sometimes raise the CPC.

Reports

Many clients request weekly or monthly reports on how their search advertising is performing. I present my services a different way. I tell clients the special benefit I offer is great copy and that, while I'm Google Certified in Analytics, going overboard into the results and dutifully reporting them is not why they're hiring me. I simply prefer to keep an eye on the campaigns and keep them functioning optimally, while I depend on my clients to tell me how the campaigns are performing. It's the bottom line.

If a campaign is successful, the client should be delighted and not pester you for excessive data. If the client is doing so, you might recommend that he or she would be happier with a data-intensive person.

If it's failing, the first place to look is the quality of your ad groups, ads, and keywords. How are they doing in the key measurements? The results you can find in Google Ads can tell you much more and you can learn even more in Google Analytics.

I find that today the usual reason a PPC campaign isn't working is the quality of the copywriting. If the ads aren't presenting the product or service optimally, the main thing the data can tell you is exactly how the campaign is failing. It can't tell you how to fix the problem.

As I often say, success comes with all the answers, and failure that comes with questions.

The Destination URL

The site or landing page you're driving traffic to can influence the quality score. In fact, if it isn't working properly, Google will disapprove the campaign.

A poorly built or poorly performing site can also precipitate a low campaign health score. It should feature the content the campaigns are featuring, all the links should be working, it should load quickly, and be based on a fluid design, so it shows up properly in all devices. Since the majority of searches now occur on a mobile device, it's more important than ever that the site is mobile friendly.

How does Google judge a website? The company has crawlers or robots that roam the Internet for content, which the "bots" judge primarily though the evaluation of the content of the sites, including the content of the headlines and copy, with special attention to the core keywords, and the metadata. Today, the data includes the title of each page, the description, and the alt tags for the visuals. Google and now Bing and Yahoo say they no longer rely on keywords in the metadata. Instead, the crawlers scour the content, as well as the quality of the links and how many inbound links the site has from other sites. Quality inbound links help the robots determine how important the site is in the category.

When we write ads to drive traffic to the site or a landing page, they should fit hand in glove with the content. We want to create our ads with the headlines, subheads, and keywords that are on the landing page or site. These are the ones that are most relevant to the searches that we want them to show up in. Second, robots have no ability to make subjective judgments. An easy way to see this is to look at the sites that accept Google Search ads. For instance, let a word like "bush" occur on a page and soon Google will place ads there for everything from George Bush to bushes for your garden.

We may conclude then that, despite the objective sophistication of the robots, they're subjectively less than bright. In positive terms, that means we should hit them over the head with relevance yet not too hard, or we'll be penalized for keyword stuffing.

Among the principles we've presented for other types of advertising are concentrating and unifying the content.

In Google Ads and other PPC ads, we concentrate the news or selling proposition, so that we can fit the messages within the wordcount of the headlines. In the process, we should make sure the most relevant keyword in the ad group is in the headline. When you exceed the character count, Google will alert you.

The landing page or the page within the website the ad takes the searcher to should fulfill the expectations the ad creates and work to develop the sales message and ask for the sale. It should be exactly the right page, not a page on the website the searcher has to navigate to from the homepage. The easy way to make the link precise is to navigate to the page you're driving traffic to and then copy the address in the address line. Now paste it in the ad as the destination URL.

The Account Manager

There are Adwords and Bing/Yahoo Search experts who run campaigns for a large number of clients. If you become one of them, you may want to sign up for an Adwords Manager Account to keep track of the campaigns and edit them more conveniently.

Getting Google Certified

If you find yourself doing a lot of Google campaigns, you'll want to get certified. Simply study the guides Google provides. But be careful. It often seems that the people at Google who prepare the tests are in a different room than the people who prepare the guides. If you're in doubt about any topic, simply enter it in the search bar. Since a lot of people have asked the same questions, you'll see answers how up as soon as you start to enter most of the topics you want clarification on.

I've presented the core information you need to create successful search and display

Banner Advertising

A banner ad can be part of a Google Display campaign or a separate entity. Either way, it can be seen as an interactive billboard. The goal is to get the headline or slogan and the visual to communicate the core message in just the right, bright way. The call to action should be exact.

Visual pizzazz, which was once usually achieved with Flash, can help attract attention when the appropriate tonality for a product or service lends itself to it.

Summary

I've presented the core information you need to create successful search engine advertising. You'll learn more as you go.

Google and Yahoo offer tutorials, which are kept up to date. To get started in this advertising mini-world, just go to *www.adwords.com* or *www.bingads.microsoft.com* and set up an account. The easiest way to get begin to understand how to work in the platforms is just to click around and see how they're structured and how each element works. Then when you're doing the tutorial, you have a better grip of what's being described.

CHAPTER 13

SOCIAL SELLING

Social selling is often touted as the most personal and effective form of selling on the Internet. When executed properly, it certainly has an important place in the media mix.

When done well, it's invitingly personal, creative, and measurable.

How is such selling achieved? You create a corporate page or profile for the client on Facebook, LinkedIn or other social media. Then you build and nourish a thriving fan base made up of people who are interested in what the client sells and are eager to click read a post and click on an offer. The result should be a high and growing volume of quality traffic to the page that will translate into more customers and leads.

Since the response is measurable, the client will be able to watch the increasing return on the marketing investment.

Facebook Advertising

Facebook and other social advertising reaches people when they're looking for new content and it's embedded in content they consider personal. So it's an especially effective way to reach them. The ads can be precisely targeted, too, because of the knowledge the platforms have collected about their users, even within the limits the regulations imposed on social sites for overreaching, particularly the excesses of Facebook.

In addition to driving traffic to the client's page, you can also drive it to the client's website or landing pages.

Since Facebook is by far the largest social site, we'll concentrate on how to market on it. The same principles apply to all social selling.

Facebook Sales Funnels

The foundation of every successful Facebook funnel is building a quality fan base that's engaged with the client's company. The fans are the people most likely to read and share a post, click on an ad, share their email and other contact information, and buy the client's product or service.

A successful Facebook funnel can be built in the following ways.

You'll want to attract fans who are in your target market with Facebook posts, boosted posts, and ads. The goal is to spend as little as possible per fan, so the budget produces optimal results.

Next, you'll want to build trust by providing content that has value to the fan base. The goal of the content is to build personal connections that will inspire them to go to the client's website or landing page and make a purchase and become a brand advocate.

You'll also want to collect email addresses, so you can reach out to them through emails. To collect the email addresses, you offer fans different kinds of value in exchange for their addresses. For instance, you can offer a free e-book or send them an invitation to register for a webinar. You can also invite them to keep up with a blog. Providing content that attracts an audience to your social page, website, or landing page is referred to as inbound marketing.

When you've built a quality fan base, you can market to them, but you should also continue to nourish them with free stuff they'll value. There's an ideal balance between selling and nurturing. Your goal is to maintain it, so your fan base grows larger and larger.

Social Media Content Creation

You attract fans through the creation of content you wish to share with them. You should make posts regularly. They can be just a sentence or two, as long as the content is engaging for the target market. You can also boost the post, disseminating it widely to your target market, much like an ad. In fact, your boosted posts will show up in the same panel where you manage your Facebook ads.

Creating social ads is an excellent communication channel for a great copywriter. But making and boosting posts does not require the highest level of marketing skill, so it is not an ideal use of your time. There are far too few great marketing copywriters, as opposed to writers who can do posts, as well as articles and blogs. You or the account group can simply provide strategic direction for the posts. The actual work is a playground for people who enjoy social interaction.

CHAPTER 14

EMAIL COPYWRITING

Selling via email campaigns requires the usual skills of a great copywriter, along with special knowhow.

Make Your Emails Personal

An email should be as personal as possible.

If you know the recipient's name, you should feature it, often not only in the salutation, but in the subject line. It helps the email avoid spam folders and separates it for the recipient from the usual plethora of junk email. Yet you must communicate and sell. So you strive for the ideal balance of personalization and commercial content. Many market-ers still do straight-ahead email marketing, in much the same style as traditional snail-mail marketing. The emails feature a sales message in the subject line, a headline before the salutation, if there is a salutation, and copy with subheads and visuals. The technique works especially well if you're sending the email to people who've opted-in to receive emails from you.

On the other hand, some marketers, including some digital agencies, are so concerned about avoiding the spam folder or being mistaken for just another sales message in a busy category that they go exceptionally far the other way, utilizing disarmingly personal subject lines and brief emails.

Such an email can have a subject line as personal as, "Hi, Jim, I was just thinking about you."

The body of the email might proceed as follows:

> Hi, there,
>
> How are you doing, Jim? I hope everything is going great.
>
> I was thinking about different business in the area and got to wondering how yours is doing?
>
> I live in the area, so I know the market really well.
>
> I have an agency, called Spectrum Digital.
>
> If the internet isn't working for you as well as you'd like it to, I'd love to talk about how I can help.
>
> If you'd like to chat, just reply to my email.
>
> Looking forward to hearing from you.
>
> Regards,
> Pete

The Subject Line

Like a great headline, the subject line should contain the most concentrated news you can create about what you're offering in terms of how it can benefit the recipient. It should be no more than 60 characters, so it appears in its entirely in the inbox. You should avoid words that activate the spam filters. These words include some venerable marketing terms, such as free, offer, bonus, save, buy, purchase, and similar words that alert the spam folders that it's a sales email. The struggle is balance selling with avoiding the spam folder.

The Copy

As noted above, begin with a personal salutation whenever you can. The remainder of the copy proceeds with the same techniques presented in the section on print advertising, but all emails should be relatively short.

Of course, you'll want to ask for the sale and, ideally, offer an incentive or two to increase conversions.

After the close, it's usual in marketing emails to include a PS, which allows you to repeat part of the offer or present an additional incentive or piece of information.

Email Campaigns

An email campaign should proceed like any other campaign, but the content should be adapted to optimize the format. It should feature the core brand message with whatever proofs, additions, or offers the campaign is intended to communicate.

The usual wisdom on the internet is that it takes an average of 5 impressions or touch points to achieve a conversion. As a result, many email campaigns tell the same core message, but the subject line is altered. The variety can be as simple as preceding the usual subject line with such alerts as "Second notice" or "Writing again." Then the first sentence or so of the copy is adapted to the variation, along with the closing sentence or two.

If you're in an agency, you can leave the look of the email campaign to your designer. If you work on your own and the client is using an email service, you can probably do a pretty good job designing the emails with the templates and tools provided.

Internet Videos

Internet videos can be especially effective. They can appear on the homepage to bring the core sales message to life. They can also appear on landing pages as video sales letters, which can be quite long. They can also appear on YouTube as part of a Google video campaign.

Some feature visuals, and when they do, the principles presented in the section on television commercials apply.

There is one different type of video sales letter, which consists of type on the screen, which appears as the announcer reads it. Such videos can be surprisingly arresting. The copywriter can think more in terms of a good print ad that's being read to the audience.

As always, we need an arresting beginning to attract attention, an address of the viewers personal wants or pain points to maintain interest, and the continuing revelation of the attributes and benefits to create desire. Finally, we ask for the conversion, usually with an offer or bonus to incentivize it.

Internet Creativity

Website design and Internet advertising have led to some renewal in advertising creativity, which is partly due to the struggle to communicate in a busy medium. So many of the principles of traditional media apply, along with the specific skills required to work in the formats unique to internet marketing. If you master what's in this book, you'll find that you'll be one of the most effective copywriters working on the internet. If you're in an agency, you'll be admired and rewarded. If you're on your own as a freelancer or creative consultant, you'll find you almost have a corner on the market for expert creative copywriting.

PART 4

Advanced Guidelines for Great Copywriting

CHAPTER 15

THE UNIQUE LANGUAGE OF ADVERTISING

The language of advertising is the most powerful form ever devised to reach and persuade people by the millions. How does the language work and how can you make it work for you?

The language evolved to meet a need and has been honed as well as human competence has so far been able to manage the task. We strive to reach, not only the brightest among us, but also the dumbest or, more thoughtfully, the most attentive, as well as the least attentive. The more people we can persuade, the more we can sell the client's product or service. As a result, the language is as simple as each occasion permits, without, however, sounding like the voice of a simpleton.

The principle of simplicity was an early discovery, and it's been expressed for decades as the KISS principle, where KISS is an unflattering mnemonic for "Keep It Simple, Stupid." Notice it does not say, "Keep It Stupid, Simple."

Various forms of linguistic simplicity have arisen. The judicious use of sentence fragments is an important part of the art of writing modern advertising copy. In fact, the language of advertising goes so far as to use a single word as an entire paragraph.

Actually, most people don't speak in complete sentences. They often use fragments. As a result, fragments have been a staple of dialogue, or writing that attempts to reflect the sound of real people talking, in all realistic drama.

Most people also express themselves in clichés, and we wish to speak to "most" people in a language that they're comfortable with. So we often use clichés, too. They create easy, familiar reading or listening. But they can be used in bright ways, usually by applying them in unexpected ways. They can add liveliness and help us emphasize points.

Let's consider some specific ways to employ the language. We can write a sentence and then make a quick comment on it with a fragment. The second piece sort of bounces off the previous one and helps propel the reader forward. A single word set off as an entire sentence or paragraph provides variety, breaks up forbidding chunks of prose, enables linguistic dexterity, and calls attention to itself.

Generally, such devices allow us to achieve, not only simplicity, but various forms of emphasis, surprises, and little intellectual rewards that help us retain the interest of the reader or listener.

Clichés can be used in two ways – in their usual meaning, to lend familiarity, and in innovative ways, to gain attention and create inviting delight. The latter is achieved by taking a cliché that is usually thought of as meaning one thing and applying it in a way that gives it another meaning. When the consumer sees it, he or she finds delight and remembers the thought and, on reflection, recalls the original application. So the new use coruscates with two facets.

Lest you have compunctions, notice that today we also find the use of fragments more widely, for example, in the reportage and editorials of *The New York Times*.

Yet the fragments are more at home in short forms. In longer forms, the liveliness they enable becomes distracting and finally annoying, like a long ride on a jerky train.

The unique language of advertising also helps us achieve another goal. In addition to simplicity, we want to be relevant to the moment and exciting. One way we can achieve these goals is to employ language that is at the forefront of usage. Words like "cool" and "zippy," once new, have now been with us for decades. So have "wow," "awesome," and "dynamite."

The ear of the good copywriter should be attuned for new expressions that will help lend a timely simpatico and freshness to the advertising.

Now, let's glance at a classic example of advertising language that was once considered controversial but the infraction is now seen in even the most august literary magazines. It concerns the use of "like" not "as," in the widely forgotten slogan, "Winston tastes good like a cigarette should." The infraction was to use 'like" as a conjunction. Yet "as" seems a bit formal in a statement that hopes to sound as off-handedly colloquial as a good slogan should. The dictionary has now elevated the use of the word as a conjunction from being "illiterate" to "colloquial."

Advertising also blithely uses prepositions at the end of sentences. The need for simple, colloquial expression often recommends it over such constructions as "with whom" or "in which." As Winston Churchill famously quipped, "A preposition is a bad word to end a sentence with."

Last, we'll discuss the wide practice of starting a sentence with a conjunction. Grammar books generally recommend against doing so because the beginning of a sentence is the second-most emphatic part of it, and it's supposedly unwise to waste it on a mere connective. The rule becomes less relevant in advertising prose, because the sentences are relatively short. So there are lots of beginnings. In addition, a conjunction can coordinate or contrast short thoughts in emphatic and delightful ways.

There are, of course, innumerable precedents outside of advertising. In no less than the *Bible,* innumerable sentences begin with "And." Adopting the technique, a creative director might write, "The creative team presented a new print campaign. And the work was good. But I thought they had only scratched the surface. So I asked them to do more work. And soon they came back with it. Yet I was still not certain they had plumed the potential of their idea. But now we were up against a killer deadline. So I approved it."

Content and Language Leverage

When we begin our search for exactly the right language, we're dealing with a lot of facts, and our first verbal expressions of what we must communicate are likely to be literal, instead of innovative. We have to get used to working with the content and the language that applies to it, until we can get some leverage on it. Basically, we become increasingly enabled as we learn to attenuate the content, so we can have language leverage over it. Then we can express, on the wings of inspiration, the essence of what we must say in an innovative way.

Metaphorically, we begin at the bottom of the tree of information, where we struggle with the trunk. We're working with so many facts we can hardly do much more than generate stiff expressions of them. As we think our way up the tree, the information thins out because the essence of what we must say comes more into focus. So our expressions can be more graceful. When we near the top, the information we require thins out to a fine point of meaning, and we can become limber with the language. We can push a little this way and that way, until we create just the right topic idea that allows us to move the entire tree with ease. We have thought our way to language leverage over the content, and the result is the right, bright slogan or headline, which sits there, like the beautiful fruit of our labor that it represents.

We can also say that there is such a thing as visual leverage, which we think our way to in the same way.

Colloquial and franker language

There is nothing more exciting in advertising than the brilliantly original, deftly appropriate, and consummately tasteful, but seemingly offhanded, expression of the recognizably correct unique brand promise. Part of the immediate effect is the use of language that is immediately familiar, or colloquial.

Sometimes, franker than usual language appears in advertising. Of course, language far franker than any that can be risked in major brand advertising occurred in literature long ago, from Chaucer's *Canterbury Tales* to Joyce's *Ulysses*.

In advertising, if we find a daring bit of language germane to the subject, we must weigh the risk/reward of the peccadillo of actually going ahead and using it.

We realize it can achieve a startling effect precisely because it is appearing in a medium where it's unexpected, somewhat like an article about prostitution which I was surprised to note, a number of years ago, in *The Atlantic Monthly*.

Timely linguistic spice offers us the virtues of impact and recall. Yet advertising represents companies that generally wish to be taken as responsible corporate citizens. So, if we opt for a piece of off-color language, or a controversial visual, we must work to present it in a way that expresses good taste. Witty, good-natured employment of it often moderates the expected uproar. On the other hand, flat-footed crudeness is never attractive.

When tempted to use a piece of risky language or a risky visual, we must remind ourselves that we are principally in the business of creating what I call risk-free excitement. Since it's what major advertisers seek, it's what agencies pay creative people the most to get.

All other considerations aside, I think tasteful people prefer to work in tasteful ways. It may often be harder, but the result is more rewarding.

CHAPTER 16

HOW TO DISCOVER THE RIGHT, BRIGHT WORDS AND VISUALS

First, let's cover how to discover the right words – the ones that express exactly what we want to say in the most effective and memorable ways. They don't just say what we have in mind; they say it in the words most related to the main claim and the brand name, so everything in the message is stitched together for maximum unity, impact, and aided recall.

How do we discover them? We turn to the resources of language collectively known as prosody, such as rhyme, alliteration, assonance (similar vowel sounds), and consonance (similar consonant sounds). There are other aspects of prosody, such as synecdoche (when a part stands for a whole, as, in the classic example, a sail for a ship), and, more to our needs, words with masculine final syllables, which are accented and emphatic and feminine final syllables, which are unaccented and trail off softly.

These resources, which can also be seen as the sources of euphony, or similar sounds, are especially valuable in minting slogans.

When we write jingles, we also need an easy familiarity with another aspect of prosody, metric feet. We usually use iambic meter, which is, of course, an unaccented syllable followed by an unaccented one. It's the most usual metrical form in the English language. For natural flow and variety, we often include some anapestic meter (two unaccented syllables followed by one that's accented). For sudden effect, we can use an occasional spondee (two accented syllables). Occasionally, we use trochaic meter (one accented syllable followed by an unaccented one; usually used to start a line with emphasis and can be seen as an iamb with the first syllable clipped off). Less often we employ dactylic meter, which consists of an accented syllable followed by two unaccented ones; it can be seen as an initial anapest with the first two syllables removed). There are rarer ones, such as an amphimacer (an unaccented syllable between two accented ones) and an amphibrach, or two unaccented syllables in an accented syllable in the middle. But these two can be seen as altered combinations of the above.

There are also more subtle values to consider, such as the similar appearance of words in terms of the letters that make them up and the number of syllables in them.

The best way to become easygoing about metrics is to read classic poetry or theater lyrics and mark the feet as you go. Shakespeare's sonnets are an excellent resource and a linguistic delight. Wordsworth, Keats, and Shelly are also valuable. The looser line lengths of Shelly will help you grasp naturally free flowing metrics. W. S. Gilbert's librettos are an amusing way to observe language organized for effect in humorous, sentimental, and other tones. Ira Gershwin's lyrics thump along loudly enough for you to hear the metrics easily. You can also learn much from the lyrics of Noel Coward, Cole Porter, Larry Hart, and Oscar Hammerstein II. In fact, poetry and lyrics are a great crash course in how various tones and goals can be achieved in language.

We also look to grammar with our needs in mind. Mastery of the basics can help make you confident and fluent. It can also enable you to make small decisions that can make all the difference.

An expert grasp of sentence structure helps you achieve liveliness, wit, and recall; for instance, understanding how to write parallel and contrasting phrases. An example of a parallel phrase is, "The more you buy, the more you save." An example of a contrasting phrase is, "You could pay more, but you can't do better."

We generally want to keep our sentences short and simple, with one thought to a sentence. We can also do two thoughts of equal importance or one with less importance that relates to the one with more importance. We'll cover sentence structure in advertising more in the section on the language of advertising.

Knowing the different ways to develop a paragraph is invaluable. In fact, you'll find it helpful to see most advertising campaigns as a paragraph. The topic sentence is the slogan, which expresses the core brand promise, or main benefit. The sentences that develop the paragraph consist primarily of the support points that prove the promise, along with secondary benefits, arranged from the most compelling to the least. The concluding sentence is the call to action and, to help unify the paragraph, may contain a play on the topic sentence or the other content that precedes it. (Basic example: "Now that you know what makes this product special, buy it.")

We have to know how to arrange the parts within the whole – the words, phrases, and sentences – because we want to achieve perfectly poised arguments for the brand. This process requires a working familiarity with appropriate emphasis and subordination, along with the deft inclusion and exclusion of material.

Since advertising consists of short forms, you don't necessarily have to become a student of the organizational principles of longer works. But keep in mind that words, as well as individual pictures, are only the moving fingers; the power is in the form, or body, of which they are a part.

Here's an example of how to think about euphony. Let's say our job is to create advertising for the pain reliever Excedrin. We prefer the word "effective," not, say, "strong." Why? The "e" that begins the word alliterates with the "E" that the brand name begins with. In fact, we could create a compact, ownable claim with just "Excedrin Effective." This construction serves as an example of another technique that helps achieve aided recall: putting the brand name in the slogan. The legal team might or might not let us use the brand name as an adjective. Coca-Cola or Kraft would never allow it. So we might redo it with the brand name as a noun, such as, "Excedrin is effective."

The Right, Bright Visuals

Now, let's consider the search for exactly the right visual or visuals to magnify the selling proposition. We want to discover the single most appropriate main visual to magnify the primary benefit. This main visual might at times consist of two parts – one visual that magnifies the problem just right and another one that magnifies the solution. For example, staying with our pain reliever, we might begin with an arresting way to demonstrate headache pain visually and then present a dramatic demonstration of the pleasure that accompanies relief. In this case, we would also search for the most appropriate secondary, or support, visual to demonstrate our "reason to believe." We might choose to show that our pain reliever contains, not just one pain reliever, but three. (Actually, Excedrin, on which I have served time, is made up of two pain relievers and one ingredient, ordinary caffeine, that functions as what the FDA considers a pain-relief "potentiator.")

If our creation is to be a commercial, the visual that magnifies the primary benefit usually begins and ends the commercial (often with a clever and reinforcing variation at the end), while the visual that provides the "reason to believe" appears in the middle. This structure is referred to as a donut, somewhat illogically, because, at least in my experience, the center of a donut is empty.

In a print ad, the visual that magnifies the primary benefit usually constitutes the main visual, while the one that supports the reason to buy appears as a smaller insert shot or in what is called a mortise.

There was a time when all that art directors, as well as copywriters who are resourcefully visual, could do is sit back and imagine visuals. Today, there is a plethora of resources for stock photographs and illustrations. We can go to stock shot sites, enter a keyword, and up come suggested visuals. The usual tactic is to enter keywords until our search leads to the right visual or visuals. If the visual concept is unusual or of a specific person, object, or location, we might still need to hire a photographer to shoot it or an illustrator to draw it.

The important thing to keep in mind is that we're not looking for a great visual or visuals. We're looking for exactly the right great visual or visuals.

The Rareness of the Right, Bright Words & Visuals

I often say that there is an imaginary little basket in the universe that contains exactly the right, bright words and pictures that go with each brand. Our job is to discover what's in the basket.

It's astonishing how many major brands have obviously never had a creative person work on them who understands the importance of expressing the message with the words and pictures most appropriate to the claim and the name. Yet such precision is the high ground of brand equity. The product or service that owns the most appropriate words and pictures in the category can dominate the brand awareness in it. The potential is enormous. A savvy creative person can still go into many heavily advertised categories and preempt the conceptual high ground.

So when we begin to work on a brand, we want to discover, not only the most compelling claim, but as much of the verbal and visual high ground that we can. We can utilize it to express the content optimally. Over the years, we can enlarge and refine our knowledge until we finally know everything that's in the precious little basket.

Why must we be this precise? We want to achieve, not just success, but maximum success. And, since we're working in such small forms, every element is, with proper emphasis and subordination, important. Even syllables and mice type are significant elements. We might say, in fact, that there is no such thing in advertising as an unimportant element or value.

Let me return to elaborate on an example of exactly the right, bright verbal magnification from my own work. It's a campaign I wrote for *The Village Voice*, the New York weekly that, when it remembered its principal mission, griped about landlords, government misbehavior, or other types of abuse that the beleaguered residents of the city are supposed to be constantly afflicted with.

I was retained by the creative director of one of the five advertising agencies that had been invited to pitch the account. I knew the way to win the day for the agency was to create a campaign, especially a slogan, that was so exactly right for the paper no other agency could hope to match it and the client couldn't possibly say no to it. I also realized that the writers at the Voice would want to have a say in the advertising, so I wanted the language to be disarmingly deft. I created the slogan, "In this city, you need a Voice." It said what the paper does in a credibly flattering way and with irresistible recall for the brand name.

The agency that retained me won the account, and the campaign ran for many years, initially as subway posters and radio commercials and later as reminder copy sprinkled throughout the paper. I especially enjoyed the radio commercials, which presented amusing magnifica-tions. My favorite began, "If you were Henry David Thoreau, lounging by the pond at Walden, contemplating the eternal verities of nature, you wouldn't need a Voice. Unfortunately, your life is not so idyllic. For instance, your car just disappeared into a pothole, etc. All of which is why, in this city, you need a Voice."

One of the media that the campaign ran on was college radio, and the president of the Voice told the advertising agency that his son love the spots and that they were a hit with students.

CHAPTER 17

A POTPOURRI OF INSIGHTS

Here are a number of disparate but effective insights that seem best presented as a group.

The Source of Appropriately Original Advertising

Unoriginal advertising generally results from approximate thinking that leads to strategies and executions that can be applied to many different products or services, just as a broadly tailored suit can fit more people than a trimly tailored one. The product or service is draped in the general idea, which obscures its unique character.

There are many ways to create original advertising. Our search is for originality that is deftly appropriate to the brand. The source of this originality is not a mystery. It grows out of sensitivity to the details of the assignment. When we search carefully, we discover something unique about every product or service. Since the content is unique, advertising that is exactly appropriate to it is unique, too.

If the unique content is not substantial enough to build a campaign around, we search for a unique claim that we can preempt. So, in a seeming paradox, the search for originality is, instead of way out there, usually "way in there." In fact, advertising that is "way out there" is often the kind in which inappropriate originality obscures the selling proposition.

Obviously, a great deal of advertising is unoriginal. The strategy, or "what to say," is often unoriginal, along with the tactic, or "how to say it."

When the uniqueness we settle on is not sufficiently dramatic to achieve an effect, we add production values.

But before we settle on razzle-dazzle, we should consider lesser values, such as the brand name, the heritage, the lifestyles of the target audience, even, at times, the price. These seemingly small values might evoke highly original advertising or, at least, a different tone than any competitors have brought to the category.

A frequent source of new tonality is the perceived voice of a new generation. Notice the edgy, downplayed, or tongue-in-cheek tonality in lots of Internet advertising. The implication is "we grew up with this attitude and lingo, so we're in on something other people just don't get."

Yet in a mass media world, everyone who's tuned into it is essentially the same mental age, because we all turn to the same sources for most of our information. What primarily accounts for our differences is the content we choose to feature or exclude and the age of the people with whom we have our usual camaraderie.

Whatever uniqueness is settled on, it must be expressed in a way that convinces the consumer that he or she can't get exactly the same thing anywhere else. When the content is so small that uniqueness is achieved primarily through image advertising, the image should still have a credible foundation.

To summarize, we find the uniqueness and express it exactly; the result is advertising that is appropriately unique.

Think Beyond Words and Pictures to the Power of Form

When many people watch a commercial or read an advertisement, they notice the words and pictures, and when many people create advertising, they think primarily about those two ingredients. But there is something far more powerful behind these ingredients – the form or the overall shape of the argument in the commercial or the print ad.

Form is, of course, everywhere. Take, for instance, classical sculpture. At its best, it embodies an exquisitely balanced combination of form and content. While every part has its individual appeal, it exists in the right place and proportion to the whole.

Form in music is proverbial, for instance, the rondo. We find it readily evident in traditional poetry, for example, the sonnet. The language of Shakespeare is rich and delightful, but the words themselves are like the fingers. The real power is in the overall shape or structure of the play and in the shape or structure of the longer speeches. They are the body behind the fingers.

So when we create, we try to see the form of our ideas whole and then place each word and picture in the wholeness so that it is in the right place and in an appropriate proportion. Of course, we generally do not immediately see the wholeness in all its detail. We cast a long imaginary line. We discover the refinements as we work to express the wholeness, much like a sculptor works to render a statue he has in mind by working and refining here and there.

Charming as some of the parts may be, the overall impact is not in them, but in the parts, shaped into a unit.

Form and Content: An Inverse Proportion

Sometimes the content, or news, in an advertisement is of ultimate importance, but at other times little real content can, or ought to be, communicated. How can we arrive at an appropriate balance?

Here is a little-known insight: form and content function in an inverse proportion. We covered the proportions earlier but in less detail in the section of television commercials.

The more important the news – for instance, a cure for cancer – the simpler the form should be. A serious-minded on-camera announcer will help emphasize the news, while a hospital drama would obscure it. Once the news is established in the mass consciousness, more form can be added, such as testimonials from survivors.

As a Hall of Fame art director I was working with once said to me, "If the headline is 'Pope Elopes,' you don't have to do a lot more than say it."

On the other hand, if there is little real news to communicate, we don't want to make up any that is transparently false or inappropriate. So the emphasis can only come from form. You can see ample evidence in the big production numbers in commercials for brands like Coca-Cola and Budweiser.

The goal is to affect the audience, and an essential part of the means derives from the right balance of persuasive stuff and inviting fluff.

All advertising, however, must be built on some significant or slight content. The advertising must communicate something. It's more effective to present at least some reason for consumers to try the brand, remain loyal to it, or rethink their disposition toward it. The real stuff is often as gossamer as a novel expression of a usual claim.

When a large form is required, we want to be especially careful that it magnifies whatever news there is, no matter how minuscule it is, not get in the way of it, because the tidbit is the unique selling proposition.

It's impossible to create the right, bright advertising with the wrong, dumb form or content.

Given a choice we should never have to make but may find ourselves in the middle of, it's better to have the right content in the wrong form than the wrong content in the right form. The first alternative is more likely to produce some success, because we're saying what we ought to, although not with optimal persuasive power. The second mishap is akin to firing blanks at the target market.

When the creative work achieves the right balance of form and content, the advertising takes a significant step toward what we characterize generally as solid, but is, more specifically, the correct package for the correct sales message.

Agility and the Problem/Solution Format

The typical commercial format is called a problem/solution. Why? If there is no problem the brand solves, what need is there for the brand?

Creatively, it's usually easier to be dramatic by staging the problem. Why? The interest value in all stories and news articles is usually about problems, or crises. So just as a crisis makes a story or the news more interesting, dramatizing the problem rather than the answer is often a readier source of excitement.

Yet we begin by asking where the greatest brand interest and excitement will come from. If we have revelatory news about a brand, we can make an exception and just announce it and bring in the problem afterward.

Otherwise, the obvious and subtle aspects of the problem are likely places to look to for dramatic ingredients to set up the entry of the product as the solution. In fact, few things enliven a campaign like locating a good "whipping boy," which usually can be found in the subtext of exactly the opposite of what you're offering. For example, if we're advertising an e-commerce solution that touts unified customer-relations management, we can create excitement by staging the drawbacks of a piecemeal approach, that is, variations on the complications a confused salesman might experience with managing his relationships.

Staging the problem can attract attention, be memorable, and serve to place the product in the consumer's life. Yet the account team and the client generally have an urge to get to the solution, or entry of the product, as fast as possible.

Can we arrive at a guideline? I think so. It's appropriate proportion.

When the product news is extensive or important, it's imperative to get from the problem to the solution quickly, so there is enough time or space to do it justice.

On the other hand, when the brand story is very simple or when the brand is well-known and the primary purpose of the advertising is to act as a reminder – by presenting the usual story with interesting variety, rather than to introduce major news – the most effective advertising may well devote a great deal of time or space to the problem. It may simply be the most effective way to involve the audience.

Some of the best-know commercials I've written – for instance, twelve spoofs for Dr Pepper – were made up of devoting most of the commercials to staging the problem, with only a few seconds at the end reserved for the solution.

When the campaign began, the beverage was popular in the south, but it seemed an odd and forbidding drink to much of the nation. It appealed primarily to young people, who, at the time, grew up watching television, including old movies, instead of surfing the internet or playing video games. To entertain them and get them over their reservations about the beverage, the spots featured one character trying to convince another one to do something that seemed related to the scene from the original movie, play, or opera, with the denouement being that the protagonist was actually trying to convince the antagonist to try it.

The twelve humorous commercials for the beverage that I wrote helped make it a national brand, as well as a minor form of national levity.

The commercials won a lot of awards. One of the ones I wrote won a Gold Lion from the Cannes Commercial Film Festival, and another one of them won a Silver Lion. Four of the ones I wrote are in the permanent collection of The Paley Museum of Media in New York.

Advertising Should Have Immediate Importance

All advertising should appear to have immediate importance. So the news it presents should sound as consequential as the maintenance of credibility allows. But something more is required. The advertising must have what I call "moment." I touched on it earlier.

What do I mean? The commercial or ad should be poised in a way that makes the news immediately relevant to the consumer's current mindset. The verbal and visual form of the argument should strike the consumer just at the psychological moment she is assumed to be in with regard to her relationship with the brand.

For example, is she likely to be aware of the brand or not? How aware? Is she likely to be well disposed toward it or not? Is the advertising riding on an emerging wave in the mass culture that we feel she is in touch with, so that we can tune her in to the brand message through it?

In summary, immediate importance grows out of the magnitude of the news and presenting it so that it is addressed to the current psychological disposition of the consumer.

Make the Tone Appropriate

When someone speaks to us, we listen to their tone as much as to the content. Tone is an aspect of character, so getting it right is one of the most important overall values.

Tone helps us tell the audience about the advertiser, as well as about the people doing the advertising. When we get it right, the members of the audience are more likely to care about what we want them to do. An overall tone also helps unify the advertising, so it enhances how impactful or memorable it is.

When we speak to different people, or to the same people about different subjects, we speak in a tone that's appropriate. The same guide is true when we speak through mass media. The tone should be right for the product, the audience, and the occasion.

The strategy usually indicates the desired "tone and manner," but the range within the guideline can be wide. So we should proceed with creative latitude, but there are borders. We discover the tone that feels just right as we work. The process is something like finding a path in the dark by going off the edges from time to time or, more dramatically, by driving down a road and banging into the guardrails.

Of course, if we're in familiar territory, we know what tone is right before we begin to create.

Nothing focuses tone like a specific assignment. For instance, if we're advertising a candy to kids, we'll probably prefer a lighthearted tone. If we're creating a public service message to raise money for a shelter, we'll want an earnest tone.

Some categories have a usual tone. Medical advertising is generally in a tone I call "the doctor in disguise." He speaks in the professional but personal manner of a doctor with an excellent bedside manner. Soft-drink advertising is usually "effervescent."

A product or service that solves a relatively trivial problem or that has something inherently funny about it invites a humorous tone. The more significant the problem is that the brand solves, the more likely the tone is to be serious.

Some major advertisers have a tone they prefer. For instance, most Kraft advertising has a family feel, and most advertising for Johnson & Johnson has a mothering feel. Advertising for Bristol-Myers/Squibb generally features attractive people, because the company, although it manufacturers many drugs, also owns Clairol and carries its predilection for beautiful people and images over even to it medical advertising.

Is there a way to become deft at selecting the right tone? Beyond referencing the strategy, here are effective ways to learn. Start to observe the variety of tones in which advertising is executed, and look over collections of past advertising, especially work that has won awards. Notice that different television shows and films also have tones.

A copywriter can increase his tonal range by observing the ways language has been used to achieve goals, from the earliest works to contemporary ones. I mentioned earlier that you can get an excellent cram course by studying the classic lyricists of the theater, because the lyrics were written to meet a variety of tonal occasions. Since they're also brief, there are lessons in compactness, euphony, parallelism, and contrast, etc. The role of the refrain is much like the role of a slogan. There are delightful lessons in precision and enchantment in the librettos of W. S. Gilbert, and the lyrics of, say, Noel Coward, Ira Gershwin, Larry Hart, Cole Porter, and Oscar Hammerstein.

An art director can explore the visual tonal palette by reviewing the history of visual achievement, from paintings and illustrations to photographs and even the motifs of the circus, which are carryovers from the showy publicity tactics of P. T. Barnum.

The Art of the Skillful Miniaturist

Advertising consists of miniature creative forms. So, like the watchmaker with his loop, we work to get every little thing right. Every word, and even every syllable, is important. We can say that there are actually no small values.

For example, we want to make sure our copy isn't softened by excessive use of words that end in "-ing," "-ly," "-er" and other soft syllables, especially in our headlines and slogans. Notice the difference between "It gets to your pain fast" and "It gets to your pain quickly."

And how memorable would Winston Churchill have been if he said, "We shall be fighting them on the beaches" instead of "We shall fight them on the beaches"?

Of course, you may opt for an occasional syllabic extravagance when a word with a soft ending just seems to fit better in terms of the smallest hints of meaning or in the overall cadence of the copy.

What about the visuals? The tiniest aspects are important, too. For example, there's something greatly appealing and artistically satisfying about having just the right highlight on an insert shot that features, say, a gelcap. And every art director with a highly developed visual sense wants to get even the smallest, or the mice, type just right.

There is a Place for Humor

It's one of the colors on the tonal palette of versatile creative people and should be used when appropriate.

While serious subjects generally require a serious tone, lighter ones invite humor.

After all, don't some of the best salesmen have a sense of humor that they use when the time is right? In the same way, advertising can sell better when it employs humor at the right time. Once in a while, it can be dared when seriousness would be the norm; for instance, in an effort to transcend the constraints of a small media budget.

The only time humor should be absolutely ruled out is when the product or service is of such a serious nature that a humorous approach would vitiate the message.

It helps us decide which tone to use if we see ourselves in the court of the king, who, in our case, is the consumer. Who are we? The clowns of commerce, who tumble in and amuse, or is it time to be the wise man who whispers sage advice in the king's ear.

By the way, seeming ourselves in the court of the king is also a helpful way to magnify other subjects. For instance, when people say America is in the service business, I wonder how they can expect the nation to continue as the most powerful nation in the world. The king is not in the service business.

How to Make People Laugh

How do you create humorous advertising? Even those with a good sense of humor can learn what we might call the craft of the laugh.

Of course, you can learn a bit by watching sit-coms and other TV shows that aim for humor or social satire. But most of the shows only achieve smiles or chuckles. What's the difference?

First, let's talk about the overall form of a funny idea. There is an important general principle that applies especially to short forms. Create a whole idea that's funny, instead of attempting to crack jokes in one that isn't. From the get-go, shift the usual expectations of the viewer to a world where incongruity reigns. When the whole is funny, the parts are. In fact, they can be hilarious.

Most laughs come from visual events. People see them and laugh. Watch the silent comics.

What about verbal laughs? If you listen to a good standup comic, and there are precious few, you'll notice that the jokes are made up of more than just words. The setup sentence or phrase creates a mental picture. The punch line describes a funny event that happens in the mental picture. When you see it, you laugh. So that the punch line comes as a surprise, the setup is usually presented in a way that creates, not only the expectation of a coming event, but some uncertainty as to what it will be. Bob Hope was especially adept at seeking out and utilizing jokes that achieved their effect with a one-sentence verbal/visual setup and a one-sentence verbal/visual punch line. A series of these setups and releases made up his monologues. Think about the visual content of your favorite jokes.

Much humor proceeds through outrage. Since the advertising is the voice of the advertiser, it's not usually germane.

So how can you create humor without upsetting a lot of people? As you know, a joke has a brunt – a person or a place where the punchline lands. The impact releases the laugh. Since you want to enchant consumers, it's unwise to make them the brunt. Also, avoid making the brunt anyone or anything your consumers may have an affinity for. Campaigns that do make the mistake of making the consumer the brunt are usually annoying and the creative people run out of relatively acceptable slams rather quickly. One egregious example was some highly publicized advertising for Apple Computers. The goal was to attract PC users, but the target audience was portrayed as a fool. So the advertising was more likely to appeal to Apple users, who could pat themselves on the back and feel superior. Meanwhile, the audience the advertising was directed at was likely to feel insulted and even less likely to convert.

We can say that advertising is, to a degree, the art of creating risk-free excitement. So I especially suggest that you avoid insult comedy. When the joke doesn't work, all that's left is the insult. The aim in advertising is mutually considerate fun for you and the audience. Where can you turn for it? A usual source for brunts is to make the joke reflexive; that is, make sure the punch lines land on the commercial itself, the product, the company that makes it, or a character in it, providing the character is not the type of person the consumer will see as himself or herself. Another source is to base the commercial on content that the consumer is unlikely to see himself or herself as part of, like a classic story or remote character, such as caveman or, for a change, a cavewoman.

There are other ways you can learn to make people laugh. For a crash course, read books of humorous quotations. Mark Twain's quotations and short pieces are a good place to start. Read collections of humorous theater sketches. Two sketches that will show you how to use an overall form that's funny are "The Still Alarm" and "If Men Played Cards As Women Do," both by George S. Kaufman. Longer comedies are also a great resource, such as the plays "The Front Page" and "Room Service," which are now, of course, old movies. Both can be seen on Turner Classic Movies.

You can learn to set up and release sight gags by watching the silent comics work, like Charlie Chaplin and Laurel & Hardy. You can learn the art of sight gags and verbal wit from the later movie comics, such as the Marx Brothers and Abbott & Costello. More subtle sight gags can be found in the films of Jacques Tati and visual/verbal ones in the roles of Peter Sellers. I don't find many recent movies well-crafted in terms of how to release laughter. Goofiness is more likely to be the source of guilty giggles.

If you'd like to go deeper into what releases laughter, particularly when it releases otherwise hidden content, you may want to read Freud's *Wit and its Relation to the Unconscious*.

I suggest you study humor seriously. Don't just note what's making you laugh. Ask how it's making your laugh.

Sometimes, when you do get an opportunity to create a funny commercial or ad, you may just not be in a funny mood. There are few more regrettable sights than people with white knuckles trying to be funny. You can suggest your intent to yourself by consciously putting a small, impish smile on your face as you work, just as you're likely to frown when you work in a serious tone.

Finally, remember that the laughter belongs to the audience, not to the joke teller. Jack Benny found that being downright dour worked for him. Rodney Dangerfield learned to be a hapless loser. Both learned that when the creators of humor are doing the laughing, chances are the audience isn't.

Leave a Place for the Audience

Most advertising proceeds from start to finish to achieve its own self-interested goal. Smarter advertising invites the consumer to participate.

How? Ask yourself, "During my effort to sell, where does the spot or ad take a moment or so to relate to the audience? Is there a space where my advertising has more to do with the consumer than it does with the brand?"

All that's required are a few words, a scene, or a photograph. This wise generosity should be at the beginning of a commercial or part of the headline and/or visual.

For instance, if you would like to sell a detergent, instead of opening up in the laundry room, you might spend a moment showing mom playing outdoors with her child and talking about something that has nothing to with dirty clothes or whitening power. Maybe the child, tossing a shovelful of sand in the air, says, "This is so much fun, Mom!" And the mom replies, "I know. My mother used to play in the sandbox with me, too."

When there's not a lot to say about a product itself, you might even devote the slogan to the consumer's life. An inviting blandishment can achieve a lot. Consider Nike's slogan, "Just do it!"

How to Use Borrowed Interest

When a product has real interest in itself, the job of the advertising is to stage the interest. Sometimes, however, we need or want to add something interesting to our advertising. We may be dealing with a frequently advertised brand that has a simple story, so people have seen the usual content and don't expect much new or with a brand that people might not be as interested in as we'd like them to be. In such cases, we must create added interest. We can imagine more creative executions. One of the resources we can turn to is what is known as borrowed interest. We relate something more interesting to the product or service.

The interest can come from virtually anywhere, usually a star, a cultural icon or a new trend. Notice how the advertising for Kenneth Cole attaches itself to cultural topics; the only product claim is implied hipness. Apparently, the client is satisfied that the goals for the advertising are being met.

More astutely, once the interest to be borrowed is settled on, the correct task is to borrow it in a way that, not only adds interest, but also helps magnify the selling proposition.

How to Create Advertising That's Bigger Than Advertising

When advertising transcends the limits of pure salesmanship and adds an interesting ingredient to the culture, it's said to be bigger than advertising. Take, for example, slogans that consumers have picked up:

"Try it. You'll like it."

"Where's the beef?"

These slogans became vehicles for people to express many of their own sentiments in novel and supposedly witty ways. While such developments often happen inadvertently, they can be helped along.

The day-to-day lives of most people are, at least on the surface, kind of routine, particularly in a mass-media society, where most of us usually go to work and then come back home, where the rest of the world comes to us. Advertising, welcome or not, is part of the incoming stream of information and entertainment. And most of the stream is kind of ordinary.

So while going about the usual business of magnifying the selling proposition, if we say something clever, it will stand out and seem fresh. If it helps people express themselves in a catchy new way, many of them will adopt it as a ready way to seem fresh and tuned in themselves. A novel visual may also get them talking.

The magnetic ingredient may also consist of a new trend, featured in advertising for the first time. So it helps to keep tabs of the doings in the mass culture, or trend spotting. Yet we don't want to get lost in trivia. It's easier to put a spin on something when we can observe it with intelligent perspective.

Using Objective Correlatives

Concrete visual and verbal items outside of your product that you select to relate to your message to magnify it are known as objective correlatives. We might also consider them cultural correlatives. They occur in all kinds of writing but today are most often encountered in lyrics we've come to consider standards.

Consider Ira Gershwin's lyric "Our Love is Here to Stay." What happens in the listener's mind when the lyric states that "The Rockies may crumble and Gibraltar may tumble, but our love is here to stay"? The words create visuals that illustrate or magnify the meaning. Or consider Cole Porter's lyric for "You're the Top." This "list song" enumerates objective correlatives one after the other, such as comparing the object of the song to the Mona Lisa and the Tower of Pisa.

As an aside, Ira said that the way he worked was to get a title and then prove it. Creating advertising is much the same. We develop a brand promise and prove it in one tactic after another.

How do we learn to use our metaphorical minds visually and verbally? We develop the capacity as time goes by.

Sometimes, when we begin an assignment, it's helpful to make a quick mental scan of the culture to see if there are elements in it that apply to the work. The tactic is usually better for one-time ads and commercials than for long-term campaigns.

Here's an example from my own work. It's an ad the great Art Director Harvey Baron and I did for Mikasa tableware for a Presidents Day sale. At the time, he was my art partner in Heavy Creative, Inc.

We were on a tight timeline and were after a quick ad. If we simply announced the sale, we'd have a one-dimensional presentation, transparent but charmless. Adapting a cultural tie-in was appropriate. It would make our answer multidimensional.

Here are two of many headlines we developed:

The sale Martha Washington would have crossed the Delaware for.

The one time a year Washington saves you money.

The last ad is the one the client bought. He liked the sub-textual cultural reference to taxes.

While working on this project, a bonus inspiration arrived. I was thinking about people serving dinner on attractive plates, drinking wine from delicate glasses, and other events in the life of a product or service that are called "use-occasions." I realized that there is a moment of appreciation for tasteful dinnerware and stemware. The thought dropped in "Mikasa makes the moment." Our long-term assignment was to develop an image campaign. So, after we presented the individual ads, we announced we had a present. Then we presented the line as the slogan for the campaign, and the client bought it.

Consumer Attention Is Usually Involuntary

Although it may pain us to remind ourselves, when consumers watch, listen to, or read advertising, they're often doing it involuntarily. The exception is when they're in the market for a particular item or have decided to pay attention to or look into a brand or category.

Part of the blame lies with advertising itself. There are so many loud, inconsiderate, and outright dumb advertisements that we come to resent advertising in general. The most usual offender is graceless hard-sell advertising. Some of the blame also lies with the number of commercials networks are currently packing into the breaks. These overloaded presentations are a disservice to advertisers and encourage people to fast forward to the program they're watching.

Even when advertising is inviting, people usually only lend their attention to it with impatience. They're certain they have more important things to do.

So, once we've attracted their attention, we have to use every resource to keep it. How? We must continue to deliver, in the tone that captivated them, what they perceive to be information of urgent or, at least, middling importance to them. To achieve their continuing attention, the message must continue as a coherent whole.

To amplify the point, I used to tell the copy trainees at Y & R to think of the advertisement as a strand of spaghetti, not separate pieces of macaroni. Once you get the tip of it into the consumer's mouth, you have to keep feeding it as an unbroken strand, until it's all been eaten.

How to Overcome Skepticism

Consumers are skeptical of advertising. We've given them plenty of reasons to be. So, obviously, the best way to remain credible is to refrain from providing reasons to be disbelieved. Over time, the brands we work on will gain an aura of trust.

If we find ourselves with a claim that seems incredible, we must make sure to back it up with undeniable proof.

Are there specific tactics to overcome skepticism? Testimonials are a proverbial method. But there are other ways.

When we make a claim, we can attempt to do so in a way that makes the truth seem self-evident; that is, we include or imply the truthfulness right in the statement. Take the slogan, "With a name like Smucker's, it has to be good."

You might ask, why waste time telling people what is self-evidently true? Sometimes the most effective thing to do is magnify a known attribute, as reminder copy or to reaffirm the claim when the product or service has ignored utilizing it or has wandered from it.

Visual proof can be effective and sometimes more effective than verbal proof. A ready way to overcome skepticism is to show the consumer what we're talking about. As an example, if we're telling them that our stores have been remodeled and are now great places to shop, when we know she doesn't remember them that way, we realize that the most inarguable proof is to take potential shoppers on a tour of one or more of them.

Using Testimonials

In the above instance, we'd also want to consider testimonials, that is, showing and hearing from shoppers who've discovered the truth of what we're claiming.

While often considered dull, testimonials are a technique and can be used in original and winning ways.

While the usual reason to employ them is to overcome skepticism, they can also serve to build more trust, to personalize a communication, gain attention with a star or characters of a certain type, or communicate an attribute, such as low prices or high quality.

Talent agents regularly circulate lists of celebrities who are available. The wiser include the attitude of the public toward the star, particularly in terms of a characteristic for which the potential testifier is ranked high. So, if we need to establish trust, we look for a spokesperson who has a high trust profile.

At other times, we may want to employ everyday people, because other everyday people tend to trust those they perceive to be similar to themselves, even more than they do experts.

If we frame, cast, and shoot them brightly, we can end up with commercials that are actually likable and innovative.

Generally, it's usually better to shoot testifiers in an environment that they can be expected to inhabit, instead of uprooting them and putting them on-camera for our own transparent purposes.

They can also be used as an aspect of a campaign, rather than as the format of its entirety. For instance, we can introduce a product without them. Then we can accompany it or follow it with a person or people who confirm that what we said about the product or service is actually true.

The Value of an Ongoing Character or Characters

Sometimes, a star or an everyday person is featured in a campaign for a product or service. But characters in commercials generally come and go. Apparently, the power of ongoing characters has not been as much appreciated by the advertising industry as it has been by TV program developers, who will hardly even consider programs that don't feature them.

Notice how shows are built around an ongoing character or, more usually, a cast of continuing characters. The developers know that people like to develop relationships with other people and that the process occurs over time.

The same applies to advertising. Consider the Maytag salesman, William Shatner for Priceline.com, plump as he has become, and George Foreman with his BBQ grille.

Continuity though character can enhance brand recognition. As soon as the audience sees the character, they're reminded of the advertising, the message, and their own disposition toward the product or service. There are also subliminal values, for instance, the consumer may decide that the company that makes the product is nice, because it continues to employ the character, and people generally like to do business with people they consider nice.

Of course, the character can also be used in all kinds of promotional materials. The unity enhances impact and recall.

Don't Climb Any Mountains You Don't Have To

You want to achieve success, and it lies on the other side of the mountain. The surest way to get there is to take the route that offers the least resistance. In other words, don't address any problems or attempt to achieve any goals that are not absolutely essential to success. So in developing the advertising, deciding what you have to say and show also involves deciding what you don't have to say and show. Specifically, you don't want to make and prove any claims you don't have to.

Here's an instance from my own experience. Once, General Foods retained me to develop concepts for new Jell-O Instant Boston Cream Pies. At the focus groups, we hit a sticking point with consumers. The cake component was prepared by opening an envelope filled with yellow crumbs, moistening them with milk, fluffing them with a fork, and then putting them in the bottom of a glass. I tried to make the crumbs and the process sound appetizing. But the word "crumbs" was a nonstarter with consumers. So I rewrote the concepts, calling them bits, morsels, and even golden nuggets – anything but the dreaded crumbs. But we discovered a cosmic truth: to consumers a crumb is a crumb. Although they had accepted graham-cracker crumbs as a way to make a crust for Jell-O Instant Cheesecake, now we were talking about a cake component they had a lifelong perception of as light and fresh.

Then the bright bird of wonder landed on my head. I asked myself if the consumer really had to know how to make the pies. Maybe the response would change dramatically if we just announced the advent of luscious Boston Cream Pies you could whip up in an instant. So I deleted any mention of how they were prepared, including any reference to the crumbs. Instant result: people loved the concept and couldn't wait to try the product.

The quantitative test results came in high, too, and the miraculous little product made its way to market. Whether consumers were able to make peace with the crumbs in the privacy of their own homes is beyond my knowledge. The point is, we arrived at whatever success we did by not climbing a mountain we didn't have to.

Don't Start a Battle You Can't Win

Should you create a campaign that is directly competitive? It depends on the magnitude of your advantage, the size of your budget, and the courage of your client. Brand land is ruled by giants, and it's easy to get stepped on and crushed, especially if we taunt one of them.

A Chinese Emperor once said that he would never go into a battle until he was sure he had already won it. He prepared so that his advantage was overwhelming. It's sound advice.

If you're a megabrand, you can find confidence in your own crushing size. And, if you're a small brand, you can also be pretty sure that the giant you're attacking won't do battle with you, because it would only attract attention to you. You can generally expect to be ignored but can never be certain.

Big brand or small, if your claim is so strong that you begin to chip away at the competitor's share of market, you may be in for a return salvo. The effect depends partly on the size of the competitor you've aroused.

If you've got a strong competitive advantage, you can be more confident that you'll do well, come what may.

Before proceeding, evaluate the risk-reward ratio. How much are we likely to gain or lose? Is the estimated success significantly greater than the one you might have simply by magnifying your claim without a direct reference to the competition? All things considered, do the odds indicate at least some degree of incremental success? In your assessment, include an estimate of the client's sentiment. Is he or she likely to be comfortable with competitive advertising if the going gets hot?

To dare or not to dare – that is the question. Tread carefully but dare appropriately.

The Truths Sells – And Gets on the Air

While advertising has less than a stellar reputation for telling the truth, the most enlightened goal of advertising is to present the truth in the most convincing way.

Despite the general perception of advertising, it actually has to be based on the truth, particularly when it appears in major media. As often noted, advertising is the most regulated form of selling in history. W. C. Fields and his forebears, touting a magical elixir from the small stage of a traveling cart, had far more leeway than any national advertiser would dare to permit.

Yet America is one of the most sophisticated media markets, If not the most sophisticated, so consumers generally expect and factor in that advertising presents the truth with a degree of hyperbole. And the practice is permitted within the range of general words that indicate superiority, like "best" or "greatest." As you probably know, they're considered puffery.

The harsh reality is if creative people don't express the truth at the maximum acceptable level of hyperbole, the agency or the client will quickly look for somebody who will.

Finally, however, most realize that the truth is the only reliable foundation for an ongoing business. Why? It's the only thing the product can live up to. If we promise something it doesn't deliver, the consumer won't buy it again. No repeat sales, no ongoing business.

We come to understand just how regulated modern advertising is when we attempt to create it for drugs. The medical/legal people have a reference book with all FDA approved claims for each drug. There's very little you can do except create an original form in which to wrap the approved boilerplate. When I began to work in the area, it was on Excedrin. I tried to humanize the overworked lingo "for the temporary relief of minor pain," etc. No chance. The copy would come back, crossed out, with the boilerplate as a substitute.

Children's advertising is another area with pages of guidelines.

Lesson: magnify the truth for all its worth, but never lie. You probably won't get away with it anyway. But you can look stupid for trying.

Never Underestimate the Power of Sincerity

Sincerity in advertising is a generally an underappreciated value. Presented in a sit-com, it would be ridiculed as impractical or the sentiment of a loser. Such is the superficial society we attempt to be intelligent in.

Yet authors from Leo Tolstoy to Oscar Hammerstein have touted its artistic merits. When you're sincere, most people will sense it and be encouraged to be sincere in how they listen and respond. Consumers actually resent insincerity. They expect an advertisement to tell them something of value, so they can make up their minds if the product or service has a place in their lives.

And, no matter what your tone, you should be sincere - serious, funny, or whatever. On the other hand, never overdo it. You'll become unctuous.

For example, few things are funnier than doing or saying something hilarious in a very sincere way. See Charlie Chaplain, as a waiter trying to carve a chicken with concentrated effort, only to have his effort send it flying off to slam into a customer. Or Jack Benny with his violin and his cultivated reputation for cheapness. You probably know the joke. A thief comes up to him, and says, "Your money or your life!" He considers the matter seriously, and replies, "Let me think about it." The audience laughs. He continues to consider the matter very sincerely, and the audience continues to laugh. In fact, sincerity is so important in humor that if you "have fun with your fun," you'll take the laugh away from the audience – the reason all skillful comics, past or present, perform in a relatively deadpan manner. The laugh belongs to the audience.

Smart Sell Works Better Than Hard Sell

Everybody wants advertising that is effective. Some advertisers confuse that goal with advertising that is known as hard sell or hard hitting. It may work. But let's remember that the consumer is usually a woman. Imagine trying to get your way by going home and being hard-hitting with your wife. You'd try to be smarter, wouldn't you?

Now, consider that mass media only serves the advertiser as an interface between someone who wants to sell something and someone who may want to listen. It's not a disguise. So a hard-hitting voice sounds as if it's coming from a hard person. We might even say an inconsiderate one. In addition, advertising that "mouths off" can make an advertiser sound as if he's among the painless brainless – not especially desirable company in which to place the corporate image.

Many think the only alternative to hard sell is soft sell. If we only consider the tone of the advertising, the dichotomy holds.

When we consider all the values, we come up with a third choice: smart sell. Since we rarely consider people who shout at us smart, hard sell drowns out the possibility of smart sell. But a softer tone at least makes smart sell possible. We might say it is the precondition of opening up a rational communication with the consumer. Of course, we do not want to speak in an excessively obsequious manner, because we will sound false and unbearable. A good metaphor to guide us is the one we often give announcers: imagine that you're putting your arm around the shoulders of a friend and giving him or her what you generally believe is good and genuinely exciting advice.

When we speak softly and politely, we indicate to the consumer that she is being spoken to by an intelligent and thoughtful person – someone who might even have something interesting to tell her. Then we can make the most of her more open response.

There is another reason to speak softly and carry a big message. Since advertising media are generally "cool," loudness pushes the audience away, while softness invites participation. In fact, silence in advertising is so unusual it makes people lean forward and perk up their ears.

Then, within that welcoming environment, we can be as brightly persuasive as we can.

Such advertising can be so effective it can drown out hard sell.

Speaking in a polite and thoughtful way has another significant benefit. Big companies, when they behave, seem proper but, to many consumers, they can also seem intimidating. Savvy consumers also harbor subliminal feelings that worldwide companies may be too big for their own good, regardless if such size is what enables their international success and ultimately America's success.

When such companies retain their composure, they make the most of the natural persuasiveness that comes as part of their imposing persona. It is not cast into the wind by a loud announcer.

Tastefulness and restraint enhance credibility and persuasiveness and create the forum for copywriting and advertising in general that can achieve the greatest success.

In his book *The Summing Up*, Somerset Maugham said that he considered the novel "intelligent entertainment." Smart advertisers should opt for intelligent salesmanship.

See the Strategy, or Product Story, as a Paragraph

Advertising strategies are written in sections, much like a PowerPoint presentation. It's a convenient way to get a handle on the various aspects of the strategy. Yet, creatively speaking, these constructs are sort of like Frankenstein yearning to be whole.

Once the material in the strategy is clearly in mind, you might find that you can think more precisely about the advertising if you see the strategy, or the product story, as a paragraph. It should begin with, rather than build to, the general, or topic, idea, which can be the goal of the advertising, if we're thinking only strategically. Then we develop the paragraph with how we're going to achieve the goal. Starting this way, however, is inevitably brand-focused, instead of consumer focused.

When we're thinking about the advertising, or the actual communication of the strategy, it's more correct to begin the paragraph with the topic sentence of the campaign, that is, with the slogan.

Now, we turn to how we plan to prove the slogan. So in the next sentence we include the primary benefit. Then we go on to develop the paragraph with the secondary benefit or benefits and the reason or reasons to believe, etc.

We can add a sentence about the target audience and perhaps one about the competitive framework. Then we conclude with the appropriate call to action.

The paragraph, visualized in the mind's eye, is a graspable, responsive unit. So it's a more workable way to imagine ways to realize the potential of the strategy in creative advertising and marketing.

Hit the Nail on the Head but with Style

The job of an individual tactic or a campaign is to drive home the main message. Seen it as a nail and notice that you can hammer all day right beside it nothing will happen. Hit it even a little to one side, and you may bend it so out of shape that you can never get the job done. At least, you won't drive it as well as you hope. The right way to drive it is to hit it on the head. What else would a good carpenter do? I don't mean to create advertising as dull as a thud. Hitting the nail on the head should be done with style and appropriate originality. The magic comes, not from a clever indirect blow, but from the sureness and style of the swing.

Make Sure There Is Something Specific for the Consumer to Pay For

When you decide to buy something, you're usually specific about what you're paying for. The consumer makes her decisions the same way, even if all she has decided to pay for is an image she likes. She has decided it's her kind of image. Yet it's astonishing how much advertising, creative and otherwise, doesn't present something specific, and appropriately emphasized, for the consumer to pay for.

Make sure all of your advertising contains it and that it's presented in the most inviting and compelling way.

Make Your Advertising Newsworthy

Mass media welcomes news. It was devised to present it in various forms, as well as to bring us entertainment. As a result, consumers are conditioned to go to media for news or, in a broader sense, newness. They expect to find it there and are disposed toward receiving it. To make the most of this aspect of media, all advertising should be newsworthy. It should feature compelling news, as much as it credibly can, that will advance the consumer's understanding of or disposition toward the brand.

To help us judge advertising in terms of news content, let's call the ingredient announcement value. Now, when you look at a commercial, print or digital ad, or even website or landing page headline you've just created, ask yourself, "How much announcement value does it have?" If there isn't any, put it aside and create something that has it.

Of course, news is the raison d'etre of advertising for a new product. But even the most advertised brands, which are condemned to present a lot of reminder copy, should have some sort of announcement value in every creative tactic – something new, even if it's just a bright new turn of language or piece of visual excitement that adds a new and inviting dimension to the product story.

Avoid Unnecessarily Loud Commercials & Internet Videos

While most of nature generally seems pretty serene, human beings, though part of it, make all kinds of racket. Paradoxically, however, noise disappears into noise. Any addition to it becomes part of the overall cacophony. So, in terms of its ability to communicate, blatant noise actually becomes silent. Lesson: excessively loud advertising is not only annoying; it also tends to get lost in the loud crowd.

It's functioning at the same intensity as a lot of its surroundings, so it blends in with the other screamers. It's also not the most desirable temperature. It's hot, or off-putting, which is different from warm or cool, which can be inviting. In fact, in media, especially TV spots and internet videos, a hot tonality usually drives people away, while a warm or cool one invites them to participate.

One of the ways to invite people to listen is by saying less than expected, even introducing that most unusual of advertising values, an extended silence, which, partly out of surprise, invites people to participate as powerfully as any other tactic.

If you choose not to be loud and the client is wise enough to agree, you've taken the first step to being heard more. The next step is to speak in a warmer tone, one that obviously recognizes human-to-human values. This is one of the rarest tones in media and the preferred way to make contact with your audience. Since a great deal of the content of mass media is created by relatively insensitive and self-interested people, it often has a pervasive impersonal tone.

A cool tone can also work; witness "cool" actors, from Gary Cooper and Marlon Brando to the latest "cool" guy. Their unwillingness to come at the audience creates a gaping hole for the audience to come at them.

Of course, there are exceptions. At times, a product or a political campaign invites you to speak in a tougher tone – perhaps when you're in a widely recognized competitive battle. Or to speak in a stuffier tone, usually for a pricey product. Yet, even in these cases, you want to proceed in such a way that you're speaking as one human being to another. Lose it and the connection will likely be lost.

There is no need to give an example of tough-minded advertising; there's always some of it around, especially in an election year, some of it scandalously tough-minded.

There is also usually a lot of the stuffy stuff. For instance, listen to the tonality of the advertising for Mercedes-Benz and Lexus. Pretty highfalutin for a fancy bucket of bolts.

Overall, when the content and form, including the tone, of the advertising seems just right, trust it. It will stand out even if you whisper it. It will very likely succeed, as well as help make our clangorous world a trifle easier on the ears of sensitive souls.

Overcoming Clutter: An Imaginary Sine Wave

How do we make our advertising stand out in the clutter? Here's a device that will help. It's an imaginary graph that represents the temperature of media. It moves along like a sine wave, with crests and troughs of various amplitudes, somewhat like our moods.

To begin, imagine the graph moving along on your television screen during a typical night of viewing. Most of the programs and commercials occur within a pretty predictable temperature range, or level of excitement. The sit-coms will have a certain amount of inane wisecracking, the action-adventure shows will rack up a dramatic but cost-effective body count, and the commercials will move through their usual varieties of form, transparent hype, and uneven production values. The graph will reflect these usual fluctuations in temperature and, as you might expect, there won't be much variation in amplitude.

Now, imagine what happens when something comes on the screen that's significantly warmer, brighter, more beautiful, cooler, or, yes, tougher than the usual content; that is, something more inviting or involving. It has a different temperature than the surrounding clutter. And its unexpected advent bleeps the graph.

If it's warmer, which is the usual case, it creates a sudden rise in the crest of the wave. If it's cooler, it creates a sudden downswing. The most important thing is that it changes the usual temperature of the screen. Then it's gone, and the graph resumes its usual amplitude. What do you think most people will remember?

Our imaginary graph also applies to print media. To experience it, imaginatively position yourself in front of a newsstand and visualize the movement of the graph as you look over the array of publications. The colorful magazines feature the usual abundance of gorgeously retouched women, men trying to represent our somewhat uncertain vision of handsomeness, oddly turned out young people, and captions trying to grab our attention with the latest of everything that's acceptably inconsequential. Turning to newspapers, a tabloid headline shouts something risqué, whether consequential or trivial, as controversially as the editors can manage, but we expect it to. The broadsheet newspapers lie there with their invitation to a more judicious consideration of the day's events. Has the graph done anything unexpected?

Now, peruse a few of the publications and keep the graph in mind. Consider the ads in relation, not only to other ads, but to the articles. After all, advertising must stand out in the total environment. The ads go about their usual business of trying to capture attention and persuade, but, you note with remorse, they're generally so ordinary that you decide they can contain little of compelling interest to you. So the graph is still pretty much moving along within a usual amplitude.

Then you turn a page and there's a really focused, bright, and appropriate idea, invitingly presented. You're struck by it, appreciate the bright competence, and note the bleep in the graph. For our own purposes, let's say the cause of the amplitude shift was an ad, not an article.

Since you're also a consumer, you can be pretty sure that other consumers will notice the ad, too, even without the aid of our responsive graph.

The graph also applies to surfing the internet.

Here is the major benefit. When you think in terms of the graph as you create advertising, you can judge the usual temperature of the media it will appear in. So you can judge if a piece of creative work is hot or cold enough to alter the amplitude of the imaginary graph markedly.

Since advertising is often primarily a visual medium, the need, more usually, the desperation, to achieve a high recall score for a commercial or to stand out in any kind of clutter can make creative people resort to what I call visual stunting. Something truly odd will happen, such as a torso being twisted, to indicate some form of gastrointestinal distress. The visual stunt is a device we must all turn to from time to time, and, thankfully, it can be utilized tastefully.

The intent of this section is, however, not to enumerate a laundry list of devices that gain attention but to provide a reliable way to judge if your work will achieve it.

Deftly Appropriate Originality Stands Out

An original and winning idea appears in media only rarely. So, even when it appears in advertising, it stands out.

Each inviting new arrival achieves its goal by utilizing, with various levels of talent and skill, the verbal and visual resources of media available for the particular occasion. People recognize the achievement, and many actually appreciate the artfulness. So they talk about it. For instance, what a pleasant surprise it is to note for the first time a bright new slogan that seems just right for its intent.

What do people talk about it? It's an event.

To misappropriate an insight of Herbert Marcuse, a sage of the sixties, who stated that in a modern society many people become "one-dimensional." According to him, they merely reflect the input of media without processing it and making up their own minds about it, so they come to define themselves by what they choose to reflect. A lot of them like to reflect ideas and products that are presented in a bright way. Doing so helps them feel bright. The more intelligent souls will, of course, process the bright advertising before they make up their minds about it. They may also admire it, unless they've attached their egos to detesting advertising categorically.

When to Risk Directly Competitive Advertising

Consumers want to be fair-minded. It's part of the sense of fair play we all grow up with. So a great many of them react negatively to directly competitive advertising, particularly when it seems to take unfair advantage of the other product. This reflexive reaction is particularly pronounced in focus groups, where peer influence encourages vocal allegiance to what the respondents perceive to be their shared standards. When presented with advertising that slams the competition, even with restraint and credibility, they reject it and insist that a product should be sold on its own merits.

Some clients feel the same way, especially at the largest companies, which generally have the luxury of remaining above the fray. Since their aim is to shepherd the leading brands through the ever-present calculations of wannabe competitors, they're usually being wise. They know that it's counterproductive to put the me-too brands up there with their own or to give them any kind of free publicity. So it takes a direct attack that begins to do unusual damage to bring their high-minded attitude into question and finally to create enough urgency for them to act.

Despite the usual attitude of consumers and major advertisers, a great deal of directly competitive advertising still goes on, and some of it works. When should you risk it? The easiest answer is when you're advertising a small brand with little to lose and much to gain. The call to be competitive is seductive if your product has an advantage over the leading entry, especially when the advantage makes up for a weakness in the leading brand that the audience doesn't know about, and you believe that pointing out the difference will do your product a great deal of good; in fact, in such cases, you almost feel an obligation to let the audience in on the shortcoming and the improvement.

Another time being directly competitive recommends itself is when you're creating advertising for a new product that has a significant advantage over the leading entry, or over all the established brands in the category, and you know that you have to succeed quickly to keep your new brand on the shelves of impatient retailers and to achieve enough sales to continue to fund the cost of the slotting allowance for the shelf space and for the advertising. A new product has to gain an impressive share of the market in the brief window allotted to it or fall from the shelf and be consigned to the lot of the vanquished.

When you decide to make a directly competitive pitch, you must, of course, be especially careful that the claim or claims you're making are on solid ground legally.

Next, you must present the claim or claims with precision. It's counterproductive to exaggerate and create undue risk. If the facts are strong enough, the clear presentation of them should achieve your goal.

One way to ameliorate the supposed antipathy of consumers who note your direct comparison is to present the advantage or advantages as if you're sharing the information only or primarily because you have their best interests in mind. You can be a hero for pointing out something to them that really is, in a great or small way, better for them. A little wit or humor also softens the blow. So does even a passing positive comment about the brand you're comparing your own to. Skillfully done, competitive advertising can actually be presented in a way that appears fair minded.

Avoid Negative Advertising

What is the difference between competitive and negative advertising? There may be positive aspects to competitive advertising. As just noted, it can allow a genuine improvement to be brought to light in a way that will help assure the brand's survival. Competitive advertising can also be done without crass disregard for the other product or for the sensitivities of those who have a preference for it and the anxieties of those whose livelihoods depend on it.

Negative advertising, as we define it, consists of just slamming another product – in the jargon, "trash canning" it. It's a tasteless tactic and it can backfire. So, even when we have every reason to be directly competitive, we should all aim to make our points like the considerate folks we are.

Involving the brand in such graceless self-interested behavior can tarnish it and undermine the effectiveness of the advertising. Many consumers, bless their fair-mindedness, will decide they just don't like you and don't want to give you their money.

Such unfeeling heavy-handedness also exposes competitive economics and advertising to criticism. Both merit our respect. So let us proceed in a way that helps enable the rightful role of advertising, as the informative and generally well-mannered voice of competitive economics, as well as competitive causes and candidates.

Brainstorming, or When the Clouds Roll in

Creative people are generally independent minded, so they aren't much attracted to brainstorming. I used to say, "When the brainstorming starts, the clouds roll in."

But in time I learned it has a place. It's a spontaneous and efficient way to plum the obvious. So it can serve as a way to collect the top-of-mind thoughts of, for example, the marketing and research people for a new product or at a new client.

Prior thinking or the interaction itself may occasionally unearth ideas that are a bit deeper. On rare occasion, something inspired may occur.

But the process has limits, and it's certainly not a substitute for individual creativity. To amplify, imagine that you've been hired to take a voyage of the imagination. In the usual scenario, you load up your boat with the proper supply of information and then off you go, on an imaginary voyage, headed for the unknown with hope and confidence. What happens with brainstorming? Every time your mind leaves the dock, you're called back to hear somebody else's idea.

The result is, the water near the dock gets turned into a froth while more distant waters remain unexplored.

Thankfully, after the brainstorming is over, you can take what was learned as part of your store of information and then embark on your privileged voyage to the far horizon.

How to Deal with Global This and Global That

Given the global nature of today's advertising and the internet, what about little me? Must we each be humbled into feeling like feudal peasants sadly tilling our little plot of land while the grand pageantry of the world goes its merry way? You may find that it enhances your confidence to tell yourself, "Global this and global that – all ideas still occur in the small space between one person's ears."

What about the wisdom of having one global campaign? Of course, there are efficiencies and, if it were a perfect world, by which we mean, in this context, flat as a pancake, the undeniable virtues of unity would win the day. But since cultures still do present the worldwide marketer with inconvenient variations, it may often be wiser to have exactly the right campaign for each market. In most cases, it may constitute the better part of bigness to seek a balance of culturally appropriate diversity within the overall unity of the campaign.

Wandering around the Halls, Creating

As we cogitate strategic and creative possibilities, many of us like to wander the halls. If you find yourself wandering without making the progress you hope to, I suggest that you pause and ask yourself the obvious. Am I doing what I vowed never to do again – trying to solve a difficult problem while ruminating at random? Return to The Creative Exploratory and isolate the difficulty. It provides a manageable way to see exactly where you've been in your thinking and to spot new avenues for exploration. While it's always an invaluable aid to ideation, it's especially helpful when you're confronted with an especially difficult problem.

Don't Weigh down the Gorgeous Bird

In advertising, small values are really the only values, so all the details are important. We want to get all of them just right. Trouble is, everybody may have his or her own version of what the details are. So suggestions for "improvement" of the advertising or website can pile up and, at a certain point, they become counterproductive.

To magnify our message, let's think of the advertising or website as a beautiful bird that has just landed on the conference-room table. We know it has wings and is capable of flight. But now one dutiful person suggests what he considers a small improvement, which translates into, "What if we just add a little weight to one of the bird's wings?" A second person suggests another little improvement, which we will consider an itsy-bitsy weight on the other wing. The first person, who may be speaking as the most senior member of the client team, announces that the last suggestion just keyed off another "improvement" in his mind. So now we add a little weight around the darling creature's neck. Pretty soon our once-proud bird is sitting there, all weighted down. What can it do when everybody says, "OK, now, fly!"

One way to moderate the process is to realize that in mass media the overall form and major content of an idea matter far more than any detail. If the advertising is based on the right idea said the right way, it will fly. If it isn't, no amount of tinkering can give it wings.

Of course, like all items intended for flight, the sleeker it is, the better it will fly.

How to Create with Confidence

We can only create at our best when we create with confidence. How much music could Chopin have let flow from his melodic mind if he had sat at the piano, rattled with self-doubt?

One way to gain confidence is to understand the source of any doubts we may allow to intrude. Self-doubt often grows out of comparing our own abilities with others, both historical and contemporary. It's important to realize that we can never hope to do what anybody else did or will do? In turn, we realize that anyone else would have a hard time, and very likely an impossible time, attempting to do what we can do. Our individual natures and nurtures are just too various. When we source our unique selves, we work it an area that is our own, so we have no competition to measure up to.

It also helps to remember that our minds have capacities that exceed our usual demands on them, and we can decide to utilize them to the max. To reassure ourselves, we can remember how there are more neurons in the typical human brain than there are stars in the universe. So there is more than enough capacity to conduct the relatively trivial affairs of advertising with supreme confidence.

Of course, the more we know about what we would like to do, the better chance we have of doing it with ease. Self-doubt can also intrude when we see the process of recording our thinking as the same thing as our thinking. Let's take "writing" in the usual sense that it's bandied about. If we see it as an end in itself, how on earth can we work with it? Writing is an effect, and we can't control effects. There is, in terms of something difficult, no such thing as "writing." There is a separate and prior activity, that is, thinking. Our goal is clear thinking. Once we've done it, we may record the result as effortlessly as a faithful secretary. "Writing" can also be made difficult when we write before we think, trying to sort out our thoughts as we go, often because we're too insecure to court the delicate voice of our minds with patience.

Along similar lines, an art director may want to draw something before he takes the time to clarify his concept.

It's OK to feel your way a certain amount. But trying to create before you think can lead to knots that are a nuisance to untangle.

The quickest, neatest editor is the mind. We don't end up with pages of copy or layouts that need to be sorted out and refined.

So rely on whatever unfathomable individual capacities you may have, relax and court your muse. When you have a clear thought in mind, type it out or draw it up. Develop your ego around how easy advertising is for you, not how difficult it's perceived to be.

To the extent that any human can, take control of the creative process, instead of allowing it to control you. Aim to be, as I mentioned before, the good secretary of your mind.

Finally, when you're creating, don't imagine how great the result will be and, even worse, brag about your hopes. When you do, you create imaginary walls that you have to jump over, and you might make them so high that neither you nor any other mere human being could get over them. It's like running in front of yourself and putting up hurdles you have to get over to get to your goal.

Let's conclude with the cliché that we should all learn to get out of our own way. Let your mind reveal its potential, instead of putting arbitrary limits on it. Its capacities are so unfathomable any attempt to measure it is bound to do it an injustice.

You can always do your own best work. It's the most you can do, and the least you should do. With enough confidence, you can do it with enjoyment.

CHAPTER 18

HOW TO SHIFT AN ENTIRE MARKET TOWARD YOUR BRAND

While most people hope to gain a little more of the share of a market in a category with an advertising campaign, there are times when you can shift an enormous share with startling suddenness.

Here's a secret that will help you.

There is, we can say, an invisible balance scale in every category. It is tilted toward the brand that has the most weight in terms of consumer preference.

We ask how much weight would we have to add to our side of the scale to shift the balance, or consumer preference, our way?

In some cases, the leading brand owns its share with such lightweight consumer preference that the amount we need to add is surprisingly small. Maybe even having a lower price or dropping a coupon can tilt a lot of consumers our way. But such a tactic would largely result in only a short-term shift.

If we're the leading brand in the category, we want to add reasons for consumer preference to the scale. If we're not the leading brand, what is available to us? We can't do much about the products themselves, distribution and the client's sales force. What can we do?

We ask, what is the high ground for claims in the category, or the most effective ones that can be made, and does the leader, or anyone else, own it?

If the advertising in the category is proceeding at the usual level of competence, it's unlikely that anyone owns the high ground. In fact, it's astonishing how rarely the leading entry in a category has advertising that says exactly the right thing in the right way. It may seem important, convincing, and perhaps even bright. But it very likely isn't the right advertising for the leading brand in the category.

For instance, take MacDonald's. The company finally has advertising that touts what people want, like 100% beef. Yet the slogan it still uses, "I'm lovin' it," is a piece of trivia that can be applied to just about any product. While it has the merit of preempting a contemporary phrase, the phrase is, unfortunately, much too broad to be exactly the right one to build the brand on. Think back to all of its slogans, as they've come and gone. Can you think of one that's exactly right for the leader in the fast-food category? Even an easy but exact answer like "It's MacDelicious!" would, I think, be superior to anything the company has had.

But now let's return to our task. We develop a strategy that captures the high ground for claims in the category, that is, the claims we know have the most weight with the consumer. Market research may be done to help us arrive at it. We make certain that our product can live up to it. If possible, we can suggest that the client modify the product or service so it will have the weighty advantage we've discovered.

Now, we create an advertising campaign that presents the claim in a perfectly poised visual and verbal argument. We sign the campaign in by saying what we know consumers want to hear most and by saying it in the most compelling way. What happens? The weightiest benefit or benefits that are germane to the category start to land on our side of the balance scale. And, because of the unusual clarity and power with which we communicate, they land there with unprecedented impact. Result: consumer preference tilts our way. When it comes to each category, we can say, in fact, that each consumer has just such an imaginary balance scale in his or her mind, on which he or she weighs brand preference. So when our advertising breaks, the consumer will note it and begin to weigh the benefits of our product against those of the leading entry. If we've done our homework right, millions of tiny scales will tilt our client's way.

If the weight of the brand preference toward the leader is especially light, the shift may happen with dramatic suddenness.

The shift can be facilitated if the advertising is introduced with a sign-in period of two to three weeks; that is, if the campaign is launched with higher media weight than the sustaining part of the campaign. The impact helps overcome the inertia of the balance scale.

We're not quite done. If we're not the leading entry in the category, in order to shift the balance scale with assurance, we should present our product in a way that makes it appear to exist in a 50/50 relationship with the leader; that is, we want our advertising to create the impression of a 2-product category. We essentially ignore the other entries. Then we associate our product with the category leader, either with a direct comparison or an indirect one that is clear enough to every viewer or reader.

To provide an example of how this might be done, I'll discuss two commercials I did as a creative consultant to Bristol-Myers Squibb. The campaign was for a new product, positioned to appeal to one of the most brand-loyal groups. You'll have to judge what would have happened by the test scores, because a complication prevented the product from going to market.

Bristol-Myers Squibb makes a number of over-the-counter pain relievers, such as Bufferin and Excedrin, but the perennial thorn in its side is the large share of the pain-reliever category held by Tylenol. The company was trying to find ways to acquire some of Tylenol's share or, in the language of our current topic, to tilt some of the business its way.

The company had formulated a new pain reliever that was similar to Tylenol but that had an added ingredient. One of the large agencies that Bristol-Myers Squibb works with had done strategic and creative development. The unnamed agency had created three commercials to present the new product. The results of consumer testing had just come in and were disappointing. The tests had measured persuasion, or how convinced Tylenol users were by the commercials to try the new product. One of the commercials had gotten a score of 3 and two had gotten a 2. The norm for a score in the category at the time was 12. Worse yet, the client's action standard – the score needed to move ahead with the product – was double the norm, or 24.

The gifted marketing person who was heading up the analgesic new-product effort at the time asked me to take a look at the results.

I was invited to an internal meeting at the company at which the research was presented. One of the graphs was composed of an X and Y axis, with safety along one and efficacy along another one. It told the tale. I noticed that Tylenol was in an area of the graph all by itself, way up in the upper right in terms of safety and efficacy. What new product could hope to land there? I knew I had the answer and the product right away.

To get up where Tylenol was on the graph, the first thing the advertising would have to say is that the new pain-reliever is exactly like Tylenol. Such a claim would be "the price of entry" onto the consumer's scale of brand preference. Only then could we go on to say that it contains an extra ingredient that makes it work better.

We could do so because the new product, like Tylenol, was made with acetaminophen. But it also contained caffeine, which the FDA considers a "pain-relief potentiator." Evidently, it helps the main ingredient work better.

I also knew that part of the price of entry would be to give the product a name that seemed to identify it as belonging to the same category as Tylenol. When I was brought in, one of the first things I noticed is that the name the agency had given it ended in "-in," as in the Tylenol market's dreaded aspirin, when Tylenol loyalists recognize, even if they aren't conscious of it, that the pain reliever they prefer is partially differentiated by ending in "-ol."

I also noticed that most pain relievers have names that consist of three syllables. Such are the details we must concern ourselves with in our miniature world.

So I set about creating a new name for it. I decided that, if the middle syllable were a vowel, there would only be five choices and, since I knew how I wanted the last syllable to end, all that would be required to complete it would be to look at "-ol" preceded by all the consonants in the alphabet. The linguistic experiment revealed only a few viable variants, among them -dol, -rol, -tol, as well as the directly imitative -nol.

All that remained was to determine the first syllable, which could be discovered by looking into all the consonants in the alphabet joined with all the vowels. I decided that the leading entry in the Tylenol category might well have the familiar foundation that the perennial pain reliever in the aspirin category has, that is, an initial "A."

I explored the various couplings and recommend the name "Avitol."

When the agency was told of the requirements I had devised for the name, someone there apparently unleashed the computer to explore the possibilities; in a subsequent meeting, the client hefted a thick tome that was supposed to contain all of them. We were amused that Avitol was not among them.

Next, I knew the clear communication that there was another product like the brand they were so loyal to would probably perk up the ears of the Tylenol audience; the fact that the new pain reliever might be better would probably get to them, if not insult them.

Now, how might we magnify the message? I decided that the product loyalists were so entrenched that nothing would get to them like having other Tylenol loyalists admit that they found something they like better. Then we wouldn't just have testimonials; we'd have a rebellion. To assure them that they were taking a step ahead by changing to Avitol, I created the slogan "Advance to Avitol."

We placed the new product with Tylenol users and, when sufficient time had passed for them to have some experience with it, we did focus groups with them, which were, with the knowledge of the participants, videotaped.

Most of the respondents, to their surprise, liked the product, and, thankfully, some were quite effusive. So we were able to tape a lot of potential dynamite.

I created two test commercials that contained the most persuasive footage, along with a middle, or donut, that compared our product Tylenol. The voiceover said, "It's made with exactly the same pain reliever as Tylenol, but it contains an added ingredient that makes the pain reliever work better."

The commercials were shown to Tylenol users just as the former three commercials had been. One of them scored a "48" and the other one a "47." In other words, they quadrupled the norm and doubled the client's action standard.

The client was ecstatic. We had a product and a communication that we knew could tilt the market our way. But we do not live in a world that always functions as we would expect. We hit what I call the rock at the 90-yard-line. At the time, caffeine as an ingredient in pain relievers was under scrutiny by the FDA, and, faced with the unprecedented prospect of having a viable entry to compete against Tyelenol, the client had to consider factors he had never taken into account.

The director of new product development and I recommended going ahead immediately. But top management made the decision that, despite how successful the new product promised to be, after a major investment to introduce it, the FDA might rule that we would have to pull it from the shelves. So, despite the astonishing scores, the product never went to market.

Then why did I use this example? It is harder to find a more brand loyal group of consumers than Tylenol loyalists, and the scores tell the tale.

Despite the many entries in the pain relief category, the advertising created an apparent 2-product category, consisting of our new product and the non-aspirin leader. This set the stage to add weight to our side of the balance scale.

CHAPTER 19

SPECIFIC CATEGORIES OF ADVERTISING

Most advertising can be done successfully with the principles I've presented in other chapters. The categories covered here have a few principles that are unique to them.

Food Advertising

Smart food advertising should make you want to taste the delectable item. The goal is accomplished with three main ingredients:

1. The Taste Shot

Someone in the commercial or the print ad should taste the product and say or indicate that it tastes delicious. There is an obvious reason. What is the most persuasive way you've been convinced to try something? When you see someone taste something, and they tell you, "Hey, this is delicious! You should try it."

2. Appetite Appeal

Every aspect of a food commercial or ad should look appetizing. After all, when you see a great-looking food item, what happens? Your well-adjusted involuntary nervous system makes you salivate, and you want to enjoy it. While this principle applies primarily to the food shots, it actually covers every moment or column inch of the advertising. For instance, the people in the piece should be in an environment anyone would enjoy eating in. Likable actors and attractive typography also enhance appetite appeal.

As an aside, notice that many restaurants apparently never heard of appetite appeal. Easy ways to spot them are garish signs, dirty windows, and an unclean floor, especially near the entrance, when it should be clean enough to eat off.

3. Emotional Reward for the Preparer

What does a homemaker – or the gatekeeper, as she is often referred to in her role as the principal purchaser for the family – want when she prepares a meal? How about a little gratitude? If she thinks preparing something will be met with it, she's more likely to buy and serve the product.

The reward is easy to accomplish. At some point in the commercial, one of the lucky diners indicates gratitude, usually right after the taste shot. For example, a husband may say, "Um delicious, sweetheart." Or a child might exclaim, "Wow, great, mom!" In a print ad, the goal is accomplished with a phase like "Your whole family will love it."

The more women work, and the less time they spend preparing meals, the more they seem to need a little praise. Watching these beleaguered ladies respond to new food offerings in focus groups, we quickly see that they become especially interested if the product allows them to hope for a family-pleasing result at the same time that it has what they yearn for most these days. It's quick and easy to prepare.

Healthcare Advertising

When most people are sick, they would like someone knowledgeable to advise them about what to do. As a result, healthcare advertising that has a serious tone is generally just what the patient ordered. I call this tone "the doctor in disguise." It's sincere, helpful, and personable. In short, it exudes a good bedside manner.

The manner need not employ a doctor. Notice the lifestyle advertising for many drugs. Yet the tone is generally sympathetic and helpful.

Advertising for aspirin or heart medicine may go so far as to utilize an electrocardiogram, and at times we find ourselves in the emergency room.

Once in a while, we note humorous or light-hearted drug advertising. It may work, especially if the condition it promises to relieve is not very serious. The classic example is the humorous Alka-Seltzer commercials of yesteryear, which invited people to laugh away their indigestion.

Yet what do you want when you're not feeling well? A friend who cracks jokes or a sympathetic doctor who tells you how to find relief? Better yet, a doctor you don't have to pay.

Advertising to physicians has the tone of one medical professional talking to another. Peer-reviewed studies are often used as reasons to believe the claims. Yet within this tone there is still a need for creative magnification of the message, not only to get busy physicians to notice the ad, but also out of the realization that he or she is also a human being, whose attention must be commanded by a dramatic visual-verbal event and who can be enchanted by a stylish presentation, as long as it is appropriate to the message. Much advertising to physicians features a dramatic symbolic visual. It is used to achieve stopping power and, when used as an ongoing icon, brand recognition.

When we write copy for physicians, dentists, or other healthcare practitioners, usually copy for a website, we should retain the sympathetic tone of "the doctor in disguise."

Technology Advertising

Today, we all do a great deal of tech advertising, mostly by writing websites and landing pages and driving traffic to them with digital ads. Regardless of the technology, the principles we've discussed apply.

The difference is, of course, that we must learn about the technology we're to write about. I've now written websites and other content for innumerable kinds of technology, including big data analytics, edge computing, the industrial IIoT, outdoor and cellphone security, crypto-currency and cryptocurrency hardware wallets, etc. I find that if I study the client's input and read competitive websites, I can learn what I must to write the material the client needs. I think you'll discover the same thing. So don't be daunted. You know more about how to express the client's message than people who know the technology better than you ever will or need to. In a nutshell, the client knows the technology; you know how to sell it.

Retail Advertising

While some retail advertising is skillful, much of it is wretched. Once, I complained about the pervasive mediocrity in the category and else-where; now I view it as an opportunity for astonishing success.

Every store is a box, and the general management guideline is to get the box right in terms of the product mix and the pricing. For instance, some large chains emphasize specials, others feature everyday low prices, and some few will tout prestige over price. The daily conduct of the store concept is up to operations.

Now, let's turn to a secret of successful retail advertising. It served as the basis of the successful turnaround campaigns I did for A & P Supermarkets – the first when the chain was in dire trouble, and the second one when the company had remodeled many of its stores and built numerous new ones.

The first campaign, which I mentioned in the section on slogan devel-opment, was built around the brand promise, "We watch our P's and Q's." It's often credited with saving the chain, to the extent that advertising could contribute to the goal. The second campaign featured the slogan, "The great store just next door."

All the work was done due to the realization by the bright and affa-ble CEO, James Wood, who was brought in to save the chain, that he needed great advertising to help him do it. He instructed his executive vice president, Jerry Good, to find a creative consultant, and I was for-tunate enough to have a marketing person at Bristol-Myers who had worked with me and recommended me.

The advertising approach I devised fits the needs of most retailers, who have two goals. They know they need a favorable brand image, but they also know they must move as much merchandise as they can, while they protect their profit margins. So there is usually a dilemma about whether retail advertising should be driven by brand image or item-price advertising. The answer is a balance of the two that is appropriate to each chain. I call the approach "two-armed salesmanship."

Let me explain its merits metaphorically. Imagine a long line of retailers who are holding out the same products with different prices on them. The consumer walks along the line and decides who to buy from. What does she do? She buys from the one who has what she wants at the lowest price. The problem is, the next time she shows up, she notices that somebody else has the lowest price, and she buys from him. Since all of the retailers have an overhead and the need for profit, none of them can afford to have the lowest price every week. When retailers attempt to operate that way, they don't "protect their margins," so they get into financial trouble.

How can one of the retailers make her a regular customer? Enter the secret. One retailer who notices the process decides to do something about it. So when he sees the consumer coming, he slips out of the line and tells her, in the most engaging way he can, that he'd like to talk with her for a moment. Due to his inviting tone, she decides to grant him a few seconds. He tells her that he has her best interests at heart, and, if she'd shop with him every week, he'd always take the best care of her. She'll get, he assures her, the best products at the best prices. And just think, he points out, if she shops with him all the time, she won't have to sort through that big line of retailers every week.

Having this cordial talk with her is the role of image advertising. Once she seems to have lent a willing ear, he holds out the featured product of the week with his other hand, telling her, "And to prove my point, just look what a great deal I've got for you this week." This is the role of the item/price advertising.

She glances over his shoulder at the prices the other retailers are offering the product for, and she notices that he is telling her the truth, at least, this time. She decides to trust him and buys from him.

Most critically, the next time she goes shopping, she goes straight up to him to see other ways he might prove to have her best interests in mind. And, though the others are still pitching their specials, she doesn't really hear them. She has developed an allegiance to the retailer who had a personal talk with her and then lived up to what he told her.

She knows in her heart of hearts that he can't offer her the lowest prices on everything every week. But she believes that he can offer her the best overall shopping experience and value.

Now, if the retailer knows that no shopper hath fury like a shopper scorned, he will continue to live up to what he promised, at least, without frequent glaring infractions, and she will grow to rely on his store more and more, while the other retailers still stand in line, shouting prices every week and wondering why she doesn't pay attention to them anymore.

I call this appropriate combination of retail advertising two-armed salesmanship. One arm is the image advertising, and the other arm holds out the specials. Neither total image or price advertising can compete with it. And, when the combination is right, the retailer can achieve unprecedented success.

Advocacy and Political Advertising

The most important first step in advocacy and political creative work is, as in all advertising, to get the poster right. This becomes the topic idea of the campaign. Everything else becomes a support point that helps prove the topic idea. The concluding line of the paragraph is the call to action, usually to donate or vote for the candidate.

In both kinds of advertising, it is imperative to create a sense of importance and urgency. The advertising must have enormous moment; it must be immediately relevant and compelling to the target audience. Fortunately, we have unusually powerful texts and subtexts to work with. So we're able to create exciting advertising almost as soon as we begin to think creatively. In fact, the real challenge is to keep thinking until we know that we have gotten to the core content that is the most compelling and that we are presenting it in the most persuasive manner.

A rock-solid, emotionally charged slogan is a necessity. Explosive visuals that are so appropriate to the message that they excuse themselves help drive the impact.

For instance, I recently did an advocacy ad against the Patent Reform Act. The U. S. Constitution provides for the protection of the intellectual property of authors and inventors for a limited time, yet Congress was threatening to compromise these rights in destructive ways without seeking a Constitutional amendment. The main headline I wrote was

"Stop Congress from Trashing the Constitution." The visual was the U. S. Constitution disappearing into a shredder. The ad ran as a full-page in two appropriate venues: The main section of *The New York Times* and *The Hill,* a newspaper widely read by members of Congress. The ad helped stop the measure.

Political advertising can be especially powerful. Why? Only a statistically insignificant number of voters actually know the usual candidate. So they must decide who to vote for based on the information they can glean through the mass media. There are basically two sources: the news and advertising.

In political advertising, it's not always correct to stage the most dramatic commercials you can think of, but the ones that will persuade the most voters. For instance, when the candidate is relatively unknown, the primary goal must be to enable voters to get to know him or her. So it would be more effective to bring the candidate to center stage. He or she could deliver a variation of FDR's fireside chats. For maximum effect, the chats would be scripted. Rudolph Giuliani, in his more level-headed years, could have used such advertising in his bid for the republican presidential nomination; instead, he ran dramatic commercials that relegated him to saying the usual signoff, "I'm Rudy Giuliani, and I approve of this commercial."

In both advocacy and political advertising, it's especially important to see the argument as a paragraph, so you can line up your proofs for maximum effect.

In the Democratic primary of 2008, Hillary Clinton had a topic sentence and a concluding sentence. She informed us that she was "ready on day one." Then she generally went straight to her concluding sentence, "Thank you for your support." Where was the paragraph that said, "On day one, I will launch the following initiatives"?

Meanwhile, the Obama campaign stuck to the message of "Change we can believe in." It was based on calculated, consistent branding. He only developed the paragraph sporadically and lightly, perhaps to preserve flexibility or to avoid alienating voters by being too specific. Yet his branding effort prevailed over the surprisingly ineffectual and wavering presentation of his opponent. Sometimes, a little competence is all that is required, even in the biggest venues.

The advertising should also leverage the candidate's strengths. In the 2016 election, Hillary Clinton had the change to base her campaign on the usual advantages that women are supposed to bring to leadership, such as "caring about you," "nourishing your best potential," and even "governing with love for each and every one of you." What did she do instead? The opposite of what she should have. Her first slogan was "Fighting for you," and her second was "Stronger together." May I ask what the keywords "fighting" and "stronger" have to do with exactly the right ones for the first woman candidate for President? The words, in fact, sound more suited to her demagogic opponent, whose campaign was really, I sometimes quip, based on the ancient slogan for Arpege perfume, which was "Promise her anything but give her Arpege." His, as it turned out, might as well have been "Promise them anything but give them the shaft."

In both kinds of advertising it's especially important to keep the call to action single minded. We tell the audience to do one thing, usually to write in about an issue or to vote for a candidate.

In political advertising, we never take a minute or spend a dime attempting to get the votes we already have. We concentrate on addressing the voters we need to get, even if we must take acceptable risks that might alienate the voters we know we already have. We know, as they do, once they get in the voting booth, there is likely no way that they will bring themselves to vote for the other candidate.

A word of caution. When you become involved in a major advocacy or political campaign – and often in a major brand campaign – a growing number of people will have influence. The struggle can become, not so much to get the right, bright campaign done but to get the idea done that various factions want to lay claim to. Why? Because ownership of such a high-profile campaign becomes a career-building achievement. My advice is to exert every effort to be the top creative person, so you can control the process and focus on what's best for the candidate.

Entertainment Advertising

Most entertainment advertising is condemned to presenting scenes and sounds from the show or to shouting snatches from reviews, so it might be hopeless to offer more sophisticated advice. We will content ourselves by saying that an inviting concept, especially a verbal one that does not get in the way of the show, can be used to position the content so that it interfaces with its audience in the most inviting way. Occasionally, a film is fortunate to have such a line to present it. Theater advertising generally occurs at such a manic level that one throws up his arms at the hopelessness of persuading the perpetrators to calm down and talk to the audience in an intelligent and reasonable manner. Apparently, few purveyors of entertainment advertising know that loud presentations drive the audience into themselves, while a more personal presentation invites their participation.

Corporate Image Advertising

The goal of corporate-image advertising is to characterize the company in a favorable way, to the public and, even more, to potential investors. Yet the goal is really to sell the company or, in the words of W. S. Gilbert, to "polish up the handle on the big front door." The tone should be appropriate to the company and the category it's in.

Direct Response Advertising

Today, direct response advertising is more pervasive than ever, primarily because most digital advertising is DR.

There are many tones to work in. The goal of getting the consumer to "convert" still leads many advertisers to do a great deal of shouting and repetition. As I've explained, creative advertising offers far more effective ways to be persuasive. I began in direct, selling books through ads and snail-mail sales letters. Over the years, I've done a great deal of it, and my DR copywriting has been featured on the cover of DM News, the leading publication in the industry.

One of the most gratifying lessons I've learned is that an idea presented with the magnifying power of the right, bright creative work can succeed magnificently and consistently. So we can be proud of such advertising.

Direct, as well as all advertising, proceeds, superficially understood, in four steps, called the AIDA principle. The acronym stands for Attention, Interest, Desire, and Action. First, we gain attention. Then we must maintain interest. Next, we're to create desire. Last, we're instructed to get the consumer to take action. Unfortunately, all of these directives are effects, which we can't work with. We need to work with causes. How do we achieve AIDA?

I was amused, for instance, to realize that the usual form of direct-response advertising can be seen as a rondo (ABACADA, where A is the recurring theme and the other letters are different themes; in our case, the recurring theme is asking for the order).

We capture attention with the core content of our sales message, including the problem or pain point and core brand promise, and then we ask for the order. We maintain interest by developing the sales message with the most important support points or benefits. Now, we ask for the order again, hopefully with a bit of variety; next we continue to build interest and now create desire by introducing the second-most-important fact and return to ask for the order; at the end, we include with our incentive to increase desire, such as a discount or gift, usually with a time-fuse to spark a prompt response; then we conclude with a summary of the sales message and ask for the order, or action, one last time. At the end, we might repeat critical information twice, but more becomes offensive. We needn't be reminded to superimpose the core information with type in our commercial and in print to display it with prominent typography, but we can use restraint and make the type tasteful.

Some hard-sell landing page or long-form sales letter copy uses bold type, underlining, red and blue type. The use results in a bit of a Barnum & Bailey effect, but in the context of the other landing pages and sales letters in venues such as Clickbank, such highlights are usual and, if you want to write in such DR venues, inescapable.

Regardless of the medium, within the innovative presentation of the selling proposition, we include the usual mandatory ingredients of DR, such as getting the offer upfront in a commercial or in the headline of a print ad, website or landing page, using natural and therefore credible excitement about the offer, tasteful repetition of key content for emphasis, incentives to enhance the response rate, and a recurring single-minded call to action.

Does this approach work? I recently did a direct-response campaign for The New York Sun, when it was New York's up and coming new daily broadsheet newspaper. It had a more conservative editorial viewpoint than The New York Times. When the paper was struggling, I was recommended to the editor and worked on the campaign with an art director who was then my partner in a small agency. He had been a creative director at Ogilvy and Bozell, so he understood strategic creative development.

We realized the Times is the newspaper of record, and most people were going to continue to read it, even if they were more conservative. So we decided it would be more doable to ask conservative readers to make the Sun their other daily newspaper.

At the time, the Times cost 75 cents at the newsstand. To make trying it easier, we priced the Sun at just 25 cents for a specific period, so the Times reader could buy both for $1. I wrote a slogan that associated the Sun with the Times but in a way that is appropriate for it. The slogan for the Times was, at the time, "Expect the world." I wrote the slogan, "Illuminate your world," and developed it as "the bright new way to get a different point of view." The advertising was launched in print, outdoor, radio, and television. Within weeks, it took the Sun from a circulation of about 17,000, going down, to a circulation of over 50,000, going up. The campaign became the featured cover story in DM News, and the commercial, which starred a man getting on the subway with The Sun, sitting down, and opening it. When he did, rays of sunlight came out and other riders began to wonder what was going on and to lean over for a look. The commercial won a Gold Telly award. You can still see it at *Adforum.com.*

Unfortunately, the editor decided the paper was growing so well advertising was no longer needed. We tried to persuade him that now was the time to "step on the gas," but he couldn't appreciate the value of our advice. Down went the circulation, and the paper is now a footnote to journalistic history.

A War Story

No matter how much we know, the usual vicissitudes of probability can afflict us. Campaigns don't go forward even when we know they're right. For example, I was invited to do a youth campaign for Maxwell House coffee. I realized it would be appropriate to emphasize, besides the hedonic values of coffee, the interpersonal values: enjoying it with friends, even if the friend you're relating to is just yourself. I also realized a happy coincidence. Coffee is usually enjoyed with other ingredients, such as sweeteners and cream. I expressed both thoughts by selecting what was, at the time, a youthful-sounding, hip word. The slogan I recommended was "The Together Drink." I was confident the idea would be bought, backed, and well known. But I noticed over the months that it did not appear. Since I can't recall a high-profile youth campaign for the brand, the idea of doing one was apparently shelved. We all must learn to live with the inevitable uncertainties of events and influence.

Is One Style of Advertising Better Than Another?

In this section, it seems appropriate to address a question creative people often wonder about. Is one style of advertising creatively superior to another? The style that wins most of the awards is the kind that appears to be trenchantly intelligent, often consisting of a voice over, speaking with authority and perhaps a tad of hardnosed wit, while a logical piece of visual demonstration proceeds under his all-knowing voice. Even humor has a hard time competing with the form. Perhaps one reason is that many advertising people feel that recognizing the intelligence and voting for it makes them feel intelligent. Given the way a lot of advertising is still done and the way advertising is still generally regarded, their need is understandable.

While what are considered creative commercials, print ads, websites or other digital fare often look and sound similar, the one thing nearly all advertising we wish to call creative does have in common is that it is, in one way or another, tasteful. We judge by it that a talented writer and art director created it. We also acknowledge that a smart account team formulated the strategy and helped present and defend the work with justifiable faith in its excellence, that a wise and deserving client decided to buy it, and that a talented and responsive production team helped realize its potential.

Yet all advertising that we might deign to call great is correct in its form and content, not only literally, but brightly. Great advertising creativity is an appropriate imaginative response to marketing information, and any form of rigidity actually seems anti-creative. We want to stay bright and flexible, so we can respond to each assignment in just the right, bright way.

Finally advertising ought to be judged the way other creative works are. We ask, what was the goal of the advertising and how well was it crafted to achieve it? Given the occasion of the creativity, was the creative response just right. When we decide it was, we can genuinely deign it creative and, in fact, great advertising.

CHAPTER 20

GETTING THE
PRODUCTION RIGHT

Once the advertising has been created and bought, it's time to produce it. In a large agency, the production department helps the creative team settle on an appropriate director, gets together the bids, makes casting calls, and oversees the logistics of the shoot. In smaller agencies or consulting firms, the art director and copywriter assume more or all of the functions.

The production of print advertising is seen over primarily by the art director, with the copywriter for the most part providing proofreading. The same goes for websites and digital ads. The copywriter's job is to proofread the work, to make sure the emphasis and subordination is optimal for marketing and to make sure no typos have slipped in during the design process.

Today, stock photography exists in abundance, so photographers aren't needed as often. But the widespread use of stock shots has led, in the extreme, to two kinds of art directors. First, there's the one who can sketch out ideas and then go to stock photography for suitable shots. Second, there's the art director who can or can't draw well but, when it's time to ideate visually, immediately turns to stock photography, entering keywords and searching among the visuals that come up in the searches. As one creative director said to me, "Nobody draws anymore." Yet I still prefer to work with art directors who can ideate with me, do quick sketches of ideas, and then turn to stock photography. If the idea is requires a highly original visual, a photographer will usually be hired to shoot it.

While stock photography has a number of merits, one problem is that the overuse of it has resulted in a lot of advertising that consists of interesting photos with semi-clever lines stuck on them, as if the art director found the offbeat shot and the copywriter knocked out a suitably witty line for it. Such ads can be quite good. But when we can sense the strangeness of the construct, they seldom achieve the effect of ads that are conceptual wholes. We can avoid these Frankenstein-like creations when the words and pictures work hand in glove to make the recognizably right point.

Correct Casting

In both television and print, the performers we choose must look so right for the role that the advertising functions as an immediately appropriate poster. The brevity of the forms makes the obvious more important. Subtlety comes from the performances.

The demand for the right look causes anxiety among many actors and actresses who don't understand that acceptance or rejection doesn't depend primarily on how well they do in the audition. Their real task is to go to enough casting sessions to arrive at some where they have just the right appearance. Then their acting can win them the role.

Second, the voice and mannerisms of the performers must be consistent with their looks (unless our intent is irony, say, a big person with a small voice).

When actors meet these two criteria, we can consider the quality of their performances. What are we looking for? Actors who are alive in the role. They're generally pros. They study the script while waiting to audition and develop ideas for it, so they can perform in a way that shows they're right for the role and add to it in ways they think will surprise and delight us.

They're easy to spot. They seem to have an immediate feel for the part and ask questions between takes, such as, "What if I do it this way?" Or "How about this?" So we realize they're unlikely to freeze during the shoot and do every take the same way. Instead, they'll provide interesting variety and grow in the role during the shoot. The result is more likely to be an organically alive performance. And they will often winningly magnify your own idea of the commercial or photograph.

Similar advice applies to selecting voice-over announcers. First, the quality of the voice must be right. Second, the announcer you choose should display a natural feeling for the proper tone and cadence of the script, so it sounds organically right, and he or she should be adroitly, or irascibly, responsive to direction. The goal is a perfectly cadenced and appropriately nuanced performance.

How to Work with Actors

We want to produce commercials that do justice to the quality of the ideas. One of the most import ingredients is the ability to spot actors who can deliver convincing performances.

How do we learn to do so with assurance? We do something very few people in advertising do. We study acting, just enough to understand how actors work and what constitutes a good performance. So bite the bullet and sign up for at least two evening courses – first, one on technique and then another one on scene study. Then you'll be better with talent than, not only most other advertising people, but most commercial directors and actors. Since 30-second and 15-second mini-dramas don't require much in the way of character development, even unknowing directors and unskilled actors can get often do quite well. The directors get by because they have a good eye, and the actors do so because they have a widely appealing look.

You'll learn that some trained actors work internally, the well-known Method school, while others work externally, (representational acting, usually associated with the British school.)

Better actors, especially American ones, usually work internally. How? They relate the role to a real event or events in their personal lives, the "as if" of Method acting. This subtext keys off authentic responses to the events, or beats, in a role and will generally result in the most true-to-life performances.

You'll also come across many commercial actors who are adept at representational acting, less kindly referred to as faking it. The most skillful ones can make "adjustments" upon request. Their responsiveness and flexibility make them different than actors who do what is called "copping an attitude." The latter tend to be frozen in one kind of performance, usually a one-dimensional one.

During casting, when you find an interesting actor who you're still uncertain of, you might try to make a suggestion. Don't ask for an effect, like "smile more." Suggest an "as if" to see if he or she knows what you're talking about; for instance, you can say "Give yourself something that will show you really like the product." If the actor seems uncertain, he or she is untrained in the Method. Then you have no choice but to ask for an effect, such as smile more, which will tell you if he or she is a skillful representational actor.

The actors who know how to study the script before the audition are working to understand the overall goal of the character and getting ideas for their performance. The ones who work internally are getting together their "as ifs" to make their performance real. Actors who work externally are figuring out what you're looking for and how they can represent it better than anyone else.

When the auditions begin, invite the actors to give you the performance they have in mind. Sometimes, you'll be pleasantly surprised by what they do. When you make suggestions, you'll find that some of the Method actors may become impatient if you begin to ask for effects, which are external events. Make suggestions they can internalize; for instance, if you want the actor to say something tastes great convincingly, you might ask, "What's your favorite dessert?" When the actor tells you, suggest, "Think of how good it tastes when you taste our dessert."

The representational actors will usually do a performance and wait for advice. You'll find that giving them specific directions works. No to shortchange their art, but they're sort of like marionettes. As soon as you give them a direction, they seem to come to life and mimic what you asked for.

When the shoot begins, allow the actors time to find the role for themselves before you, or the director, start to make suggestions. After all, you hired them because of the life they brought to the role. It's time to give them space to make their own unique contributions. So give them the opportunity to get in touch with the role and give you the spontaneous, convincing performance you're hoping for.

When you find yourself with directors who don't know as much about how actors work as you do and they start to ask for effects right away, you can take them aside and ask them to give the actors a little space to do their things first. The time to make contributions is when you detect that an actor has plumbed his or her potential. How do you know? You're getting the same or about the same performance take after take.

You can resort to specific instructions when you're just not getting what you want or when you're really close to it and just want the actor to make a minor adjustment.

If you don't get the performance you want with a Method actor, you can begin to ask for specific effects, like "laugh more." With representational actors, you can only try to figure out more ways to communicate exactly what you're looking for. Sometimes, a suggestion that is a mixture of external and internal advice works, for instance, "Can you say that with a little more natural enthusiasm?"

Giving exact directions are OK later in the production, such as "Can you emphasize the word 'relief' a little more?" But if you begin with them, pretty soon the actors will have so many strings attached them that they'll be lurching from one to the next and the performance will be, at best, stiff.

In the worst case, the actor will become the mirror reflection of the mannerisms of the director, the copywriter, or the art director, depending on who has attached the greatest number of strings. How often we've watched a commercial and noted that every performer behaves a lot like the person who's proudly showing us the creative work.

Occasionally, heavy-handed advice does become necessary. As politely as possible, we say, for instance, "I want you to think you've just experienced the happiest moment of your life."

The easiest crash course you can give yourself is to read an excellent book on acting. Rather than wading immediately into Stanislavsky's books, such as *Building A Character,* I suggest you spend some time with *Respect for Acting* by Uta Hagen.

How to Work with Directors

Many commercial directors began as art directors. They can give you visual excellence and, due to the poster-like form of the commercial, they can often have enormously successful careers. If a commercial looks ravishing, it's generally considered excellent. The brevity of the form is very forgiving.

A few commercial directors have actually studied directing. They can be a pleasure to work with. My own feeling is that directors, as well as copywriters and art directors, should take at least one course in directing. The acting schools teach them. You'll do scenes with actors. If you do make the effort, you'll usually find that you're the most skillful production person on the set.

You'll learn to think of the form, or overall shape, of your ideas, instead of just the individual words and pictures that make up a commercial, and you'll become more aware of values like proportion, tone, and pace.

Commercial directors who know professional directorial values can do a much better job. The same knowledge can help copywriters and art directors be more circumspect in selecting directors.

If you find yourself with a director who just isn't getting the performances you need, you'll know how to help. Do it as courteously as you can, but make sure you end up with a commercial with authentic performances. Do not settle for a picture-perfect postcard that's as false as the performances in most commercials. You want it to make authentic contact with the audience.

Thankfully, some talented directors are affable and open to suggestions. These are the ones you're looking for. It's best for the actors to get all of their direction from once source, and they're used to the director functioning in that role. So you want to work through him or her as much as possible. But, before you award a job, determine the director's openness to input from you. Assure him or her that you always give the director plenty of space to get the performances right. Then ask if he or she has a problem with you talking directly with the actors if you're not getting them. In return, you can pledge that you'll ask to do it first. When the director or the actors realize you know what you're talking about, they'll generally be open to your suggestions.

In return, go about your work as considerately as possible. You owe it to directors to let them get as far as they can with the actors, as long as the process they're using doesn't vitiate the possibility of getting good performances.

When you feel suggestions are necessary, make them to the directors and continue working through them as long you note that they relay the instructions to the actors in an accurate way. Unfortunately, many insist on putting your suggestion into their own words, and most directors are not the masters of verbal expression. When you feel you must, it's time to ask to talk with the actors.

When the production is going well, the best time to step in is when the performances are close to what you envision. Then all you have to do is make a small suggestion or two to bring them right to where you think they ought to be.

The account executives and the people from the client's side who are at the shoot should offer their advice to the copywriter and art director. The director is busy and prefers to talk only to the copywriter and art director. The directors is also usually a less-practiced diplomat, and, if they all start to give him advice directly, he's likely to get upset.

As the shoot progresses, make sure the director and the script person know which takes you like the best, so they're selected for the edit.

In post-production, if the director wants to do a director's cut, let him. Then show up, look at it, and make, hopefully, the few suggestions required to make the spot just right. If the edit is going to be done by the editor, let him or her do the same. Then show up and make your comments. You'll not only invite their best contributions; you'll be looking at their work with a fresh eye.

How to Work with Announcers

Since announcers are usually actors, many of the same suggestions we've already made apply to working with them.

Who do you cast? Since even a voice is part of the mass-media poster, first hire an announcer whose voice suits the spot. Second, hire one with the talent to express it in an authentic, artful way. When the recording session begins, give him or her plenty of takes to find the right way to read, or perform, the script. Talented announcers will grow into the role and ask to do more takes. They pride themselves on finding the way the script should be presented and, when given the space, will go for the optimal reading with enthusiasm. They can be demoralized by too many directions, especially when they're made early in the session. If you do have to offer advice, make your initial suggestions ones that apply to the overall performance. Only get into specifics when the announcer has gotten as close to the reading you want as he or she seems to be able to get.

When you do make suggestions, first try to give them the same way you do with actors, as something they can work with internally that will elicit the adjustment you want. If one of them looks puzzled, you'll realize you've got an announcer who works externally. Then the way to get what you want is to ask for it directly, as in, "Can you emphasize the word 'incompetent' more?"

Last, if your script is so long that the announcer is enslaved to rushing, cut it until he or she can read it at a credible pace and provide the texturing required to present the various points in a believable and compelling way.

How to Work with Photographers

The same esthetic principle that applies to commercials applies to photography sessions. The goal should be to capture a sense of truth in the most telling way. We're looking for what the photographer Henri Cartier-Brisson called "the decisive moment." We should seek to capture the sentiments of everyday life, such as joy or sorrow, love or hate, in a genuine way.

Art directors are, of course, more naturally visual and need little advice from me. Copywriters can train their eyes by looking at the photographs in award-winning and other good ads and magazine articles and by perusing photographers' portfolios and websites. A look into an amply illustrated history of photography helps, as does a visit to The Museum of Photography in New York.

Of course, taking your own photographs can help, too.

Although there are different types of commercial photographers – such as people photographers, still-life photographers, and fashion photographers – most of the good ones are painterly. They can compose and light shots well. Studying great paintings can help you understand these values. For instance, when a photographer is lighting the subject, you'll know to ask yourself things like, "Where's the window," or source of the light? It's often single-source sidelight, softened with layers of gauze or silk.

The best shooters develop their own approaches. I've worked with a well-known people photographer who uses seven layers of silk over the single-source strobe light to soften the flash. I've also work with a well-known still-life photographer who employed toothpicks with little aluminum-foil reflectors wrapped around them like flags. He placed them in various locations and rotated them to reflect light at whatever he was shooting to create inviting highlights.

The best thing to do is hire photographers who are right for the job and let them do what you hired them to do. Many are not, however, trained in dramatic art, so you may have to advise the actors, models, and even the people or fashion photographers that you're aiming for a sense of truth. Then you're less likely to end up with a beautiful shot that's agonizingly false.

How to Work with Composers

Large agencies have a music department to help the copywriter and art director along. The rest of us need to develop our own taste in music, so we can hear what style is appropriate. As usual, the more we know, the easier life gets and the better the results.

If you listen to music with an ear toward knowing the various styles and understanding how various moods and other goals are expressed tonally, you'll begin to understand the kind of music that is right for each occasion. You also might want to take a music course or two and learn, if you didn't as a child, to play an instrument, even if in a rudimentary way.

When you're looking for the right stock music, make sure you explain to the source of it what you're looking for as exactly as possible.

If you need original music, how do you choose a composer? You look for one whose style is appropriate to magnifying your message. In the actual composition, the music should, as composers have said for centuries, express the truth in the words. This goal covers meaning, metrics, syllabic length, and overall spirit. The music and words should complement each other, and the result should seem bigger and more pleasing than either would alone. The combination should sound and feel like just the right auditory enchantment to amplify the meaning.

Production Values, High and Low

Should every commercial, print ad, website or digital ad be produced as gorgeously as possible? It's usually smart to invest in high production values, no matter whether the budget is enormous or relatively minuscule, because it's better to look first-class and be seen less frequently than to look second-class and be seen often.

The need for great production is especially pronounced in certain categories; for instance, food advertising, where visual appetite appeal must be communicated; beverage advertising, where the goal is often to exude glamorous refreshment; financial services, which must represent financial success; fragrances, which ought to breathe enchantment, and any luxury item.

We may say that high-production values are preferred anytime there is the need to communicate quality. There is an exception. When the advertising for a product or service is intended to convince the consumer to believe a low-price claim, it's smarter to prefer comparatively plain, though still tasteful, production values. The consumer realizes somebody has to pay for the advertising and suspects she and other shoppers are the source of the funding. As a result, high production values can actually undermine a low-price claim.

It such cases, create bright advertising and then produce it simply. It ought to look nice but not lavish. Then the message will persuade while the modest look helps reassure the consumer that the advertiser just may be penny wise enough to deliver the promised bargain prices.

PART 5

The Creative Exploratory and Solving Tough Creative Problems

CHAPTER 21

THE CREATIVE EXPLORATORY AND SOLVING TOUGH CREATIVE PROBLEMS

Is there a smarter way to go about creating the copy and design on which to spend the budgets clients entrust to us? After all, their business and personal success, along with the wellbeing of their employees, depend to a great extent on how well we tell consumers about the products they make or the services they perform.

Let's begin with how the usual creative people work. Once they understand the strategy, they begin to rove over the strategic content, out of which they hope to make an appeal to the consumer, to see what creative ideas might spring from it.

As they proceed, they may make notes. But the questions they have to deal with multiply as they continue to create. What they do not have is an orderly way to explore the possibilities.

For instance, are they sure what ideational areas they looked into? Did they miss the most valuable ideas in any of the areas?

The uncertainty helps us understand why the advertising creative process has generally been inconsistently successful. How can we go beyond the usual haphazard conduct of it?

First, we must understand exactly what we're looking for – the perfectly appropriate verbal and visual magnification of the brand promise, or unique selling proposition. We intend it to include appropriate originality. To magnify our own description, let's look at a few examples.

We'll begin with a classic example of copywriting, David Ogilvy's headline for Rolls-Royce, "At 60 miles an hour, the loudest noise in this new Rolls-Royce comes from the ticking of the electric clock."

What is the source of its power but the verbal magnification of the selling proposition, which was, we assume, an incomparably quiet ride, with "quiet" implying, as advertising's so-called "end-end benefit," consummate luxury. Since the visual shows the car rolling along as majestically as possible, we'll consider it a relatively workaday way to compliment the headline with visual magnification. We might have magnified the meaning more if the car was driving through an area that contained some sort of noisy event, like a marching band, while the occupants remained pleasantly undisturbed.

Now, let's look at a few classic examples that seem to violate our description. For instance, how can we say that the "Lemon" and "Think Small" ads for Volkswagen are magnifications of the selling proposition, when they seem to gain their appeal by a charming denigration of the car's appearance?

Let's look more carefully. Given a car to sell with an appearance that would earn it the nickname of "The Beetle," we might well decide that the best, if not the only, hope of making it appealing is to have fun with the look – that is, to magnify the odd shape, thereby to excuse it and make the car, not only acceptable, but lovable – an ugly duckling that admits it has no hope of becoming a swan and adjusts to its appearance with inviting self-deprecation.

To bring us up more current, let's turn again to the long-time slogan of Federal Express, "The World on Time." Can you see how the slogan is a deft, inviting verbal magnification of what the service endeavors to provide, which is timely delivery of packages anywhere on the globe. As another more contemporary example, let's take the early slogan that expressed the brand promise of YouTube: "Broadcast yourself."

Let me also refer to a passing slogan by *The New York Times,* which has figured out how to navigate the digital landscape with growing success. I'm not referring to its traditional "All the news that's fit to print," but to the relatively recent but now abandoned brand promise, "Expect the world." I do it to illustrate that an effective slogan can be created by adroitly transferring the meaning of a colloquial expression to a new application and thereby refreshing it. The phrase becomes new and remains familiar at the same time – a laudable combination when our goal is to win over a lot of people readily. This technique is a frequent advertising resource for communicating with clarity and wit.

Now, that we've covered the preliminaries, let's go on to the overall way to develop creative work that I call The Creative Exploratory.

I developed it when I began to do creative consulting to some of the biggest marketing companies, including Kraft, Unilever, Johnson & Johnson, Bristol-Myers Squibb, and Pizza Hut. I wanted a way to succeed for them every time. When we present ourselves as experts and people have the insight to hire us, we want to be especially careful to deliver an optimally successful answer.

Advertising Age wrote an article about me as a creative problem-solver for major companies. You know the creative problems were considered tough, or I wouldn't have been retained.

The media planner I was using at the time was included in the interview. Here's an excerpt you might enjoy:

"With no fanfare or publicity, these ad sleuths [the author and the media planner he retains as needed] are assigned projects to solve and then they slip away – sometimes without even the knowledge of the primary agency ... their work is virtually always kept from the public."

– ADVERTISING AGE MAGAZINE

What is the Creative Exploratory?

It's a way to go about any aspect of the advertising creative process in an organized way, so that we are in control of it. As a result, we can significantly increase the likelihood that we will create branding and advertising that is not only invitingly bright but also inarguably right; that is, creative advertising that is the most successful advertising the brand can have.

In fact, The Creative Exploratory will enable great copywriters and designers to solve even the most difficult problems in an inspired but orderly way.

If you're an account person, understanding it will help you work with creative people more effectively, and, if you're a client, the understanding will help you feel confident about your ability to choose advertising that will do the best job for you.

First, I'll describe the procedure. Then I'll develop it with examples. It works for development of the brand promise or slogan for development in traditional or digital media, as well as for the development of campaigns, and enables us to maximize our own creative capacity and the potential of the creative process. It also works for new product concepts and name development, as well as product ideation.

There is a crucial difference between it and the usual advertising creative process. There are two ways to do it, which we might call deductive and inductive.

The Deductive Approach

Let's begin with the deductive approach. Before or shortly after we start to ideate, we take some time to think about the strategy or other input we've been given and write down the various strategic areas in which we might work creatively. This is the first step to maximizing the effectiveness of the creative process.

We can describe the areas in a word or two. For instance, if the product is a berry-flavored beverage and the taste is the primary benefit, we would simply write down "Taste." Then we could develop ideas about the great taste. But what about the various ways to get at taste? How about "Berry-Specific Taste?" Or "Natural Berry Taste?" What about taste in terms of refreshment? Does the strategy allow for a combination of benefits, such as a category we might call "Taste/Refreshment?" Or, to reverse the emphasis and subordination, "Refreshment/Taste?"

We continue to explore the areas in which we might get creative ideas until we feel we've thought of all the relevant ones. We might add an area or areas as our thinking evolves. We don't want to get carried away. While the Exploratory enables us to think more exactly, it's not an end in itself. We treat it as a flexible instrument, responsive to our own way of implementing it.

Once we have a pretty good grasp of the areas that seem ripe for creative development, we're ready for specific ideation. We begin to do verbal and visual experiments – thinking up slogans, headlines, visuals, commercials, print or digital ads.

Each time we get an idea, we place it under the area in which it belongs, so we can keep track of our ideas and free our minds to continue ideating.

At first, we'll generally come up with creative ideas that are pretty basic, although we could get just the right, bright inspiration early and even before we launch the Exploratory. But now we'd just place it in the Exploratory in the appropriate area for ideation and continue. As we get past the basic concepts – which can be seen as the ideas at the bottom of the mountain, we head for the top, where, hopefully, in a moment of inspiration, we can snatch the right idea off the crest. We find our imaginations moving on to more original and exciting ideas, and we continue to note them in the appropriate areas.

We discover that, since we're keeping track of our ideas in an organized way, we can now move from area to area with ease, as the free play of your imagination leads us.

Once we've looked at the various ideational areas that refer to the taste of the beverage itself, we might expand our thinking. For instance, we might consider the target audience. What is their established behavior? How can we utilize it or change it? How about their new, or emerging, behavior? When we get a creative lifestyle idea, we can place it in the taste category that it fits in, called, for example, "Taste/Lifestyle."

The same applies if we decide to consider, for instance, taste in terms of the competition. We initiate an area called Taste/Competitive." We ask, what are the competitive taste claims? How does our taste fit into the beverage category? How does it relate to the taste claim, as well as the actual taste, of the leading entry in the category?

We put each inspiration in the ideational area it belongs.

We ask again, are there other ways to get at "taste"? What about the various ingredients? What if we create a subarea or new area called "Taste/Ingredients"? Does the brand name lend itself to a tie-in with taste? What about the heritage of the brand? We create as many areas as we like. Oh, and let's not forget about the client's preferences? Does that lead to an area or areas?

And how big is the budget? If it's big, we might concentrate on ideas that will require more elaborate productions. If it's small, we'll be wise to develop ideas that are simple to produce. The size of the budget can also guide us in deciding how dramatic the advertising has to be to impact the market. Obviously, if we can afford to run the commercial or other advertising with a robust budget, we can present the story differently than if we know we have to make our point with fewer impressions against the target market.

The great thing is, no matter how far our minds range, we have an easy way to keep track of our ideas.

If we come up with a great creative idea that is not of primary importance in the strategy, we can make a note of it. We might want to discuss it with our supervisors and the account team. After all, we're at the front lines of the interface with the consumer – the one place where only the creative people can go ideationally. So we may well unearth questions and opportunities that are still latent or have yet to be expressed in the strategy.

We explore at will and continue to group and, if we like, to subgroup our ideas, so we stay in control of the creative process.

Now, something amazingly valuable begins to happen. As the slogans, headlines, visuals, commercial and ad ideas mount, the areas we're working in start to reveal their potential. Some areas are alive with creative possibilities, while others produce very little that's exciting. So we can see the fertile area or two where the right advertising is more likely to come from.

After a while, something else important happens. We begin to sense that we've explored the creative possibilities pretty much to the horizons of the assignment. We have covered all the likely areas in which the right, bright marketing communications may lurk.

Now, our thinking becomes more sophisticated. Since we're viewing the creative options in a coherent way, we're in a better position to recognize the right, bright creative idea when it flashes into mental view. Because we appreciate its unique value within the panorama of the creative possibilities, we can get intelligently excited.

Our minds have reached up and plucked exactly the right bright idea from the pinnacle of the creative mountain. Or, to say it another way, it has fallen out of the higher reaches of our imaginations and landed in our laps, like an exciting present.

When we define the areas to ideate in first or soon after we begin to think, I call the process working from the top down. It can be seen as a form of deductive reasoning and is usually preferred when we have a strategy to work from or just know the terrain the brand lives in pretty well. It's also a ready way to begin when we find ourselves with a relatively simple creative problem. In fact, we might be able to map out the areas in our minds without even having to write them down.

Now, let's get tougher on ourselves. What if we haven't been provided with a strategy? Obviously, to create the right bright advertising, we need the correct information, and we generally assume the marketing people at the agency will provide it. Yet sometimes we may find ourselves without a strategy, especially if we're consulting directly with a smaller advertiser or if we're doing the creative work to promote our own business. We can help make up for the shortfall in various ways. We can give the client a creative brief to fill out and study it. We can study whatever information the client provides and develop our own best version of a strategy. Then we can go to The Creative Exploratory with the information we have and map out what appear to be the relevant areas in which to ideate. There is, however, a third answer. We can "work from the bottom up," or inductively.

The Inductive Approach

We begin just as a relatively unsophisticated copywriter and art director might – by randomly creating whatever headlines, slogans, visuals, commercial ideas, and ads we can. But here's the difference. As we do so, we keep a watchful eye out for how the ideas begin to group themselves. In other words, we use the individual ideas to lead us to the areas that will define the creative terrain of the project. As the areas develop, we begin to group the creative concepts under them.

The result will be the same. In time, we'll begin to get the feel of the possible areas to work in, the relative value of each area, and the value of the ideas in each area. And, when we hit on just the right idea, our grasp of the possibilities will allow us to see it for what it is and get excited with credible confidence.

The latter approach also recommends itself when the brand and the world it lives in are relatively unfamiliar to us.

Benefits of the Creative Exploratory

As you can see, a key benefit of The Creative Exploratory is that it prevents us from diving into the creative forest and losing our way. When we work "from the top down," we're able to map the terrain before we enter it, and when we work "from the bottom up," we're able to map it as we go.

There is another enormous benefit. For the first time, we can make our creative recommendation, not just with an explanation of why we think the work is great, but with a knowledge the options. This unprecedented view helps us frame the recommendation. And, if we're challenged, we can share the creative possibilities to clarify why we believe our recommendation is the right one.

Which brings us to another benefit. We can print out The Exploratory and take it to the presentation, just in case we need it. It's an especially good tactic if you're on your own as a creative consultant. It's best to make a cover sheet and bind the pages. Make copies, too. Then, if you run into any resistance, you can take it out, pass it around if you want to, and review it with the people you're presenting to.

Your audience, accustomed to the usual sort of presentation, will often be astonished by its very existence. More critically, for the first time in the history of advertising, it lets them see the creative possibilities as you've discovered them, so they, too, can judge your recommendation in light of the likely creative options.

Now, you have the basic idea of The Creative Exploratory. Simple, right? But invaluable. It doesn't get in your way, but it optimizes your creative capacities.

The More You Work with it, the Better You'll Get at it

In time, you can make it the automatically intuitive way you go about creating advertising. In fact, you can become so skillful at it that simple creative problems almost solve themselves. You can quickly imagine the likely areas of appeal, ideate to the right answer, and present.

Today, when I'm doing brand-promise development, I simply start typing up the ideas I get, as I roam imaginatively over the possible areas of appeal, as market-ready slogans – until I think I've covered the likely areas and sense I've hit on just the right, bright promise. Then I arrange it as a recommendation, other favorites, maybe ten to fifteen, and just more that I came up with on the way to the recommendation that I believe still have merit. Clients often buy the recommendation, but at times they may even reach down into other choices for something that works for their business for a reason they'll explain.

Since I can do The Exploratory in a relative flash, I'm often able to get the right creative idea even when I'm being told about the problem – a skill that has allowed me to be invited to help solve tough creative problems at leading ad agencies when time is short.

Of course, I may or may not tell the client I've already got what I think is very likely the answer. Whether I do or not depends on the time constraints to develop an answer and whether I think the client is knowledgeable enough to appreciate it. I've also learned by experience that it's wiser to look more extensively into the creative possibilities before I settle on a recommendation.

Lighting up the Room

What are you actually doing when you proceed according to The Creative Exploratory? Let me offer a metaphor.

When most people attempt to create great advertising, they run into a dark room, feel around until they find something that seems especially valuable, and then run out, ready to share their discovery.

The wiser activity is to enter the room, light it up until you can see what its creative contents are and choose the most valuable items. Then you can share them, not only with enthusiasm, but with the knowledge of what else is in the room.

Here's another metaphor I often use. If you try to thread a needle in the dark, you can only poke and hope. But when you light up the room, you can thread it with ease.

Thinking in Three Coronas

When you're in the midst of the creative process, it helps to see creative ideas in three coronas. What do I mean?

First, there is the near corona. The ideas here are pretty obvious, but you'll still want to look at them. You may discover something highly original and immediately valuable; for instance, you may find the brand promise, campaign, or new product that should always have been there but somehow never was. I call these ideas the gold at your feet. It can be tough to bend your neck down to see them.

Second, there is the middle corona. You'll find most of the right, bright ideas here. They have two commendable characteristics. They're new at the same time they're not so far out that they're hard to sell or may seem strange to consumers.

Third, there is the far corona, where the far-out ideas reside. It's always a good idea to let your imagination roam here for a while, just to see what's there. Occasionally, you'll discover a surprisingly creative answer that somehow makes such infinite sense the client buys it and consumers are attracted to it. At the very least, you may find some exotic spice to enliven the presentation.

An Example of the Power of the Creative Exploratory

The Creative Exploratory has allowed me to make a living as a creative consultant and freelance copywriter for many years – and for some of the biggest marketing companies and advertising agencies, as well as for a great many SMBs.

Let me provide a specific example of how effective working with it can be. Once the legendary Steve Frankfurt, then the creative director of a major New York advertising agency after his distinguished career as an art director and then the youthful president of Young & Rubicam, invited me to help create television commercials for a Colgate product. As I worked on the project, I learned that Colgate had asked five agencies to participate. The client's goal was to pick one TV spot for production. The account people who presented the work for the agency said that the client looked at seventy-five storyboards. You know I wouldn't be recounting the event unless the commercial the client selected was one I created and recommended.

I had the same advantage over all the other creative people that you can have. The Creative Exploratory allowed me to see the creative horizons of the project, so I could recommend what I believed was exactly the right, bright TV spot.

CHAPTER 22

MORE ON SOLVING TOUGH CREATIVE PROBLEMS

Most advertising creative problems are relatively easy to solve, but some are considered tough, and once in a while a real brain-breaker does come along. What accounts for the difficulty? The usual reason is that a large number of demands have been placed on the assignment. Such a situation can be seen as an opportunity to provide an especially welcome answer. It's a chance to put a creative solution on the table that, dismayingly, meets all the demands placed on it. When it meets them, everybody generally recognizes the rightness of the work immediately, because whatever demand he or she has put on the assignment has been met. You've fashioned the key that fits the lock.

Sometimes, however, demands can be illogical or contradictory. These have to be addressed. Some can be finessed but others must be confronted, especially contradictory demands. A clear explanation of the conundrum with the client generally leads to a satisfactory resolution and opens the way to the right answer.

While incisive intuition is the basic faculty that is required to see through a tough creative problem, the greatest aid is knowing exactly what you're looking for and how to get there.

We know what we're looking for: the right, bright creative solution. And we know how to get there: The Creative Exploratory.

When the assignment is truly tough, you'll want to be especially precise about your analysis of the information, and then you'll want to survey the creative terrain with sufficiently orderly ideation to make sure you get to the right answer. On such occasions, you'll generally want to do an entire Exploratory, because it will help you do justice to your potential to succeed.

How to Solve a Genuinely Tough Creative Problem

Once in a while a creative problem comes along that even you, with all of your innate talent and learned skill, find genuinely resistant. Labor as you do, you realize that it's difficult to discover an answer that you know is exactly right – the immediately recognizable simultaneous answer to all the demands that have been put on the project.

There you are, working away with all your conscious insight and voluntary imagination, in an orderly way, developing areas for ideation and ideating within them, but you know that you just haven't put your pick in the mountain where the gold is.

You acknowledge that you've got some good and maybe even great ideas. You had a pile of them minutes after you started to think. Yet a voice within is telling you that you just haven't gotten to exactly the right, bright answer. Listen to that voice. While some of the work may be better than the client has seen, you'll usually fail to convince your audience that you've got the answer they were hoping you'd bring them.

What can you do? When my mind seems to have hit this kind of wall, I've learned to tell myself something very straightforward. Think harder.

The solution to such a resistant problem does not lie in trivializing the assignment. The right answer just happens to be deeper than you've ideated or someplace you haven't gotten to yet.

But how can you think harder? Sit back and think about the overall terrain. Trust your insight and imagination. They've proven themselves. Let your mind roam. Have you looked into all the possible areas that may apply? Note any new areas that seem relevant. Now get more specific.

Ask yourself if you could you have missed something in one of the areas?

Readjust your perspective. If you've been breaking your brain trying to think at the far horizon, maybe the answer is closer in and you've looked right past it. Bend your chin down as hard as you can and look for the gold at your feet. Very few people know to or have the ability to do this. Yet the obvious answer that should always have been there, but somehow never was, is one of the most valuable discoveries. It has immediate, recognizable value. Consumers can adopt it as though it's something that always belonged in their lives.

Maybe the right claim is in the heritage of the brand or the company. Become simplistic. Could the answer be as innocently disarming as an adroit pun or other witticism that grows out of the name or a keyword in the claim?

If you don't see the answer close in, raise your vision just enough to look over the middle ground again. You know that's where most of the right ideas come from.

If you still don't hit on the solution, try to peek into the smallest aspects of each area. Sometimes, the gold is under a pebble you still didn't turn over. At such times you're really into the art of the miniaturist, somewhat like a watchmaker.

Oh, my, how much you know and yet the right answer still eludes you. You're sure of exactly what you want to say, but you still don't have what you know is the perfectly correct magnification of it. Wherever is the answer?

You're frustrated and a little mad. You begin to fear that this is one of those very rare times when even you may not hit on the right answer. How is such a thing possible?

Does the way the assignment has been defined preclude a deft solution? Are you dealing with such a convoluted problem that the answer would require a multiplicity of creative solutions or constitute a contradiction in terms?

Well, gifted and savvy as you might be, we're all human, and once in a while we won't get to exactly the right answer. We begin to fear we'll have to get by with what we consider approximately the right answer. Thankfully, the idea and backup ideas you may present will likely be better than anything else that the client has seen. But we dearly don't want to disappoint the people who have decided to depend on us or give them less than what we know is the work that will do the best for the brand or the service.

We know that thinking harder entails not only continuing to think big but thinking small, too. So we decide to get even more deeply into the endeavor. We become downright Lilliputian. We look over the strategy or other information with an imaginary magnifying glass.

We move the magnifier to the brand name once again and think of the word or words that go with it. Is there by chance some kind of play on the brand name, such as an added meaning it might have? Consider the forms of euphony – rhyme, alliteration, assonance, consonance, and synecdoche. (We'll go into these tools more when we get to the resources of language.)

One of my guiding principles is, never think about what you can look up. So it's time to get out a pocketbook dictionary and go to the section on the letter that the brand name begins with. Leaf through it and see if you find an appropriate alliteration. Now, take out or click onto a rhyming dictionary and see if you can find a rhyme that works.

Examine the words in the primary claim. Consider the use of the dictionary or rhyming dictionary. Take out a thesaurus and search for workable synonyms.

Is there some remarkably irresistible way to stitch the name and the claim together? The aided recall such a fit can provide can prove irresistible.

Art directors can do their own microscopic work by searching stock-photo resources with a range of keywords. Whatever is just the right bright visual or visuals?

Once again, let's stop thinking primarily about the product for a while and turn our attention to the consumer. Imagine different ways than you already have about how the product can fit into and enhance his or her life. What visual places it in the consumer's life so that the product is of the most benefit? Imaginatively place it on the kitchen table or in the consumer's hands. What can he or she do with it or say about it?

Now think about the culture at large. Is there an established or an emerging trend you might relate the brand to that's just the right tide to ride?

Reconsider the competition. Could the right verbal-visual argument still lie hidden there?

More Tips on Solving Tough Creative Problems

First, here's a tip on solving tough creative problems from an unlikely source, the French philosopher Rene Descartes. He tells us that when he woke up in the morning, he would lie in bed with his eyes closed, without moving much, and think for an hour. When you're trying to solve an especially difficult creative problem, you might try the method. You'll find that, before you move your muscles or have your mental freshness inundated with input, your mind can wander over the aspects of the project in a free and judicious way. I suggest that when you plan to do so – and actually every night – keep a pen and paper, a notebook computer, or a smartphone with an app that lets you write on the screen on your night table, so you can jot down your ideas without having to get up and disturb the peace of your contemplations.

Second, if you can manage to, it's always a good idea to start a project early enough to get through The Creative Exploratory two or three days before the presentation. If you harbor any doubts about the work, you'll still have time to think more and, just as importantly, to see what other inspirations your unconscious mind might synthesize and drop into your conscious mind. This period of reflection can be invaluable, because by now your mind has a thorough grasp of the advertising problem, and you never can tell what your conscious creativity or the higher faculties of your mind might synthesize as a welcome present. It's certainly better to have the inspiration before the presentation than the day after it.

Now, here a tip that's almost embarrassing to provide but it can save the day. Explore the possibility that the problem has a really dumb answer, the kind of answer, say, that you might expect to get from a perky junior writer, for example, a superficial wordplay or visual tie-in that just happens to express exactly what you want to in a bright and inviting way. The combination of silliness and charm can prove irresistible.

Finally, here's a way to help your afterthoughts along during the day or so before the presentation. Look over the marketing and creative materials in an easygoing way. Just leaf through them, without getting caught up in the details – the strategy, the research, the creative work in your Exploratory. The survey is easier if you mark what you think is important when you study the marketing and research materials for the first time.

How to Deal with Failure

On rare occasions, your knowledge of exactly what you need will prompt you to suspect that you still don't have the right answer. So you may want to postpone the meeting, or, more likely, considering the pressures we all work under, go to it and recommend the next best thing.

Yes, as we all must come to terms with, nothing is 100%. Talented as we may be and a much as we know our craft, once in a great while, we won't get to the right answer. It's an upsetting comeuppance. How, we demand, is such a thing possible? We may not have thought of the right area, but that oversight is a pretty big mistake and hardly likely. It's more probable that we missed something in one of the areas. For some reason, our mind just didn't get to it.

Occasionally, the most distressing thing happens. We're in some sort of competition, and the confirmation that we didn't get to the right answer arrives when we learn what the winning idea is. Somehow, somebody else got to the right advertising, or at least closer to it. Maybe it was just luck. We're left with one reassurance. Such misfortunes will intrude less often if we go about our creative work as I've recommended.

While The Creative Exploratory will not get to you the right answer every time, compared to every other approach to advertising creative development, it's almost an exact science. It's also realistic to know you're fallible. In an important way, it's also reassuring, because the awareness helps enable you to do your best and know that most of the time you will get to the right answer.

The sort of difficulties dealt with here can happen, not only in advertising, but in name development, which is fraught with small values and maddeningly evasive answers. (I'll share my powerful approach to the art in the section on new product development.)

Yet, if you're acutely logical and have an exceptional flair for creative imagination, you may one day consider even the most difficult advertising creative work relative child's play. You're just one of those special people who have the requisite combination of abilities and have taken the time to equip your faculties with the right tools. You've become a master craftsman of the happy little art of great copywriting. As you'll discover, it's delightful and rewarding to make your living in a way that is apparently difficult for many but easy for you.

Getting across the River

Sometimes I think of ideating to the right answer in terms of a great many people who arrive at the bank of a river with various supplies. They begin to discuss how to get across it. Many of them just don't know how. Those who just wade in often founder in the current. One of them points to a series of rocks that may permit a safe passage. Another one suggests that they might attempt to build a bridge. What they need is a guide who can help them get across it in the surest way. It's The Creative Exploratory.

CHAPTER 23

PRESENTING CREATIVE WORK

There are two parts to a correct presentation: the framework and the creative work itself. The framework is set up so that the creative work will appear to be what it ought to be: the answer to the creative challenge.

When more than one campaign is being presented, some people prefer to build to the recommended work. But the approach entails showing the wrong work first, so there is a risk of distressing the audience, and by the time you get to the recommendation, there is the additional challenge of reinvigorating the meeting.

I generally prefer to present the recommendation first. If the work is as right as I think it is, the meeting becomes immediately exciting and satisfying. Then I can make the decision if it's necessary to show any other work. If the recommended work isn't received well, I can still turn to the other interesting possibilities I've brought along.

When the creative problem is especially difficult, you may, after showing the recommended work and any other ideas you may have done up, take your audience, at the agency or at the client, through The Creative Exploratory. It only needs to be typed and, if you like, bound, with copies to pass around. The vision of the possibilities may help the client see that the recommendation is right. Sometimes, the client prefers something else that is in The Exploratory. Since you only show work you think is exactly or approximately correct, whatever the client chooses should be acceptable.

Many agencies prefer to show only one idea, because they're concerned that the meeting may become too open ended and the uncertainty may undermine the credibility of the agency. While the attitude has merit, especially for less sophisticated clients, I think it underestimates the judgment of the more sophisticated ones. I've often been able to win the day by sharing The Creative Exploratory, especially when I've been retained as a creative consultant.

I title the first section "Recommended Area" and put the recommended work here, along with the other work that has been created in the area. I include the recommended work so that The Exploratory can serve as a complete summary of the work presented. Sometimes, it's helpful to preface the recommended area with a short introductory paragraph about why it's right for the strategy. I mention that the recommended work has already been seen and then go straight on to the other creative material. The other work might be broken down into separate sections, such as "Recommended Area: Other Campaigns" and "Recommended Area: Other Slogans."

When you've presented all the work in this section, move onto the other areas and present the scripts, slogans and any other materials you've included. You can group them as "Other Favorites" and then simply as "More Ideas." Be confident. It's commendable to have more than one possible answer to a creative problem, especially when the problem is one your audience felt they might never see an answer to.

To make going through TV scripts that haven't been done up as storyboards, I suggest a simpler format than the usual advertising form of two-columns, with the video on the left and the audio on the right, which condemns everyone to look back and forth to coordinate the material. Instead, type the script like an ordinary document but separate the video directions and the audio with spaces and make the video directions in capital letters and the audio in sentence case. Keep the video directions as simple as possible. Maybe even the title of the commercial will serve to set the scene. Then the read down each page is easy to follow.

When you're done, the audience has not only seen an intelligent creative recommendation; they've also been taken through a range of work they have never seen from any other source. Most importantly, they can see your recommendation in light of the likely creative possibilities. So they can better understand why it's right for them. The Creative Exploratory actually provides the opportunity, for the first time in the history of advertising, to allow a client to choose, not just from a recommendation, but from a knowledge of the likely options.

Finally, this admittedly extensive way of presenting can be especially effective in a new-business presentation, that is, if the prospective client will give you enough time to show the work. At the very least, the client will understand that you're dedicated to getting the business and are unusually fertile with ideas.

Winning More New Business

There are usually two sources of new business: existing clients and new ones. The first comes from doing successful work, and the second either from recommendations or from people who have a talent for getting on the phone and getting meetings. Some agencies don't like to do spec work, but it can be the surest way to demonstrate how much the agency has to offer.

Once a meeting has been arranged, it's good to request marketing information from the client, if you can get it. Then you can present marketing insights and creative ideas that, in your judgment, are self-evidently superior to the work the client has.

Over the years, I learned something that may prove helpful. As I was presenting, I realized that what is actually shown in a meeting is, to a certain extent, what we might call substitute content. The real event is the people on the client side trying to decide if they like the people on the agency side enough to want to work with them. While I think it's still more effective to go in with what seems to be the right work or, at least, the closest thing to it that the client is likely to see, and to have effective leave behind material, my advice is not to let inanimate things, like a computer with a PowerPoint presentation, get in the way of establishing a personal, affable relationship with the client.

I usually talk about The Creative Exploratory as a unique approach that gets to the right creative answer. The mere mention that such a tool exists and a short description of it with its benefits can be extremely persuasive.

PART 6

What You Should Know about Testing and Media

CHAPTER 24

ADVERTISING TESTING

Many creative people dread advertising research, but it's actually your friend. If you've created the right, bright advertising, the research provides the opportunity for you to prove that your approach works.

The Internet has revolutionized market research. Today, almost all kinds of digital advertising is direct response, and the "research" is based on how well the sales go. Concepts, which used to be presented to focus groups, are now present in concept screens to consumers who agree to opt-in and rate concepts for a modest financial reward.

Whether we're talking about the Internet or traditional market research, it is the empiricism of advertising. There are, after all, limits on how certain we can be by putting our hands on the philosopher's stone. No matter how much we know, time teaches us that the consumer can surprise us, usually in small ways but occasionally in major ones.

We'll concentrate on research as it's used to check and/or refine the creative work.

Since some uncertainty lies ahead, you'll find that The Creative Exploratory is especially valuable. Why? Most people go to the consumer with a "great" idea or two, hoping something works. If not, they go back to the drawing board. But with The Exploratory, you know you've covered the creative possibilities, at least, as thoroughly as you can, based on your current knowledge. So you don't have to swing across the crocodile-infested river on one rope.

Sometimes more than one campaign seems so promising that you feel it would be improper to make a final recommendation without more information. We'll look at traditional market research and then at online A/B testing.

Traditional Market Research

We decide to make intelligent use of what we don't know and recommend or assent to consumer research. This apparently risky but wise decision will actually help affirm the value of the recommendation or point the way to the right advertising. So we do up the contending instances of creative excellence.

Focus groups, or qualitative testing, are usually the first step. We go to them for three main reasons: to confirm our beliefs about what the most appealing and persuasive creative work is, to discover what actually is the most appealing and persuasive work, and to refine the work. The range of the creative work will provoke consumers precisely and diversely, so the responses will help focus your thinking. So focus groups can be your friend.

Due to The Exploratory, the respondents get to look at the advertising for the brand from various angles, sort of like walking around a piece of sculpture and telling you from what angle it looks most appealing to them. The process can be facilitated if the moderator is straightforward with the attendees and informs them, before any work is shown, that the advertiser has a number of approaches to advertising and would like to know what they think about them. He then encourages them to be brutally honest.

Next, comes quantitative testing. Most clients demand it before deciding to go with the creative work. They want to see what happens when it's shown to a large enough number of consumers to project how well it will do in the marketplace.

Once you've made the adjustments you've learned to make from the focus groups, all you can do is cross your fingers and wait for the quantitative results to come in, ready to respond to them as intelligently as possible.

Thankfully, you can be more confident than most of a good score, because you've aimed to say the right thing in the right way and submitted the work to focus groups for selection and refinement.

Generally, the quantitative tests will confirm your expectations. The work you've created, selected, and refined will score well. And, instead of discovering the work is way off target, you're more likely to learn ways to tweak the copy or the visuals.

Occasionally, although you seem to have done everything right, the quantitative score doesn't meet the client's action standard. I call it the rock at the 95-yard line. Somehow, it was there, and you tripped on it. Very likely you didn't know it was there because no one else had ever taken the advertising that far. No touchdown, yet. Your process may have been right, but your information couldn't take the unprecedented complication into account. It's a new wrinkle and requires a fresh approach.

Here's an example. Once I was asked by Bristol-Myers Squibb to help out with a commercial for a new cough capsule. I learned that the spot the agency of record had created did not score, and the television was scheduled to break in three weeks. The agency had created a concept print piece for the product that had achieved a high score. Why didn't the commercial score, too?

The problem was that the concept had an unfocused headline and a number of facts that were presented in the copy without emphasis and subordination, so it was difficult to determine what accounted for the score. The marketing people were confident, however, that the product would do great if a commercial could effectively communicate the unique selling point of the product: the capsule provided 8-hours of cough relief, so there was no awful-tasting syrup to swallow.

The timeline was so tight that I asked if I could call a production company and schedule the shoot, even before I went away to think. Thankfully, I was so trusted to deliver the right answer that I was allowed me to make the call.

I began to think about cough-cold commercials. You know the usual scene. A guy with a cough can't get to sleep. His knowing wife gives him just the right medicine, and we leave the couple dozing comfortably. How could I make the simple point, in a dramatic way, that the capsule provided 8-hours of relief? What if, I asked myself, just the opposite of the usual happened?

I wrote a commercial starring a guy who couldn't get to sleep, because he was so excited about the product his wife gave him. There he was, running around the bedroom in his pajamas, exclaiming to his wife, "Can you believe it? Eight hours of cough relief in one simple capsule!" Meanwhile, she was saying, "Will you please just come to bed?"

The client loved the spot, I produced it, and it went on the air in the test markets. A few months later, when I was at the company on another assignment, I asked him how the product was doing in the marketplace. The research had just come in, and I was surprised to hear not very well. I asked if he knew why.

He told me that consumers were getting the message that the capsule provided 8 hours of relief. The problem was, due to their lifelong experience with cough syrup, they couldn't understand, at the time this commercial was done, how something that didn't coat their throats could stop them from coughing. The problem was based on new learning – the rock at the 95-yard line. Ever resourceful, I quickly suggested a demo shot for the middle of the commercial that would show how little cough suppressant there is in a dose of cough syrup, which is less by volume than most people imagine, and then put the capsule down beside the remainder, with a voiceover announcer explaining that the capsule works as well as syrup, because the capsule contains, dose for dose, the same amount of exactly the same cough medicine.

But it was too late. The short window the new product had to reach its sales goal, if it were to be taken beyond test market, was already closing.

The point is, because the 8-hour claim had never been communicated with compelling clarity, the resistance on the part of the consumer had never been elicited.

Now a few notes about focus groups and quantitative research.

With regard to groups, we all realize that the small number of people who see the creative work doesn't represent a projectable sample. The groups are for guidance only. Yet it's a rare group of observers in the back room who don't make decisions as if the groups represent the final say of the target audience. Illogical, but invariable.

In addition, the environment of a focus group is very basic. It has none of the bigger-than-life attributes of mass media. As a result, basic, or more literal, ideas are more readily accepted and praised than highly imaginative ones, which can seem out of place. Consumers love to show one another that they're far too sensible to be taken in by clever advertising. Yet if they saw the same creative work on television or in a magazine, they might very well like it and be persuaded.

The lesson is, ideas that are bigger than life are best tested in a form that's bigger than life, such as a test commercial presented in a theater environment, with the audience questioned afterward on an individual basis. The medium is more appropriate for the creative execution, and the consumers are making a private response, with no need to impress others with their unshakable sobriety.

While they are disposed to calling more imaginative advertising things like silly, corny, or stupid, some big ideas elicit a surprisingly enthusiastic response. Why? They're usually ideas with nothing stupid or irrelevant about them.

Groups are also a tough place to test advertising for products that have a deeply personal subtext. Toothpaste tests fine. But try something like hair color and tell the lovely women some blandishment like, "You're beautiful and always want to look your best," and they'll snap back with such things as, "Don't tell me what I look like. I know what I look like. Just tell me what the product does."

The way to get a more honest response to questions that touch on the personal lives of consumers is, as most advertising professionals know, one-on-one interviews, which consist of just the moderator and one respondent at a time.

Finally, in regard to print advertising, it helps to remember that in focus groups brevity is the soul of approval. It's astonishing how little patience people have with long copy. They'll tell you things like, "You expect me to read all of this?" Actually, though, it's a reflection of the real world.

By the way, I never cease to appreciate that a consumer economy makes the mightiest corporations fall on their knees before the consumer to try to figure out how they can please her or him.

When the focus groups are done and what has been learned has been used to select and refine the creative work, the next step is usually quantitative research, which is what passes for the more precise empiricism of advertising.

The hope is that the advertising will achieve a recall and/or persuasion score that meets the client's action standard, which is based on the proportion of people who recall the commercial, along with, at least, the main message, and/or the proportion of them that say they "definitely will buy" the product or service, along with, at times, the proportion who report they "probably will buy" it.

Since quantitative testing measures the response of a large enough group of people to represent a projectable sample of the target market, the scores usually result in a decision to go or not to go with the advertising. If the advertising meets the action standard, the client can be pretty confident it will help the brand achieve its sales objectives.

Given that a great deal is at stake, at least to those involved, the work should be produced in a way that's best for the type of research that lies ahead. For example, an animatic, or a drawn version of the commercial, is fine if the goal is to test a commercial that relies on basic facts that can be communicated in cartoon form. But if something has to be communicated in a more realistic way – such as a look or mood – the work should be produced as, at least, a photomatic, which, as you probably realize, is made up of photos that are videotaped or assembled on a computer in sequence to mimic a commercial.

Neither of these forms, however, communicates certain values adequately, despite what testing services tell us. Among them, we find warmth, character, and the true excitement of beauty in motion. If a commercial depends on one of these more intangible values, it's better to videotape the commercial. Film is usually too costly at this stage but may occasionally suggest itself with impressive authority when justice should be done to more visually delicate values, like romance in soft light or a resplendent outdoor scene.

Similar suggestions also apply to preparing print advertising for quantitative testing. Some can be done up with drawings, while others need gorgeous photography.

These sublime values will, after all, be available should the advertising score well enough for the commercial to be produced for broadcast.

Of course, sometimes flashy advertising that gets in the way of, instead of highlights, the most appealing things about the product or service can score well. Here's the problem. Since it is not the right advertising, the measurement is based, at least for the most part, on the appeal of the commercial, not the merit of the product, which is what the client is in business with. This caveat applies less to brands that have little, if anything, concrete to offer the consumer, such as a new fragrance.

So an accurate measurement of how the commercial will do can only be attained when the creative work features the merits of the brand. Consumers may talk about the commercial, but why would they buy the product?

The advertising and the product must be just made for each other. From this viewpoint, the right advertising can be seen as the perfect package for the package in which the product comes.

At the very least, the commercial should not misrepresent the brand. Woe awaits when the consumer buys the commercial, only to find that the product delivers something far different. There will be fewer repeat sales, so what are the prospects for the long-term? Worse yet is when the commercial egregiously exaggerates what the brand can deliver. As the saying goes, nothing kills a bad product faster than great advertising. More people try it faster.

Online Research

Most online advertising is direct-response.

The internet enables almost instantaneous feedback. True, if you create a campaign or new Ad Group in Google or Facebook, you want to wait a couple of weeks to confirm how it's doing. The key measurement is simply sales, but factors like cost per acquisition come into play, too.

The fact is, the results that can be attained on the internet dwarf in time, cost and actionable learning the rigors of research before the arrival of digital media.

CHAPTER 25

THE RIGHT MEDIA

Great copywriting and all successful advertising must appear in the right traditional and digital media to reach the target market optimally.

If you're in an agency, the media will be taken care of for you. If you're freelancing, on the internet, you'll often be in charge of the media, in terms of doing PPC advertising in the various platforms. But even on the Internet, when budgets are large and display advertising plays a major role, media people can play a key role.

It's wise to involve the media department or person in the early stages of strategic and creative development – to get their top-of-mind input and to get them thinking about the campaign to come, because the entire effort – strategic, creative, and media – ought to be synergistic.

The usual goal of online media is to achieve 5 or so touch points with the target market, while in traditional media the usual goal is to achieve 3-plus impressions against it. We'd like the advertising to appear with enough frequency. In digital media, we just kind of keep knocking on the door, hoping to get an answer within the five knocks. In traditional media, here's the usual rationale for 3+ impressions. Theoretically, the first time consumers see it, they note it. The second time, they decide, if the message evokes their desire to own the product, to do something about it. And the third time, they resolve to make the purchase.

The above norms are the media weight intended to achieve impact. It is particularly important to achieve it, or to get as close to it as the client can afford to, during the first three weeks of the campaign, or the sign-in period.

If the budget is tight, it's usually better to achieve impact weight in a limited area than to spread the advertising too thin. Then, as the campaign succeeds, enthusiasm and growing sales can fund wider reach.

Should you ever decide to go for more reach at the expense of the usual frequency? I think the decision depends on what your goal is. If you need to persuade, you might well need the recommended touch points or impressions. So it makes sense to opt for a smaller marketing area, maybe one channel like Google Ads with location targeting or traditional media purchases in the top ten markets. On the other hand, if your goal is to announce something so immediately appealing that you feel little persuasion is required, you might well decide to go for a wider audience, even though you'll have fewer impressions against the target market. Although you can't afford impact levels widely, you can let a lot of people know that your product exists. Since it has such great appeal, you might sell more of it than you would by reaching a smaller audience at the usual impact levels. The advice has particular relevance to new or newly advertising products with a strong unique selling proposition.

Is there way to help you make a decision? Here's a way I thought up. It's another, if you'll indulge the nomenclature, Attea Idea. I call it "media flash-value." Simply ask yourself, if you take the product or service and put it on a flash card with a headline that presents the essence of its appeal and turn it toward your intended audience for just a moment, will a lot of them want to buy it? Or do you think you'll have to explain some details, overcome some objections, and make some reassurances?

If you decide that a great many of them will get up off the couch at their first glimpse of the benefit, you may decide to go for all the reach you can afford. If you see them still sitting in their seats, waiting to know more before they commit, then you or the media department may decide you need more frequency.

PART 7

Landmark Books, the Creative Revolution, Advice, and Perspectives on Advertising

CHAPTER 26

A BRIEF REVIEW OF LANDMARK ADVERTISING BOOKS

To become a complete copywriter, you should know the landmark contributions to intelligent advertising.

While innumerable books have been written about advertising, only a handful have made lasting contributions to the understanding of what it is. My review is not intended to be inclusive. These are what I consider landmark contributions.

The first book is the pragmatic but insightful work, *Scientific Advertising,* by the early copywriter Claude Hopkins. His most significant contribution was to say that a claim has to be specific and unique. He provided an example. At the time, the advertising for many beers was apparently based on the claim that they were "pure beer." He developed a specific expression of the claim: "steam cleaned bottles." (The missing hyphen in "steam-cleaned" is from the book.)

Rosser Reeves created a more exact expression of Hopkins' principle. In his book *Reality in Advertising,* he presented his foundational phrase, "the unique selling proposition," abbreviated as "The U. S. P." His most-noted advertising campaign is usually considered the one he created for M & M's. The legendary slogan is, "The milk chocolate melts in your mouth, not in your hands." While such an attribute can be considered a U. S. P., the melting point of chocolate would be an unlikely candidate to qualify as the main claim of a candy today. However, his nomenclature still serves as the main guide for strategic development, or the quest for the right thing to say. I do think, however, that it is more about selling than it is about communicating with the consumer. So I prefer the nomenclature of the unique brand promise.

Next, David Ogilvy's *Confessions of an Advertising Man* arrived on the scene. Despite his elegant appearance on the dust jacket, dressed impeccably in a suit from a major client, Sears', and the lofty tone of the prose, the book presents pretty much a nuts-and-bolts treatment of the craft of advertising. He was one of the early creative people who turned to market research to help him decide what to say about a product or service. He was also a champion of long copy, an advocacy that has endeared him to direct-response copywriters.

He provided the valuable reference point that, when you write the headline, you spend 80% of your money. The reason? Most people don't read body copy. Today, the caution also applies to the headline on a home page or landing page. On the other hand, he boasts that he can write a headline that will compel you to read an entire page of newspaper copy. His headline is, "This ad is all about you." The example is, of course, his way of saying that we get a consumer involved in an advertisement by making certain that it contains as much self-interest as possible in his or her terms.

Apparently, he will be forever remembered for writing the headline, "At 60 miles an hour, the loudest noise in this new Rolls-Royce comes from the ticking of the electric clock." We are to understand this claim as meaning the car has a quiet ride, although we might also infer that the clock is unusually loud.

Many creative copywriters do not consider this ad and the other work he is known for as mainstream creative innovation, such as putting a black patch on a spokesperson's eye, which he famously did for Hathaway shirts for no apparent reason, or casting a jolly and somewhat eccentric Englishman as a spokesman Schweppes, a tactic that, I suppose, can somehow be justified by the brand heritage.

There is also a book called *The Art of Writing Advertising,* which consists of interviews with five legendary copywriters. One of them is Bill Bernbach, who was the first copywriter to advocate and write humorous or clever advertising. He also co-founded the first major advertising agency that stood for what we usually consider creative excellence: Doyle, Dane, Bernbach.

Today, we remain less than overwhelmed by the creativity of the ads he himself created, for instance, those often-cited examples of print ads for a long-defunct New York department store called Orbach's. One of them features a cat in a stylish hat.

Yet, as a result of his foundational insistence on creative excellence and his having co-founded what was for decades one of the most creative ad agencies, he is in a category by himself. In fact, we can consider him the father of creative advertising.

In terms of technique, he said that expressing the most important feature of a product well constitutes "the alpha and omega of advertising." This last comment was, at the time, the most exact way to think about advertising and, though relatively general, it's still a pretty good description of the process. I assume he took for granted that expressing it well meant with appropriate creativity.

Among the copywriters in the book, we also find the pragmatic copywriter, Leo Burnett, who founded what became the largest ad agency west of the Hudson River, with its main office in Chicago. He gave us the concept that still serves as a workable justification of so-called image advertising: "When there is nothing unique about the product, you have to create a unique world for it to live in."

This approach is useful when "what" you can say about a brand is so well known or of such minor significance that little effect can be achieved by devoting the advertising budget to communicating it in a straightforward way. The best-known example of this tactic from the agency he founded is, unfortunately, "The Marlboro Man."

Let me reveal the unknown secret behind his idea. We can say, more precisely, that form and content exist in an inverse proportion. The more content we have to work with, the simpler the form can be. We do not need a big production to announce a cure for cancer; in fact, an elaborate production would get in the way. It would be more effective just to give a straightforward script to an announcer who has a consequential manner.

On the other hand, the less content we have to work with, the more we must depend on form, or razzle-dazzle. The razzamatazz of Coca-Cola and Budweiser commercials are examples. We adjust the proportion of form and content so that we can achieve our intended effect, which is, of course, to sell the product or service, inspire donations, or get votes. Hopefully, we will achieve it in a way that is inviting for the consumer.

The other copywriters in the book mention nothing that, at least to me, rings down the ages. One of them, George Cribben, was an early copywriter at Young & Rubicam, where I did my longest big-agency stint, and he is considered by many to have been a great one.

We should also note John Caples, a legendary expert at direct-response advertising, who wrote about the discipline. To achieve success, we must learn to do such things as ask for the order. Today, we refer to it as the call to action, abbreviated as the CTA. The rate of response goes up if we include an incentive, preferably something free. His best-known headline is, "They laughed when I sat down at the piano but when I started to play! –" [The exclamation point and dash are from the original ad.]

Descending now from the Mt. Olympus of advertising advice, we turn to Messrs. Kirshenbaum and Bond, who believe that advertising should "fly under the radar." They maintain that the wary consumer has developed a defensive apparatus to avoid the intrusion of advertising into his or her personal space. We find that a more effective approach is to create advertising the consumer can readily identify as a friendly craft.

I'll also mention, as a tip of my hat to the affable author, who is a former client, the book on advertising creativity by Doug Hall, *Jump Start Your Brain.* When he was a marketing exec at Proctor & Gamble, he retained me to do creative problem-solving on new products a number of times. He went on to create the Eureka! Ranch, which serves as a retreat where major corporations sent executives to learn the ways and wiles of creative marketing and inspired to reenergize their creativity.

The content of his book, penned with great enthusiasm, contains a blizzard of tips and encouragements. During the course of it, he was kind enough to refer to me as "a wizard of a copywriter." I'm also the only naming expert he mentions.

There have been innumerable other books. Among them we find books by direct-response writers who are considered legends in their discipline. They generally made their reputations on the internet but, to my knowledge, none of them ever darkened the hallways of a great ad agency. They gave us such ideas as addressing the reader's pain points and guidelines for writing long-form video sales letters, the frequent length of which would even make David Ogilvy blush. Yet almost all digital copywriting is direct-response writing, so I'll cover how to do state-of-the art DR copy in the chapter I dedicate to it.

To my mind, we've now covered the historical contributions I've found most helpful.

Of course, there are excellent textbooks on advertising. They usually present a great deal information in organized ways and serve as credible introductions. But they specialize, not in explaining the flame of creativity as it burns across the page, but in analyzing the ashes to understand what it was.

I was pleasantly surprised to receive my first request for permission to include some of my creative work in a textbook when I had only been in advertising for about four years, and I was invited to make my latest contribution to such a book relatively recently. I provided an extended comment on brand building as erecting the tallest building in the category by first putting in the right foundation. I'll share it later.

Today, the "news about the square of the hypotenuse," in W. S. Gilbert's phrase, is digital copywriting. It has, to an extent, provided us with a new wave of creative copywriting and design.

It has certainly changed my copywriting life. I've gone from primarily writing commercials and print ads to primarily writing websites, landing pages, email campaigns, Google Ads, and other digital fare.

I was fortunate to get into the internet early. In fact, I helped Steve Case advertise the company he would later name America Online. It was called Gameline, and it delivered video games through the phone line. Steve, who I had met when I was doing new-product ideation for Pizza Hut, called a few months after he joined the company and asked me to come to the corporate location, Vienna, Virginia, for lunch. He explained that he needed advertising for the company in all media. The slogan I gave him was, "Get online with Gameline." Since the internet had not really gotten going yet, it may have been the first time anyone wrote "get online." I also edited a book on how to do Google Adwords when the platform was just a couple of years old, and another one on strategies of Internet marketing.

Before we conclude this review, we should look at a classic definition of advertising as "The truth well told." It's a seductive definition but too inexact for reliable guidance. One clue is that it also applies to other forms of writing, such as journalism and history. Our job is not only to communicate the truth but also to persuade to purchase.

Of course, if we wish to stay out of jail, we must tell the truth. Today, however, we're relatively safe by default. If we attempt to transgress, most of the mainstream media will disallow the appearance of the advertising until we make appropriate changes. Despite its colorful reputation, advertising is, as the saying goes, the most regulated form of selling in history. But what do we mean by "well told"? Most of this book is devoted to making the answer specific.

To give an overview, our role is to be given or discover the unique selling proposition, or brand promise, which should be the most compelling truth about the product or service in terms of the consumer. In our approach, it's the correct "what to say." Then we must imagine the deftly right verbal and visual magnification of it – more generally, the right dramatization. This achievement is the correct "how to say it." Thus, we might say that a more exact statement is that advertising consists of the truth well magnified, with the intent to persuade to purchase, but only magnified to the extent that it remains credible. Then we need only assure that the message is told in the right places – the media that reach the appropriate audience with maximum efficiency, so our budget goes as far as possible.

To reach these goals, we must have guidelines specific enough to help guide our creative imaginations and get it from our minds into our fingers as material we can work with.

Finally, I should mention Samuel Johnson's famous but typically superficial quip that "Promise, large promise, is the soul of advertising." To a degree, he's correct, but if the promise is too large, it will create skepticism or expectations that the product can't deliver on. As a result, the consumer will dismiss the claims or be disappointed in the product. In the first instance, the result will be little increase in sales, and, in the second, insufficient repeat sales, which usually means that in a short time the product will fail.

I prefer to remember Dr. Johnson, not for his inadequate summation of advertising, but for his lexicographic achievements, as well as for his boisterous response to David Hume's notion that reality may not exist. You probably know, courtesy of Boswell, how the world-historical blunderbuss attempted to refute the contention. He kicked a chair hard enough to hurt his foot, and announced, "I prove it thus!"

Now that we've surveyed the past, we arrive at the book in your hands. I hope to demonstrate that you will find it provides the first complete, workable approach to the reliable creation and recognition of what we may justly call great advertising.

CHAPTER 27

PERSONAL AND CAREER ADVICE

I've learned some lessons along the way that apply to working in advertising, and I'd like to share them. I hope you find the advice helpful.

For Copywriters

How can you achieve your potential as a copywriter? I don't think it's helpful to talk about talent, because it's too indefinable. I also believe we can all discover enormous resources within ourselves. So I'll stick to what each of us can manage.

Many copywriters seem to be able to get by with a bit of a way with words and some street smarts. The advice I'm going to give is for people who want to do their work more artfully.

Obviously, it's good to read and watch widely, but, if you plan to make a living with the creative use of language, you'll want to read and view for more than content, or "what" everyone is interested in. Begin to ask "how" language is used to achieve goals, not just today, but historically. As a wordsmith, you'll find the study enjoyable.

Next, it's vital to understand how language works, so over time you can learn to work with it more and more adroitly. Since all values in advertising are small, you want to master even the small aspects of grammar and usage. Sometimes knowing the smallest rule about, say, commas, or what you can expertly judge constitutes a permissible infraction can help you make a masterstroke. To become a master of your craft, you want to get together, as I sometimes call it, your basic toolkit.

I don't mean that you should struggle to learn grammar and composition. I mean you should memorize it cold. Then you can work and play with it. How?

Here's a straightforward, workable way. Choose an inclusive textbook of grammar and composition. The large ones address almost all of the issues you'll confront in the precise use of brightly colloquial English, and they provide examples to help make the rules clearer.

Originally, I wasn't content with *The Harbrace Handbook,* but it's been enlarged over the years and it's easy to locate. Read it through once and grasp what you can. Read it again to grasp more. Over time, read it maybe 25 times – often enough to understand and remember each section well. So you can fit the task into your schedule, you might decide to make it your bedtime or transportation reading for a couple of years.

When you know it cold, you'll be forever free of any functional limits your expressive abilities. When a tiny question about copy presents itself, you'll be able to execute the answer with confidence and grace. And, in grammatical terms, you'll be more than qualified to supervise the copy output a major agency.

Such a book will, of course, also help you master the basics of composition, from sentence structure to the paragraph and the whole piece. You'll become more dexterous, for example, in the use of parallel and contrasting structures in sentences and in your selection of the various ways to develop a paragraph. You'll also begin to sense the wholeness of what you write, so you can work on even the most miniscule part with an exact appreciation of its place within the whole. This latter benefit will help you become more of a conceptual thinker, instead of just being clever with snatches of language. One way to bring your thinking in line with your writing is to spend some time thinking before you speak, arranging your thoughts in complete sentences and in complete paragraphs. Then over time, writing copy will be as easy as speaking it.

And you'll be a bit imposing. When a supervisor or a client suggests a grammatical modification in your copy, your mind's eye will go to the section of the book that applies to the comment, and you'll be able to reply in a shockingly convincing way.

Yet your knowledge mustn't lead to stiffness. You want to go beyond any struggle with language to adept manipulation of it. Your goal is to get beyond laboring with language as if you're assembling rattling bones to working with it as if it were a living creature – the exact and easygoing expression of your own vibrant thoughts.

When you take this meticulous approach, you'll learn to write copy so skillfully that you'll naturally write with nouns and verbs in crisp, energetic phrases and in sentences that march like a disciplined troop of soldiers from the beginning to the end.

With such linguistic insight and grace, you can add or delete an adjective here or an adverb there; make precise decisions about when to use a noun or a pronoun; decide if you might get away without a conjunction, notice the momentous difference between employing the definite article "the" or indefinite articles "a" or "an"; avoid such common redundancies as "the reason why"; never separate verbs from their subject with a comma, unless to include parenthetical material; select the clearest and briefest prepositions, for instance, "in" instead of "inside of."

Generally, you won't want your sentences to be much more complex than a couple of thoughts coordinated with an "and" or contrasted with a "but" or a "yet." One dependent clause with one independent one can help you with emphasis and subordination without the sentence becoming too complicated to invite continued reading, even by an unwilling audience. Here's an example: "Now that you know all about our great service, sign up today."

You might also indulge in the occasional extravagance of two dependent clauses or an independent clause or two. But compound, complex sentences – ones made up of an elaborate mixture of subordinate clauses and phrases combined with independent ones have little place in mass communications. They result in copy that only your most devoted readers will take time to trudge through.

Now, for a bit of relief. If you have become wary of the need to become as accomplished with language as I'm suggesting, you could be right. Very few copywriters know what I'm advising you to learn. My goal is to make you a truly great copywriter.

If you just can't seem to get past the feeling that grammar is an especially daunting undertaking, here's an imaginary account of the development of language you might find helpful. It's a tale I devised to help the junior writers in the copy-training program at Y & R understand that grammar isn't a confounded invention but the principles we learned as we labored to make language work.

Let's say you're a caveman who decides you're tired of grunting at your fellow cave dwellers and want a better way to communicate. So you go off by yourself and cogitate. You realize that a great deal of the world you'd like to have a way to talk about is made up of items you can see – concrete entities like people, other animals, trees, and the rock you may be perched on. You can think up a sound to indicate any of them, but what are you going to call the category? You decide on the sound "nouns."

Now, you ask yourself, what are the shortcomings of my nascent language? You realize that the world you want to talk about doesn't just sit there. Many of the items in it move. So you realize you need something to describe movement. Once again, you can think of sounds that will stand for various types of movement, but what will you call the items as a whole? You invent the word "verbs."

Hey, you're feeling pretty good. Since the world is basically made up of nouns and verbs, you can describe it to a certain degree with just those two things. But, canny caveperson that you are, you also notice that the nouns aren't all the same. They have attributes like color, size, and number. You need to take this feature into account and decide to call the words you add to the nouns "adjectives."

You also note that there are different kinds of motion, like fast and slow. Obviously, you'll need a way to take that reality into consideration, and you decide to name what you'll add to verbs "adverbs."

Your new language is certainly coming along. Now, you can consider the fine points. You notice that there is such a thing as position or the way things are related to one another. You're sitting "on" a rock, "outside" the cave, with only the sky "above" you, and right now you're not thinking "along with" anybody else. You decide to call the words that describe positional relationships "prepositions."

Well, you've had a pretty productive day. But you still note a few shortcomings. It's going to get monotonous if you and your fellow cavemen and cavewomen have to repeat the same noun over and over when you're talking about what it stands for. So you take your first step in the interests of linguistic grace and decide to invent a group of words that can substitute for nouns, as long as you make it clear what nouns they refer to. You pronounce them "pronouns."

Now, it's time for a bit of detail work. You know that sometimes you'll want to talk about a specific person or other noun and at other times you'll want to talk about a person or thing in more general terms. You opt to call the words you use to denote this difference definite and indefinite articles, and you're delighted to discover that at least some aspects of your task are simple. You realize you only need three of them – "the" for definite nouns and "a" or "an" for indefinite ones.

Guess what? You realize that now you have all the kinds of words you need to make complete, accurate statements. You can't wait to run and tell your tribe. But then you realize that you don't even have a name for complete expressions. In a moment of inspiration, you decide to call them sentences. But you quickly see that you need a way to indicate the beginning and end of them, and you devise a symbol to start them, which you name "a capital letter," and a way to end them, which you deign a period. Now, your mind is running on, filled with your grammatical achievements, but you become aware that every sentence lets you say only one thought. You need a way to connect more than one thought per sentence. You opt to name these useful little words "conjunctions."

And you notice that the three you need most frequently the ones that let you add one thought to another, the one that lets you contrast the thoughts, and the one that lets you alternate them. You call the first one "and," the second one "but," and the third one "or."

Then you realize that all your thoughts are not of equal importance. You have main thoughts and other thoughts that relate to them. You begin to think about how you can arrange sentences to express these differences. As a start, you decide to call your main thoughts independent and the thoughts that relate to them dependent. Independent and dependent what? you ask yourself? And you decide to call the main ones "independent clauses" and the other ones "subordinate clauses or phrases."

We'll obviously need some words to indicate what the dependent thoughts are, to indicate such things as time, as in "when" or qualifications, as in "although." But we decide we've thought our way through quite a lot for one day and we're ready to run back and share our discovery, just when a larger thought dawns.

We'll need a way to arrange our thoughts so the sentences that refer to one thing go in one group and the ones that refer to something else go in another group. We decide to call these groups "paragraphs." And, wow, we instantly realize that we can group paragraphs to all of our thoughts about something.

Now, you're really getting excited. You've devised a way to describe your world accurately and, you'll realize in time, even beautifully.

On your way back to share your invention, you realize you need a name for all the parts of the language you've devised and maybe a separate name for how they work together. You decide on "grammar" and "composition."

A note of caution. Learning the structure of language and trying to work with it exactly can make your writing stiff at first, sort of like learning to play the piano and poking at one key after another. Just practice. Then, just as in piano playing, you'll gain more skill, until you can perform linguistically with, as Albert Schweitzer described the goal of organ playing, "perfect plasticity." In time, your knowledge can become, not a source of stiffness, but a source of confidence, daring, liveliness, and wit.

We all go through the process. When I was trying to get my first agency job, Charlie Culp, an award-winning copywriter at McCann-Erickson, was asked to look at my portfolio. He asked to see me and told me he was going to recommend that the agency hire me for the copy-training program. Then he advised me, "All you have to do is get the library dust out of your prose."

Moving on from the nuts and bolts to the glory of language, I also recommend that you study a book of prosody. You very likely know that the subject deals with the resources of language as used in poetry and explains such techniques as rhyme, alliteration, assonance, and consonance. You'll also learn to hear the strength of words with masculine endings and relative softness of words with feminine endings, for instance, the difference between the power of "stop" and "stopping." As mentioned early, the techniques also help us achieve aided recall.

Obviously, having these resources at your fingertips is especially help-ful in crafting slogans and jingle lyrics. When the jingle requires more than singing the slogan, your easy fluency with metrical patterns, rhyme schemes, and stanzas will let you "pearl" the lyric, instead of creating something that thumps along.

What about the disciplines that apply to shaping longer forms? The brevity of advertising can save you from having to know much about them. Yet you'll be better at creating appropriate compact forms if you're familiar with them.

To learn the forms of argument, you might study, or restudy, Aristotle's *Rhetoric*. After all, what is advertising if not an argument for the product? You'll want to note, for example, the various forms an argu-ment can take, such as argument to the people or argument to the man, once known, when we were closer to the Roman Empire, as *argumentum ad populum* and *argumentum ad hominum*. Consider how these forms apply to "orations" in advertising; for example, argument to the product, argument to the target audience, and argument to the competition. What is a testimonial but a variation on argument to the people? And what is a competitive political commercial but argument to the man?

I also recommend that you read a collection of great speeches. It will help you learn how to build your own arguments, specifically, ways to begin, build, perorate, and conclude, often with a call to action. You'll note that there is so much bombast in the tradition that the concept of a great speech often seems a contradiction in terms. Of course, the hand-ful of inspiring exceptions make up for the rest, such as Pericles famous address to the Athenian people and Lincoln's *Gettysburg Address*.

If you wish, you might also read Aristotle's *Poetics*. The study will help you grasp and apply, even in our miniature world, the dramatic uni-ties of time, place, and action, and appreciate the basic formal principle that every piece has a beginning, a middle, and an end. You'll also learn, as you will in your study of prosody, how to magnify meaning through the various techniques that produce word pictures – similes and metaphors, as well as others, like synecdoche, where a part may signify a whole, as in how "Mrs. Jones" might stand for female consumers.

I also recommend that you review a textbook of logic. Once you're in command of the contents, you'll find that the precision of your reason-ing sets you apart. The challenge then becomes not to become overly annoyed by the illogic you're bound to confront. Imagine the amazing advantage of being able to sit in a meeting with the capacity to define your terms exactly, keep your categories separate, reason inductively to your recommended slogan or deductively from it to the commercials you're presenting. You might toss off an easygoing syllogism, such as, "All the brands in this category claim to cure acne. Our brand is in the category. So, at least as our price of entry, we should claim that it cures acne."

Finally, you'll want to develop your ability to think in pictures. Studying our visual tradition helps: painting, sculpture, architecture, and photography. You can also improve your visual taste and creative capacities by observing the work of art directors and photographers, even the environments they create to work in.

An Aside for Art Directors & Designers

We cannot become what we are not without appearing silly, so I have much less advice for art directors and designers. I assume you're dedicated to the tradition of visual excellence and that you're well along the way to working with the goals of appropriateness, impact, and beauty. I can, however, encourage you to become as skillful as you can working verbally. The best art directors are exquisite visually and sometimes quite capable verbally.

As you know, many art directors and designers look at type more than they read and comprehend the meaning of the words. So, as a bit of a wordsmith, you'll be among the elite. You'll be more careful that typos don't slip into your designs.

Learn strategy, too. Then your designs are more likely to present the words and pictures with the proper emphasis and subordination for optimal marketing.

Arthur Beckman, a talented art director who worked with me for ten years, heard what I said about writing so well that he became a copywriter and a creative director.

He has remained a friend and was among the first to encourage me to write a book about advertising creativity.

Working With and Without Your Creative Partner

My intent is not to proffer general advice about what are inherently individual working relationships between copywriters and art directors. But I would like to recommend something I find invaluable: setting aside some time to explore the far horizons of our individual imaginations.

When we ideate together, we enjoy the benefits of creative interaction and can source our spontaneous imaginative potential. But when we ideate alone, we can explore areas of our imaginations that we can only get to through uninterrupted contemplation. When we get back together, we can share our individual inspirations.

Doing as Much Great Creative Work as Possible

How can we do the best creative work? Some projects have more creative potential than others, yet many creative people and agencies exhaust themselves attempting to do the same level of creative work for all their clients and, in the process, lose the clients who prefer more workaday advertising. The wise approach is to make a judgment about the creative potential of each assignment and do the highest level of creative work that is appropriate to it. You'll do as much great creative work as possible, while you retain the clients who demand more usual advertising. Better your agency should have the income than an agency without high creative ideals.

There is also the reality that all of us only have so much creative capacity. It's counterproductive to burn ourselves and other creative people out on assignments where great creative is not what is being demanded.

Not appreciating the merits of this pragmatic tactic has been the ruin of many a creative agency. Doing work that pays the bills is not selling out. It's surviving to create as much great work as possible.

Supervising Other Creative People

When you're offered the opportunity to supervise other creative people, I recommend that you accept the job, even if you'd rather keep on creating full time. While you'll burn up a lot of creative energy improving the work of others, you'll often be able to pick occasional assignments to do yourself, save yourself from reporting to people who would otherwise be above you, be able to spread your knowhow more widely, get more respect, and receive greater financial rewards.

There are different styles of creative management, and they're the same two main ones that apply to all management: "command and control" and "commitment-style" management. The first is generally considered more old-fashioned and applies more to hourly wage earners. You issue commands, and people are supposed to follow them exactly. Creative people don't respond well to such treatment, and you can plan on a high turnover. The second is considered more contemporary and works better with highly motivated and capable workers. The goal is to enable people to feel that we're all in this together, collaborating to do our best as individuals and team members. Creative people usually respond well to this style of supervision, and you can expect a much lower turnover.

If you're a control freak, you'll probably opt for the first style. I'm more of a believer in individuals and their self-motivated potential, so I prefer the second style. I also find that the second style usually works in a mutually rewarding way. You end up liking the people who work for you, they end up liking you, and the work grows out of the happy creative environment you all inhabit.

Of course, you'll come across writers or art directors who do need to be told flat out what to do. Since you know what both styles are, you can easily shift to command and control when they upset you enough.

When you become a creative supervisor or creative director, you also face an ethical choice that requires you to decide, in terms of the people who work for you, who you are. Should you put money or human values first? I don't mean in an extreme sense, where you're either greedily consumed by the first or self-destructively blinded by the second. It's a competitive business, and you have to be practical, or you'll be replaced by someone who wouldn't even consider these questions. "Ananke," the ancient Greek for necessity, finally rules the waves, and the worst thing is for people with the right intentions to lose power.

Thankfully, there is quite a lot of space between the things you can decide to do and the things you must do. I recommend that you put human values first, to the extent that you can. I think you'll like yourself more, and my experience is that people will actually compete to work for you.

We also have to deal with the realization that, as soon as a group of people begin to work together, politics ensues. Before I knew this, I thought of opening an agency called Nice & Smart. In fact, for years I said there are basically three kinds of creative people: nice but dumb ones, who you might like but couldn't give a difficult assignment to; smart but nasty ones, who you could give a tough assignment to but, as soon as they brought you the answer, you were happy to see them leave your office; and nice and smart people, the magic combination. Then one day I shared the categories with a sarcastic writer, who said, "Tom, where have you been all your life? You missed the biggest category of all. Dumb and nasty." My mind had never sunk that low.

To help you deal with the reality of politics, you might want to read a book on group dynamics, and to protect yourself from the occasional nasty folks you can come across, you might want to read, with disdain, Machiavelli's *The Prince*.

The truth is, every value exists under the bell-shaped curve of normal distribution, including advertising people. Enjoy the people who belong on the right side, avoid the ones who belong on the left, and make peace with the fact that most belong in the middle. This reality is not a cause for despair. It helps you appreciate the great and talented souls who have somehow found their way into advertising and who you will, if you are as fortunate as I have been, have the privilege of working with. Second, it helps build your own confidence. I once read a review of a book in *Time* magazine in which the reviewer said that a book wasn't a great achievement in itself but stood out because of the flatness of the surrounding countryside. I used to complain all the time about how many "dumb" people there are in advertising. Then one day a bird landed on my shoulder and said, "Dummy, those are the people who help make your special." Since then, I never complain. I assume this perception makes me sound elitist. I think it helps me make peace with reality and be happier.

When You Become a Creative Director

If you become the creative director of a large agency or are currently one, you must deal with the fact that every client doesn't want the same kind of advertising. If you refuse to submit to the demand for variety and cling to your own focused vision, the rejections will pile up, the creative department will become exhausted doing work on the same jobs over and over, the account people will become desperate for something the client will buy, and the clients will get more and more impatient. The water will keep backing up behind the dam, and, unless you open the gates and let some of it flow out, you'll find yourself drowning in unhappy account people and departing clients.

Once you've made peace with the need to respond appropriately to the diverse needs of clients, you'll find that less-experienced creative people may consider the flexible style you've adopted selling out. They will learn the lesson in time; right now, you're saving their jobs and likely your own by keeping the clients.

The decision actually enables the best work that can be done for each client and saves the energy of the best creative people for work orders that have the most creative potential, instead of exhausting them on ones that have comparatively little.

Dominic Rossetti, the art director at Y & R I worked with on Dr Pepper, once said, "Trying to give clients great advertising when they don't want it is like trying to teach people to dance who don't want to learn." He was right. You just keep stepping on their toes, until they get upset and walk off the floor and into someone else's arms.

Bob Wall, the head of the art department at Y & R during the glory days, whose standard of creative excellence was as high as anyone's, would at times succumb to the force of reality in his affable way. When what we considered great advertising had been rejected by the client, he'd get a sly smile on his face and say, "Well, now, let's see if we can inject a little mediocrity into this campaign."

At the risk of offending the advertisers who have accompanied us, the reality is that the care and feeding of a variety of clients is a bit like being a zookeeper. You know to feed the rabbits lettuce and the lions meat. If you happen to wander into the lion's cage with lettuce, you get eaten.

What if your longing for uniform creative greatness can't be moderated? Be wise. Present the work you think the client should buy, but make sure you've also got work tucked in your presentation that you know he or she will like. I call this approach "one chance for greatness."

If the creative you recommend gets rejected, consider it an unalloyed pleasure to take out the work you know the client will love at first sight. Then, as the complex blend of idealism and practicality that you have somehow found the resources to become, you can delight the client, preserve your place, and, in your quiet moments, console yourself with the thought that by keeping the income in the agency you have helped provide the resources to continue, as we variously injured souls have learned to call the effort, to support the creative habit. Any other adjustment is downright self-destructive.

Yet, no matter how flexible we become, once in a while a client may demand work that is so dreadful that you and the rest of agency management agree that providing it will seriously diminish the agency's reputation. It may be one of those times when the most difficult of all decisions must be made: the agency resigns the account. Fortunately, such a standoff can usually be avoided. My experience is that many tough clients actually do have a sound sense of the kind of advertising that will work best for them. If you're brightly responsive, you can work out a campaign that will satisfy their needs without disheartening you too much. You can even be proud of yourself for a job well done and know that you have become the creative cornerstone on which the agency may reliably build its business.

One last piece of advice: build layers of approval – copywriters and art directors, creative supervisors, and creative directors. Make sure work goes through the layers before it gets to you. Then you can manage even the largest creative department in a surprisingly relaxed and enjoyable way.

Managing Your Career

Many of us are better at doing and supervising creative work than in managing our careers. Yet being able to do our best creative work depends in part on managing them as best we can. I've learned a few lessons that I'd like to share.

If you get offered an enormous job and have concerns about the energy you might have for your overall life, you might want to bite the bullet and take it for a few years. The income will free you to do more of what you want and may free you for a lifetime.

Is it good to hop from job to job or should you stay in one agency? You can move ahead faster in the early stages of your career by changing jobs, especially if you're winning awards. Yet other people seem to settle in at one place; some move to the top and others finally leave or are let go.

A good rule is, if you jump as high as you can and hit your head on the ceiling, it's usually time to move out from under it.

A certain cynicism seems to have become pretty standard operating procedure in large agencies, as well in many other large companies. It has to do with a belief that the structure will survive just about any personnel changes. Obviously, it's based on a cynical estimation of the value of people. As a result, your search is not so much for an agency that values all of its employees as much as you wish it could but for a great position, in whatever agency you can find it.

By the way, creative people can benefit by presenting themselves, not only as creative, but also as solid. In the early stages of my career, when I grew a beard and wore jeans and sandals to work, a great art director, Harvey Baron advised me, "Tom, your challenge isn't to look creative. After people talk with you for ten seconds, they know you're creative. Your challenge is to look solid, so they know they can depend on you."

Since advertising has become more of a worldwide business, getting to the top of one of the major agencies or agency groups may exhaust you, but you may also find rewards that exceed what you can do in a smaller agency or on your own. In the agency world, the loaves of bread are now on the big tables, and only the crumbs fall off.

If you hope to rise to the top, artistic soul that you are, try not to be too temperamental. You must demonstrate, no matter how difficult it may at times, that you're one of those rare people who is not only creative but easygoing and reliable. Then the welfare of the agency can be trusted to your care.

I also suggest you moderate your scorn for agencies that don't do work that rises to your standard of creative excellence. There will always be clients who identify with the kind of work such agencies do. Never underestimate how much money can be made by doing the kind of work that appeals to the usual run of advertisers, especially when it's presented with a veneer of competence.

Last, I suggest that you keep your philosophical distance from all unnecessary perturbations. We all need to find some island of inner peace to create with clarity and joy. When reality that doesn't much involve you roars, don't let it get to you too much. Put in your philosophical clutch and let it roar until it quiets down.

The Role of Talent

Creativity is the ability to take known facts and synthesize them into new and appropriate answers. Seen this way, people in any field can be creative, even accountants. I often say that what you're talented at depends on what part of your brain you have a grey lump, or more neurons. Its abilities attract you to areas you're good at. If you give your brain all the tools you can, you can maximize the potential of your talent.

What constitutes advertising talent? It grows out of a combination of intelligence and sensitivity. A brilliant but insensitive person will often do the wrong thing faster than anybody else. A sensitive but less intelligent person will feel what needs to be said but often won't be able to get it right. When a person is sensitive and smart, he or she can feel what the consumer needs to hear and imagine the right way to say it.

Can you increase your talent? Some advice is impossible to act on, such as "be more intelligent" or "become more sensitive."

Yet the human mind, with its universe of neurons, is capable of far more than advertising demands, so, regardless of the talent you begin with, through hard work you can become better at copy or art and perhaps even great. It's always wrong to limit our estimate of talent. The only way to judge it is by what a person does during his or her career. One of the few times that Carl Jung was, I think, more perceptive than Freud is when he cautioned him that psychoanalysis could never hope to explain the human personality completely, because it's just too deep.

So is talent. It's a subtle inner voice or the flash of an image. It's a delicate broadcast that we strive to hear without the static of self doubt. Yet its transcendent power of synthesis, trustingly received and recorded, is the source of all the great works of the imagination.

The most and the least you can do is maximize your potential. Some just have to polish their cars harder to make them shine optimally.

If you're a copywriter, it's obviously better if you have a natural way with words, and, if you're an art director, it's better if you have a good visual sense. The more natural talent you have, the easier creative work is. There's no substitute for it. Yet we can each make the most of our natural talent.

And there's no sense thinking about how much talent you have, because the only way it can be measured is by what kind of work you do during your career. It can't be approximated; it can only manifest itself. Don't try to be the creator and the critic. You'll just keep getting in your own way. Do the best you can and leave the judgment of how talented you are to other people.

How to Live and Work with Your Talent

Curiously, most people who discover they have a talent for something – from art to athletics – find a way to make it a curse, instead of a blessing. Decide to make your talent a blessing. It seems to be the rarest achievement of all.

Conduct it so that you can make a nice living with it. You'll preserve yourself from stresses that can take away your goodness, diminish what you can achieve, and even cost you your life.

When you do something great or when you're getting through something especially rough, grab yourself by the chin and tell yourself, "What a guy!" or "What a girl!"

Do not buy into the cliché of the tormented artist and find ways to be miserable. The attendant stresses will diminish what you can achieve and take away the essence of what you have to give, which emanates from your sweetness and fellow-feeling.

When you want something badly, see yourself as a child, standing in the crib, crying for milk, and grow up. In other words, take a lesson from the Stoics and moderate our needs. Infinite need knows no satisfaction. And pleasure is incremental. The more we get, the more we need to be satisfied. Pretty soon, not much pleasure to be had. How many famous people have nailed themselves to this cross?

To the extent that you can, head off any unnecessary difficulties that would arise if you can't do your job well by learning your craft and becoming as fluent at it as you can. Given talent, ease comes with skill, and from ease, confidence.

Surprisingly, you also have the power to tell yourself that you insist on creating in a relaxed and confident way, so you can actually delight in the process.

Be a good brain farmer. Don't just reap. Rest the soil. And nourish it with good books, theater, films, music, art, other entertainments, social intercourse, and love. Then when you shake the tree of your imagination, a lot of fruit will fall out.

Finally, advertising, with its inevitable ups and downs, is basic training for becoming a manic-depressive. Retain your philosophical distance. Never subordinate the wholeness of your life to any aspect of it. First, you'll do an injustice to the wholeness of your life. Second, you'll sort of create a handle that the world can grab you by and shake you. Important as it seems to you, talent, success, and any opportunity or problem is only part of your whole life. By keeping individual events in their proper place, you can actually enjoy most of your life in advertising and float through the rough times by keeping a lot of water between you and the rocks.

Aim for the Ego-Free Pursuit of Excellence

As in all walks of life, many gigantic egos lumber about in advertising, just as in other pursuits. Sometimes we wonder, in fact, how the great globe itself can support all the egos without sinking out of its place in the solar system.

Yet many of the most capable people in any profession are actually pretty modest. They have enough confidence so that they don't have to pump up their leaky tires every day, often at the expense of others, and they have the character to appreciate the place and fragility of others.

We encourage you, as your achievements mount, not to become just another egomaniac. The pomposity reveals that self-aggrandizing people are not as sensitive as the most adept are. You can make yourself a self-centered annoyance, when you could be a generous hero to many.

Insecurity based on relative ineptitude often brings out the least generous aspects of people. It can actually drive them to undervalue talented people and, at worst, to push them out of positions of influence. After all, the stars only shine when the sun is gone.

Of course, we all want to have a healthy ego, in the sense of being confident in our capacities and proud of our achievements, but when it inflates to the point that it encroaches on the space of others, it's time to rein it in.

Actually, we wish you so much confidence and achievement that you can distinguish yourself with an unusual but achievable goal: aim for the ego-free pursuit of excellence. Shine on your own merits and enable others to shine on theirs.

Peace of Mind

We can all drive ourselves crazy with concerns, but we do want to enjoy our talents and our lives. So the usual advice is to be philosophical and take the long view. Recently, I was invited to edit transcripts of seven days of seminars by a famous mindfulness guru. During the last session he had the participants mediate on values I thought were commendable. Acceptance, forgiveness, unconditional love, and gratitude. The advice was, basically, that we should accept people as they are and accept ourselves as we are. in. We can't change other people anyway. We should forgive any wrongs others have done to us and forgive ourselves for any wrongs or mistakes we think we've made. We all make mistakes. It's part of striving for success. If we don't forgive, we just remain upset. We should even strive to send unconditional love to them, as well as to ourselves. Finally, we should feel gratitude for all the people who've come into our lives. They've made up our experiences. We should also feel gratitude toward ourselves for what we've done that we feel is commendable, as well as gratitude for the other people in our lives who are close to us and the good things that have been and are part of our lives.

While I've never felt that it's necessary for me to meditate to find peace of mind, I sometimes think of these four values when I may be a bit upset about something. I've even been known on occasion to do the scientific approach to meditating, which is simply to pick a letter of the alphabet and repeat it to yourself or out loud. The mind has one switch, and the process blocks further processing. You can even concentrate on your breathing as you repeat the letter and, if you like, turn your attention to one part of your body after another to take your mind off what's troubling your or, when you're trying to sleep, keeping your mind busy.

The Best Crash Course in Advertising Creativity

When you want to get into advertising or after you have your first job, how can you accelerate your learning curve? You lack years of creative experience; here's how you can get it.

Go to The Art Directors Club of New York or to a mercantile library and review as many issues of *The Art Directors Yearbook* as you can. The series began as *The Annual of Editorial and Advertising Art and Design*. For a time, the club also joined with The Copy Club of New York to create *The One Show,* along with volumes that contain the award-winning work.

Each volume lets you see what was voted the best creative work done in advertising during the year. The most dedicated among you may want to go clear back to the mid-fifties, when creative advertising began, with the appearance of, most memorably, the first clever Volkswagen ads. Since the body copy in the print ads, as reproduced in the books, is often so small it's hard to read, you might want to keep a magnifying glass handy. I did.

You can also review the winners of other annual awards shows, such as the Clio Awards and the Webbie Awards. AdForum.com is an excellent resource for reviewing and keeping up with advertising creativity. Of course, you'll want to look into *Advertising Age* and *Adweek* magazines to see what's happening creatively.

Confidence as a Beginner

When I ran the copy-training program at Y & R, I not only had to teach trainees how to create advertising and write great copy; I also had to do it in a way that built their confidence.

One of the things I used to tell them is, when you get your first creative assignments, it's usual to experience a lot of uncertainty on your way to the right answer. In fact, you may feel as if you're standing in front of a forest and can't see a path through it. You know the answer is on the other side, but you're just not sure how to get there. All you can do is head toward it and cut the best path you can. You'll wander off in wrong directions and at times feel that you're going in circles. But don't give up. You know you're talented and that all of us have learned to get through to the other side. You will, too. And guess what? Somehow, you'll make it, even if you need a little guidance along the way.

When the second assignment comes along and you confront the forest, you'll be able to make out just the beginnings of a path. After two or three years of getting to the other side, you'll have worn a pretty clear one. And one day, you may know what you're doing so well you'll have a highway through forest. You'll be able to load the marketing information into your creative pickup truck and pretty much drive straight to the right answer.

Time and Talent

During my career in advertising, I've learned certain lessons about time and talent.

The blue sky is deep and indefinite. Every time we court it, it measures us. In the beginning, be patient and give your talent time to grow.

There's no need to be insecure about what you might achieve today or tomorrow. You can always do your best; not somebody else's, but yours. It can be nourishing to look to the side and see what others have done and are doing. But the secure way to source your own talent is to go straight down into yourself and your own unique combination of genes and growth. Nobody else can go there as well as you can.

To make the most of your young years, you need to build a good creative reputation. You can do it by creating great advertising and winning awards. It's fun and financially rewarding to be a whiz kid. I think I was.

As time goes by, you need to move up to agency management, start your own agency, or consult to agencies and clients. I know I'm more of a whiz at advertising than I ever was, but I've had to modify how I approach the business. I have my own digital agency, which allows me to present my credentials and get as many copywriting jobs as I can do while still conducting a relaxed and happy life.

Contrary to popular opinion, advertising isn't just about bright and bushy-tailed enthusiasm, with the conviction that everyone over forty or so is better off gone. This superficial attitude makes the business a potential career disaster for everybody. Meanwhile, in most other disciplines, older people are conducting major corporations, making billions, and running a great deal of the government. It's also true historically that new ideas have come from people of all ages.

Yet we must deal with reality. Today, advertising, which is still largely innocent about the more sophisticated ways it can serve clients, obsesses about being represented by the voice of youth and jumping on the latest trends. This attitude is partly justified by the need to capture brand preferences of malleable younger people. Yet it's a bit misguided, especially today, when the majority of consumers and the major hunk of buying power is in the hands of baby boomers.

The profession actually requires a combination of brash innocence and creative experience. The two result in executions that are often foolishly daring and wisely daring. The former ones are often wrong strategically, but the shortcoming can usually be corrected by more experienced creatives.

Actually, in a mass communications society, anybody who keeps up is pretty much the same mental age; we all get most of our information from the same sources, although we each select what we wish to identify with and who we associate with.

We should also appreciate that there is a difference between being young in years and being as new as the times. Many young and old people are old-fashioned in their thinking, while all of us can be of the moment. Talented people who've mastered their discipline should be treasured at any age. Nature doesn't create enough of them.

An agency that wishes to function at its best maintains a balance between sophisticated veterans and young people. One benefit of this wisdom is that the people on the client side are of various ages, too, with many of the top people being older. So the agency-client relationship is more broadly based.

Many advertisers look for expertise at any age they can find it. So in time you can also look to the client side for employment. Some advertisers have in-house agencies. Or you can also become an advertising executive on the client side and supervise agency work.

Client openness to expertise is also a reason the consulting business has grown. It's a situation the agencies have created. Many of them write off experts of a certain age, but the experts have not obediently left the scene. They have become competitors and very highly qualified ones.

May the ad game grow in wisdom. But, more importantly, may you create as well as you can for as many years as you want to.

Advertising People

If you're considering a career in advertising, I would encourage you to go ahead. A lot of advertising people are actually extraordinarily bright, nice people. I've been fortunate enough to find them in every aspect of the business. Since there is a need to communicate in appealing and dramatic ways, the business provides a relatively pleasant, if at times shaky, career for many writers, artists, musicians, and filmmakers. In fact, I know of no industry in history that has supported so many artists and artisans.

Of course, like any other endeavor, some souls function with perfectly focused self-interest and see us all as mere means to their own ends. When I'm in an environment where there are a few of them, I call the experience sharp lapels and flying arrows. When one of those types just passes me in the hallway, I imagine that I can look down and see that part of my tie has been clipped off. The more insecure and territorial souls may resent your talented presence, even if your work saves their jobs. I suppose you incriminate their self-esteem. When I function as a freelance problem solver and I feel resentment build, I ask myself, if I stick my imaginary white hat out of the door of my office, will I get more than ten arrows in it? If I feel I will, I know it's time to move on.

There is another group whose level of self-awareness is almost comical. They specialize in creating a crisis only they can solve, despite the toll it takes on others. Then, after all of the damage has been done, they become their smiley selves again and think everything is just fine, while the people affected adversely sit there, in disarray and tempered fury.

But, I'm happy to say, my experience has been that the good people far outnumber the others. There's a sound reason. Advertising must communicate with people, so it requires and attracts people who are sensitive to the needs of others and bright enough to communicate with them intelligently. So the business attracts many people who are sensitive, intelligent, and often very nice.

CHAPTER 28

WHY THE CREATIVE REVOLUTION FELL SHORT

Today we're enjoying a bit of a creative revolution on the internet, but in this section I'd like to discuss the halcyon time in the 50s, 60s, and 70s when agencies courted creative people and clients were enthralled with creative advertising. It was the great new way to advertise.

Yet the creative revolution faltered. Why? It failed to deliver success with superior consistency. The reason is that, while the advertising was often innovative, it was not reliably employed to magnify the selling proposition. Instead, it often subordinated it. Often, there was nothing specific for the consumer to pay.

So we ask ourselves, what if all or even most the creative resources I've discussed had been used properly? Since it can do it with more verbal and visual resources than hard-sell advertising, I believe creative advertising would have proved itself beyond anyone's expectations and continued to be sought by clients.

A compelling reason to buy something magnified in an appropriately dramatic way has more inherent power than a compelling reason to buy presented with the relatively modest resources of hard-sell adverting, including such off-putting items as shouting announcers and a barrage of awful type.

The reason account people and advertisers supported and even indulged all the creativity, including the frequent cantankerousness of the supposedly inspired savants with a talent for it, is that they, hard-nosed businessmen that they were, believed it made advertising more effective. The advertisers would sell more product and the agencies would get more business.

A handful of the best creative people knew exactly or approximately what to do, and their work usually performed admirably. But we are all condemned to live under the usual bell-shaped curve, even if it is applied to bright creative people. The group in the center, which included, in its confidently erring ranks, some high-profile participants, didn't really understand what the goal of their creativity was and, when their flashy but empty work bombed in the marketplace, the disappointing results undermined the marketing community's faith in creative advertising.

The Good Ship Creativity crashed on the rocks of incompetence and we, who once helped steer it, must now be content to function as repentant slaves in the steam room. Some creative advertising still gets done. A lot of bright stuff is being created in traditional adverting and in digital advertising. But do major companies clamor for it the way they once did?

The bottom-line minded folks, whose rightful place is in the steam room, have taken control of the agencies – and they've proved their worth by building ones, through expansions and acquisitions, that dominate advertising worldwide. In fact, the agency conglomerates have gotten so big they can almost be seen as advertising utilities?

They only have one weak point: advertising is best done in a nation by the residents of the nation. While the worldwide agencies can hire and train locals, the knowledge provides some hope that small creative agencies still have a place, particularly in countries where the clients and consumers are savvy enough to get the wit and wisdom of creative advertising.

If enough advertising that is creative as well as solid comes along, we might at least get back to a more distinguished balance between inspired advertising and bean counting. What are the chances for another creative revolution? It depends on how many bright creative people understand how to use their creativity to maximize the power of the selling proposition in inviting, stylish ways.

CHAPTER 29

PERSPECTIVES ON ADVERTISING

Has advertising done a professional job presenting its own image? Has American business, or capitalism, as a whole? Hardly. The merits of both are appreciated far less than they should be, even in America, the country they have brought the greatest benefit to.

As the usual representative of business, advertising is the most visible target. Advertising grew out of the needs of business, as well as everybody else who needs to speak with the public in a persuasive way. While its usual intention is, of course, to sell products and services, it also serves political candidates who persuade voters, along with charitable organizations in their efforts to raise money.

At its best, advertising speaks credibly, responsibly, and engagingly for the benefit of those for whom it is speaking. The most capable of its practitioners know that people usually patronize, elect, and donate to those they not only remember but those they also think well of.

Let's address some of the criticisms of advertising. First, we must consider it as part of American business. Has free enterprise been explained well to the public? Do most people know that it is the foundation of individual freedom and that when the state owns your meal ticket you're likely to be a silenced slave? Do they know that by its nature free enterprise seeks out cheap labor and therefore spreads wealth, certainly more than the cozy bureaucrats of a centrally administered economy? More to the point, did advertising invent free enterprise? No, free enterprise invented advertising, as its dutiful representative. Is advertising superfluous? If so, it wouldn't be funded.

We may, in fact, appreciate advertising more if we understand how it is funded. Where does the ad budget come from? Many will say "from the client." But exactly who is the client? The executives decide how much to spend and what agency to spend it through. But the money they allocate is part of the profit produced by all of the employees of the company – management and labor. They get up every workday morning, go to their jobs, and labor to make a product or deliver a service. In our ever-changing and often challenging economic and social environment, they try to raise families, make ends meet, and enjoy life when they can. They need steady employment, along with raises and bonuses – things they can only do if the company does well.

Enter advertising. Out of all of their labor, a certain amount of profit is allocated toward telling the public what the company makes or provides and sells. These precious funds are a trust.

Now, the majority of the employees of the company, who might actually be surprised to learn what good souls many advertising people are but who will probably never meet us, nevertheless depend on us to spend the funds wisely.

When we see the ad budget in its human implications, we can actually see it as a sacred trust. To the extent that we fulfill our responsibilities as skillful and caring professionals, as well as fellow human beings, we distinguish ourselves.

What about the criticism that advertising creates demand for products that people don't really need? How many inhabitants of the mass market earn enough to buy products they don't need? Of course, there are luxury items and, when remarkable success enables private wealth or the tax structure enables income distribution that gets unconscionably out of hand, egregiously excessive ones. But luxuries exist with or without advertising; consider, for example, the lives of the pharaohs. No advertising was required to raise a pyramid and form gold mask for

Tutankhamen or to construct Versailles for the Sun King. It's also problematic to draw a line between the things we need and the things we just want. It seems to me astringent to consider modern enhancements such as toothpaste, deodorant and dishwashers as totally unnecessary. The fact is, necessities and reasonable luxuries are part of the natural joy of life – a benefit not to be dismissed in our often-tragic world.

Now, let's consider advertising as an ingredient in mass media. The most credible news media do have allegiance to responsible journalism. But many an outlet depends on maintaining an ongoing sense of crisis and outrage.

Meanwhile, entertainment media often feature violence and life-demeaning oddness. Many members of the mass audience obviously find it easier to relate to a physical crisis and moral outrage than they do to such values as life-enhancing physical activity, interpersonal tenderness, intellectual achievement, or credible spiritual uplift. Now, in this uninspiring environment, who keeps popping up with affable, responsible human behavior and messages about how to enjoy life? Advertising.

While persistent cheerleading implies a degree of mindlessness, the messages of advertising generally do have some basic values in place, if only to present the advertiser as responsible; that is, parents are usually nourishing, children grateful, and single people sweetly thoughtful. While the world advertising depicts may be seen as somewhat ideal, the more important point is that it helps balance the madness and mayhem that characterizes much of the rest of media.

Superficial as much of the behavior may be and self-interested as the source of it is, advertising is, in fact, the most usual source of life-affirmation in mass media. It reminds us that, despite everything that's going wrong, life has value and can be enjoyable. This positive message is a vital reminder for beleaguered adults and for our uncertain children, who may wonder, in the often-distressing world in which they find themselves, if life is worthwhile and if happiness is possible.

Here's an example of the necessity for the positive messages of advertising. When a car passed me on the highway, I noticed a white hand-written sign in the window. A kid was holding it there, and two of his friends were leaning around it looking at me, waiting for my response. The sign said, "Honk if you're happy." I decided to honk. They all started to smile and laugh. To me it was a heart-wrenching indication of just how much we need to remind ourselves that the Utilitarian ideal of "the greatest happiness for the greatest number" is not only commendable; it's a necessary guide to the conduct of society.

Yes, people know they have to pay to enjoy the products and services proffered by advertising. And what true friends charge for anything? The overlap of commercial and personal values is impossible to avoid. We can only hope that people remember that the ads are for products and services made by and presented by people just like them.

The advent of the internet and the innovative character of it seems to have generated more enthusiasm for business, including advertising. I often say that it began as technological wizardly but grew into advertising wizardry. After all, what business is Google primarily in? Advertising, with search as the medium. More and more people of all ages but particularly young ones continue to be enthusiastic adapters and may conduct the starship enterprise with greater enthusiasm than any Americans before them. True, many consider financial gain as the consuming end, rather than the logical means to an enjoyable life. I suppose it will take another generation or so before people learn to take computers, smartphones, and tablets for granted and renew our need for the primacy of human values. Perhaps another reason for America's current workaholic ways is anxiety about international competition and our welfare in the global economy.

Finding ourselves sensate in the naturally miraculous epic of life on earth, may all of us in advertising do whatever we can in the service, not only of our clients, but of life.

The Merits of Free Enterprise

Before we wrap up the section on advertising, let's consider the merits of free enterprise, beyond those discussed in the previous section. It balances the power of big government. We have seen the travail that befalls a country when the government conducts the economy.

A confident and independent citizenry can only exist when its members can make livings that are, except for taxes and necessary regulation, free of government influence.

Many prefer to dwell on the shortcomings of free enterprise and present themselves as trenchantly independent thinkers. Apparently, they do not realize that in a society where the government controls everything, they would be among the first to be silenced. I would much prefer freedom with abuse to the absence of freedom.

When we do our jobs, we ought to do them with consideration for our clients, our fellow consumers, and the environment. When we are merely the creatures of self-interest, we do a disservice even to ourselves.

Advice to Consumers

As we approach the end of the main part of the book, let me offer advice to any consumers who may have read this far. It's rewarding to know you have enough interest in advertising to have taken the time to join us.

I advise you to understand advertising in terms of its place in our economy, appreciate it when it's inviting, dislike it when it's tasteless, and, to the extent you can, forgive its excesses. I also hope you can appreciate it for the knowledge it brings you and the amenities with which it helps enhance your life.

PART 8

New Product Concept Development, Product Ideation, and Name Development

CHAPTER 30

NEW PRODUCT DEVELOPMENT

As a copywriter, you may be called on to work on new products. Why? In our market-driven economy, many successful new products grow out of thinking about consumers and what they may need or want. It can still happen, even on the internet. For example, I recently was retained to do concept development for a new line of digital cameras. The concepts were screened with consumers over the internet among people who had opted-in to the service to give their opinions. The product became so successful that The Wall Street Journal wrote a feature article about the line. When we're first asked to work on new products, our first reaction may be to tell ourselves that we're advertising people, not the kind of people we usually think of as inventors. Yet our unlikely new role finally makes sense to us, and we go about the job as best we can.

The newest example of this sort of inventiveness is on the internet. Most new product ideas are creative concepts about new ways to serve consumers, such as Priceline.com and YouTube.com. There are, of course, a multitude of new products that smaller merchants sell, either by creating them or simply by sourcing them from private label manufacturers and branding them. Many of these are sold on Amazon, Shopify or Etsy.

Major companies still test their products, while smaller ones just see how well they sell. When a new product concept scores well with consumers, making the idea a reality is the role of scientists. In addition to their own efforts at invention, they do the technical development.

New product development is an important aspect of advertising creativity. As the saying goes, new products are the lifeblood of a company. They are also an important source of new business for advertising agencies.

We should be expert at it. So I'll cover all the relevant aspects – concepts, names, product-ideation, focus groups and quantitative testing.

Creative Director of Concepts, Young & Rubicam's New Product Unit

I became more involved with new product development than most advertising creative people when I was at Young & Rubicam. In addition to writing copy for major brands, I performed two ancillary jobs. I ran the copy-training program, and, when the head of the unit asked me to, I agreed to become the creative director of the agency's new-product unit.

The work usually consisted of writing headlines for concept boards and thinking up names for new-products ideas, which were assigned to the agency by hopeful clients. Then the product ideas could be shown to consumers in focus groups and, if the did well, in quantitative testing.

Since I was usually busy creating television or print advertising, I often assigned the new-product work to the junior writers in my group. But when the assignment was described as especially important, the head of the unit, a bright and pleasant woman with a Ph. D. in psychology, would come to my office with and ask me to write some headlines and/or provide some working names. I always obliged, and in return she made the job as effortless as possible. She would sit in my office with the marketing information, share the key facts with me, and wait while I typed up a selection of headlines and names, until we felt I had expressed the benefit or benefits of the new product in ways that would allow her to measure its appeal with acceptable accuracy. Fortunately, she had an art person in her unit who could make up the concept boards. I would be told when the client was coming and would present the work.

If this approach to new product development seems less than ideal, remember that advertising agencies see their primary role as creating advertising. Even though new products are part of the growth of an agency, a new product usually only gets prominent attention when a client decides to advertise it. In the early stages, thinking up new products or generating names is the kind of assignment that is often passed along to secretaries, who are asked make suggestions. By comparison, Y & R's approach was responsibility incarnate.

The experience provided an unforeseen benefit. When I decided to become a creative consultant, I called the head of the dessert division of what was then General Foods, later swallowed by Kraft. His name was Peter Rosow. I knew he would remember me, because I had done a couple of quick television solutions for him while I was at Y & R, and both commercials had scored well and done well in the market.

"There must be some way you can use me besides making me come through a big agency," I suggested.

"Sure," he replied. "Do new-product development. I have an assignment for you right now."

The product turned out to be a new salad dressing for which he needed concept boards and names. So, in addition to starting to do creative problem-solving for agencies that were kind enough to retain me, I had another way to make a living. Since I've done new-product work ever since, I have more experience at it than most creative people.

I've also been able to bring clients a lot of success. For example, I was asked by two marketing people in the Post Cereal division, Margo Lowry and Erin Burgoyne, to think of the various things people have for breakfast and imagine what kind of cereals they might be. Margo and Erin referred to the intended new products as breakfast analogues. I went through my usual creative process and came back with about 120 ideas, expressed in crisp content-based headlines, working names, and, when not self-evident, a brief description of the flavor system. Margo and Erin liked thirty-five of them well enough to take to focus groups. Twenty proved appealing enough to consumers to consider taking to quantitative testing. Margo called and said that the research plan could only accommodate ten. So we selected what we thought were the most promising ones. In the quantitative test, Waffle Crisp won. The cereal became a $100-million business in year one and continues to sell. Why, of all the imaginative ideas we tested, did such an obvious idea win – and go on to do well in the marketplace?

The lesson is subtle, and very few people learn it. The product is an obvious idea but it wasn't yet available – an instance of what I call the gold at your feet. Besides being new, it had a basis in the familiar. It seemed to be a product that should always have been there but some- how wasn't. Or, to express the advantage metaphorically, it was not a totally new island that we were asking the consumer to swim to. It was a new island with a bridge from the familiar that the consumer could just walk across.

Of course, totally new ideas succeed, too. But when we overdo such words as "revolutionary," and "amazing, we actually reinforce the idea that the product is a separate island, so consumers are less inclined to go there readily. It's more immediately achievable to fit it into the consumer's lifestyle than to attempt to change it to accommodate the product. We strive to make it part of the lives of the target audience as easily as possible. Sometimes, an entirely new product can be given a degree of instant familiarity by attaching it to something that is already part of the consumer's everyday life, for instance, a familial setting, a usual use-occasion, or a likable celebrity.

The Secrets of New Product Success a Free Sample

Now, let's move on to a piece I once wrote to solicit new-product busi- ness for my consulting firm. We used it as a leave-behind, a mailing piece, and as a small-space ad in *Advertising Age*. Brief as it is, some exceptional people found a special place for it. Margo, when she was one of the top new-product-development people at GF, used to keep it under the glass on her desk, and one of the gifted art directors I worked with at an Interpublic agency, Gary Geyer, made copies and passed it out to everyone in the creative department of the large agency where he became a creative director. He told me, "I did it because what's in there doesn't just apply to new products. It applies to advertising, too."

To capture the spirit of new products, I presented the information as a free sample. Some of the information will sound familiar from thoughts I've already shared with you.

1. Great Ideas Aren't the Answer

Just as a good idea may stop you from going on to discover a great one, a great idea may stop you from going on to discover the right one. After you get a great idea, continue to look for the right idea.

2. Exact Appropriateness

Every product has a small group of words and pictures that are exactly appropriate to it. When time is taken to discover them and weave them together expertly, recall goes way up and top-of-mind awareness in the category is pre-empted.

3. News, with Style

The excitement of a concept board or test commercial must come from the clear communication of news about the product. Style comes from clarity and precision, not cleverness that subordinates the news. Even when image is all-important, it takes the form of news, not so much inherent in the product, but invented.

4. Efficiency in Communication

Maximum efficiency in mass communications is one word – a name that says everything. Second is a slogan that contains the name. After that, people have to remember two or more things to know your message. Efficiency goes down, and media expenditures lose impact.

5. The Disappearing Concept Board

Most people test concept boards and commercials. The right concept board or commercial tests the product – by allowing the consumer to see right through it to the product shown in its best light.

The Creative Exploratory and New-Product Development

In new product development, we can read the marketing materials and then start to think, hoping great ideas will drop into our minds? Or can we go about the process in a way that is more likely to lead to success. We discover, not surprisingly, that our familiar friend, The Creative

Exploratory, can be our guide. While there are some differences in the way we go about it, the overall structure remains the same.

Phase One: Input – What You Need to Know

Our first task is to obtain whatever marketing and research information we can about the product. To help direct our strategic thinking and creative imaginations, we also want to understand the client's new product goals, along with, at times, his production capabilities. In the latter case, the client may want to make more use of a manufacturing process that's already in place but is underutilized or the client may have limitations about the extent to which the company is willing to invest in new production facilities. The client may, in fact, be planning to let someone else manufacture whatever we come up with and just market the product.

We'll also ask for a look at any development work that has already been done on the project, because we don't want to spend time reinventing the wheel if we don't have to. We can use prior work to take us to a more advanced starting point, so the project becomes a relay race. By starting much farther along the track, we have a better chance, as well as an easier time, of getting to the finish line. If we suspect that the client may know more than has been shared, we might suggest a day of brainstorming, so that everyone on the client side who's involved, including the marketing and technical people, and the people on our side of the team can collect everyone's top-of-mind thoughts.

We'll also want to wander into a few stores and look over the category. It's time to study the labels, so that we can understand the current claims, including the language and visuals employed to express them, as well as note the varieties of packaging. These on-shelf materials have been developed over the life of the category and contain a state-of-the-art presentation of how it interfaces with the consumer and what needs are being met. We can also Google the product category and study the products that come up in search.

As we look over the materials, we may notice an unmet need in the category or a need that might be met better, because we're aware of the mindset of consumers in the evolution of their needs in regard to the category, not only because we've studied the marketing materials, but also because we ourselves are consumers.

Phase Two: The Creative Exploratory

Once we feel we have enough information to think about the category at its imaginative frontier, we're ready to begin ideating. But, instead of looking for advertising ideas, we'll be looking for new products, new product concepts, or names.

Of course, when the client supplies the new product or new-product idea, the only work required is for the marketing people to think strategically about how the product might be presented to consumers, while the creative people need only develop concept boards to present the products to consumers, often along with a selection of appropriate working names.

Concept Development

No matter whether we're creating new products ourselves or developing ideas for a product the client has provided, we'll want to express the attributes and benefits with deft, news-driven headlines, suitable brand names, and, for now, rough artwork. Our goal is not so much to enchant consumers with stylish advertising but to introduce them in persuasively direct ways to products they know nothing or comparatively little about. As a result, the excitement in our headlines grows more out of news than style. The headlines function much like the concentrated ones in tabloid newspapers, such as *The New York Post* or *The Daily News.* We might, in fact, see the work as the art of the compact fact.

Our newsy headlines, in their most basic forms, will be made up of positioning statements, that is, frames of reference and points of difference. For example, before Aleve or extended-release Tylenol came along, a headline might read, "At last, a pain reliever that works all day." As you know, "pain reliever" is the frame of reference and "works all day" is the point of difference. We prefer this to a more stylish expression, such as, "When your pain reliever doesn't work all day, how can you be pain-free all day."

When we highlight the news, we enable the consumer to respond to the product in ways that will let us measure the appeal of it, instead how much she likes the expression of the benefit. Yet, along with the literal thoughts we must give first preference to, we also want to develop a selection of headlines that magnify the news with a little flair. By doing so, we may well increase the appeal of the product without excessively distracting interest from it. What's our justification? We know that if we're fortunate enough for the product to go to market, the presentation of it will have the benefit of some advertising style.

While adding our more creative or image-driven headlines, we may, in fact, unearth a surprisingly appealing approach. Of course, in more image-driven categories, like the latest irresistible fragrance, we may find ourselves creating nothing but image-driven headlines and visuals, simply because there is often a lack of solid content. Then our job is to enchant in new ways, usually by creating inviting new worlds that we think the consumer will want to spend some time in, or simply new experiences we imagine and present invitingly.

If you're an art director, you also want to jot down some of your ideas in words. When the time comes to present the work, you'll do up rough concept boards, either with type and stock photos, type and rough sketches, or a combination of both. The level of finish depends on how much visual appeal, instead of just visual information, is right for the occasion. Naturally, the main visual should do its best to present the primary benefit and the support visual, if there is one, should serve to help explain or prove why the product will live up to the claim being made for it. Or, if the presentation is of necessity a more image-driven one, your visual representations should capture, not so much literal content, but enchantment that will enhance the claim.

New Product Ideation

How do we think up products themselves? Since the ones we're talking about are usually marketing driven, they arise from the contemplation of consumer needs. We study a category, such as toothpaste, and ask ourselves if there are any unmet consumer needs. These may be needs that have been there since someone sprinkled the first tooth powder on bristles or they may be needs that have evolved due to changing consumer behavior and developments in the category. These are called emerging needs.

New products can also be created by thinking about how to redo old products. For example, consumers have known the benefits of baking soda and peroxide in tooth care for quite some time but both seemed old-fashioned. Unilever combined them in a product called Mentadent in a way that appeared novel but the dispenser was pricey. Soon, however, competitors discovered ways to introduce such combinations in tubes. The traditional packaging allowed these manufacturers to meet the recently evolved consumer need for a lower-priced combination of baking soda and peroxide, as well as to protect their shares of the toothpaste category from further incursions by Mentadent.

The surprising thing is, once we detect an unmet need, we discover that we can pretty readily imagine a new product that will satisfy it. When we detect an unmet need that is big enough, the new product we imagine might even have the potential to become the leading entry in the category. On those rare occasions when, with all our input, sensitivity to the consumer, and resourceful imagination, we are unable to detect any unmet needs, we must satisfy ourselves with imagining products that will meet the same needs in better or, at least, in more appealing ways. Our search must still be for products that have, to the extent we can invest them with it, a specific and substantial attribute or so that we feel the consumer will pay for.

We let our minds imagine as freely as we can. When a new product idea comes to us with a possible name for it, we jot down the inspiration as at least a working name.

What role does The Creative Exploratory serve? It helps us organize our thoughts, so we can ideate more freely and exactly.

As in advertising, we may work either from the top down or from the bottom up. That is, we may begin by mapping out possible areas of appeal and the needs that may occur under them. Then we begin to imagine products in each area that will meet those needs. Or we may proceed from the bottom up, by ideating freely and then grouping the new products as we begin to realize the areas they fit under.

Since make-work is the anathema of every intelligently occupied mind, in simpler assignments – ones with a very focused goal or need to be met – we might simply write down our ideas as we go and then group them for presentation into our recommended new-product ideas and additional ideas.

How should we express the ideas we're writing down or sketching out roughly?

If we get a thought about packaging, we make a note or rough sketch of it, too.

At any time, we can opt to turn to sources of information that we think might help inform and inspire us. Most basically, we may decide to leaf through the marketing information the client has provided, viewing it from our perspective as it has evolved though the input and creative work we've done. We can also elect to go further. For instance, if our job is to think up a new liqueur, we might peruse *Grossman's Guide to Wine & Spirits* and other reading materials that apply to the category. To investigate other flavors that we might introduce to the category, we could decide to go through a cookbook. If the drink will function as an after-dinner treat, we pay special attention to the dessert section. Even though our ideas will feature a new and inviting taste, we also know the liqueur category is highly image driven. To discover a new piece of enchantment to build around, we might look into the romantic tradition; for example, we might ask, "Can we use anything from the play *Cyrano de Bergerac?*" Consider well-known love stories in any form and the poetry of love. We might include leafing through a history of music or art to see if we can find something enchanting to base a product on or to lend an image to a product idea.

We continue ideating until we begin to suspect that we have plumbed the potential of the assignment, at least, to the extent that we can imagine it now. Perhaps our minds may get a better grasp of the terrain in time and present us with additional ideas.

As always, we do our best to finish our conscious creative work early enough to allow the involuntary, synthesizing powers of our imaginations a day or two to mull over the assignment and see what additional ideas we get.

Now, the time has come to share our ideas

How to Create Deft Concept Boards

We present our ideas to the account team, the client and to the consumer as concept boards, which are something like basic advertisements. What goes into a deft one? Above all it should, as mentioned earlier, seem to disappear, unless, of course, we're presenting a highly image-driven product, in which case, the concept board should retain more presence.

Yet both should function as such clear presentations of the product itself that they let the consumer see right through them to the product in its most appealing light.

How do we create concept boards that seem to disappear? Primarily, the headline and main visual must function as a news-driven poster that communicates the primary benefit of the product or service. We must also take great care to see that the concepts are made up of all of the right inclusions and exclusions, with each element, verbal and visual, properly emphasized and subordinated. Both the content and the proportion allotted to every aspect of it should be just right.

Now, the account team and the client will be able to judge the value of the product ideas accurately but, most importantly, consumers will be able to. The answers they provide, whether in focus groups or in quantitative testing, will measure purchase interest in the product itself.

When a concept board fails to disappear, or to be perfectly transparent, it clouds her view of the product. The unfortunate result is that none of the measurements that come back provide an accurate indication of how the product may actually do in the marketplace.

Concept boards we create for more image-driven products must capture the benefit in a more stylish way, but they must still be transparent, in the sense that they must primarily present the product as the thing to be desired, instead of a piece of verbal or visual enchantment that distracts the consumer from the promise instead of enhancing it.

There is creative satisfaction in knowing that the concepts we have created are perfectly suited to their function, and, if we create a product that scores well and goes to market, we've created a new account either for ourselves or for the agency it will be assigned to.

Phase Three: The Consumer Interface

If enough of the new product ideas and concepts boards are approved by the client, we take them to the court of the consumer. If traditional research is in order, it begins with focus groups. If one or more of our ideas do well, we take it on to quantitative testing, such as mall intercepts, where the interviewer shows the concept or concepts to consumers and asks a list of questions. By the results we, and the greatest marketing companies in the world, watch new-product ideas thrive or perish.

Sometimes, especially when the test results are unexpectedly disappointing, we may, for our own edification, request that the questionnaires that the results were drawn from be forwarded to us, so that we might examine them.

Marketing research people do their best to develop and select ways to measure consumer appeal. The overall indications that come back are generally accurate and the information may provide a guide to improving the product or the communication of the benefits so that the score is better next time out.

Amid whatever uncertainties we may face, we have the reassurance of knowing that, as a result of our imaginations, guided by The Creative Exploratory, we've discovered the best possibilities of the project and presented them correctly. As a result, we can be much more confident of success than people who utilize the usual random ideation to create new products and concepts. On the best occasions, we create a new product that exceeds the client's expectations.

Leveraging Global Brand Equity

While we're often asked to invent entirely new products, the largest marketing companies want ways to leverage global brands. We are asked to create products that extend the brand equity. To accomplish this goal, the products must be compatible with the brand image, and, ideally, seem to be inevitable extensions of it. These can be literal line extensions or consonant new products.

For instance, Unilever devised the brand Mentadent partly, we may assume, because the company was not at the time the steward of a global toothpaste brand on the level of, say, Crest. Notice, however, that when Proctor & Gamble, the owner of such a worldwide brand, introduced competitive products, it did so as line extensions of Crest or another of its brands, Scope.

If our job is to leverage the equity of a large brand, we begin to think about consumer needs in the category in terms of the ones the brand already meets, how well it meets them, and what other needs, established or emerging, it might meet. To focus our efforts, we'll want to keep in mind the brand image with consumers, how its true attributes and benefits fit with that image, and what modifications or additions might have a place, both in terms of ones that might be easy and cost-effective and those that would require a more extensive effort by the client.

How to Create Products that Will Retain Their Uniqueness

When we create a new product, we hope it will be unique. But how can we help assure it will retain its uniqueness, especially in a world of quick imitations? No marketing company can afford to develop and introduce a product that can be imitated before sales produce a payback.

Of course, there is less concern about products that can be patented or, in the case of software, also copyrighted.

The usual tactic is to require that a viable new product have what is called "technical insulation." The uniqueness must be based on technology that the competition will likely need at least six months to copy.

Today, however, even the most sophisticated companies have had to come to terms with the fact that many of the new products they would like to introduce don't have as much technical insulation as they would like, such as a new juice-based beverage that features an appealing new group of flavors. Some new products may be no more than attractively presented "me too" items, and the only difference is the brand image.

There are still companies that cannot bring themselves to go ahead with such ventures, especially when the only uniqueness is the packaging. They are often wise.

Yet excessive caution can lead to missed opportunities, especially when a small improvement has wide and immediate appeal or the particular image seems comparatively irresistible.

On such occasions, our goal is to dress up the product with superior image advertising. Our intent is to provide, in place of technical insulation, what I call image insulation. Another way to express the goal is that we seek to make up for the lack of unique matter by enrobing the product in a unique manner. The tactic can be seen as providing an insulating package for the product.

There are surprisingly positive aspects about such insulation. It will help create a unique world for the product to live in. It won't expire in six months or when the term of the patent is over. If the manner is inviting enough, the public comes to prefer it as much as matter. And image insulation is more difficult to imitate. In fact, over time image insulation can grow stronger and stronger.

It's important to appreciate that image insulation is pretty much all that some of the world's strongest brands have. What is the technical advantage Coke®, Heinz® ketchup, or Hershey® Chocolate?

So, while we always prefer to introduce a product that has technical insulation, we can go so far as to say that image insulation, when skillfully implemented and maintained, can turn out to be the most enduring uniqueness of all.

There are very few people who know exactly how to create it, so the skill can be especially valuable. All you have to do is find clients who know to appreciate it. Given the lack of wide awareness of the values we're discussing, the effort can often be even more difficult than having great ideas. But such complications are often the case, and we can best adjust to them with the smile that only philosophical distance and the consolations of probability can provide.

How to Create Whole New Categories

So far we've discussed creating new products in categories that already exist, but occasionally we realize that much more is possible. We sense the opportunity to create, not only a new product, but a whole new category – and be the first entry into it.

What begets the happy event? You note that the product does not fit comfortably in an existing category. In fact, it's different and substantial enough to form the basis of a new one. A likely precipitant is that the product is based on new or emerging behavior.

For example, take the evolving consumer need for healthier eating. What if you were thinking about it when concern for agricultural chemicals has just begun to be widespread enough to support a national brand? You would get the radical idea of going back to growing food without their use. Would consumers, you might wonder, go for such a thing as naturally grown tomatoes? You would realize that the tomatoes would be the first entry in a new category. To help define the category and to lend image insulation to your new brand, you might decide to call them organic tomatoes. Or the moniker for the category would evolve later.

Here are two examples from my own work. In both cases, the new category was imagined by the clients, and I served as the copywriter.

First, I created, with my art director at the time, Arthur Beckman, the introductory advertising for Lifetime cable television. The new category was television for women. Today, Lifetime is so successful it is sometimes ranked as the number one cable channel in prime time. I have talked more extensively about the introduction elsewhere.

In the next case, the client, Citibank, imagined the possibility of the category. The marketing people there were wondering if there might be a new category of financial institution that was different from a bank or a loan company. It would be a financial institution that would, along with the usual banking services, offer financial counseling to people who usually don't think much of it is available to them: upper-blue-collar and lower-white-collar workers. It would not be intimidating to them, as Citibank felt a bank or investment company might be, or demeaning, as a loan company might seem.

The assignment was given to the agency where I was then a Vice President & Creative Management Supervisor, Rosenfeld Sirowitz & Lawson. It was founded my two creative stars out of Doyle Dane Bernbach – the great copywriter Ron Rosenfeld and the innovative art director, Len Sirowitz – along with an account person out of Ogilvy, and it had just been named The Advertising Agency of the Year by *Advertising Age* magazine. My art director on the assignment was Lenny.

Our job was to define the institution and initiate the category. To give the new financial product a personal feel that would make it appear welcoming to the target audience, I named it simply Person-to-Person Financial Centers And I described its various services in a people-friendly way. To magnify the personal feeling visually, Lenny created an animated logo of two silhouetted male figures that walked up to each other and shook hands. The logo appeared at the end of the commercials, while a static representation of it appeared in the print advertising.

We decided on visuals for print advertising that would be made up of simple illustrations, so they would reproduce well in local newspapers. The kickoff ad flagged the new category with the headline "Introducing Person-to-Person Financial Centers. A new kind of financial institution." The copy developed the idea by first offering expert financial advice to people who might think it is usually only available to wealthy individuals and then it presented the usual array of financial services. One ad, which was for a home equity loan, featured a man, sitting on his roof and contemplating, with the headline, "If you need extra money, maybe you're sitting on it." Another one featured a man being fitted for a suit by a tailor, but the suit was made of a fabric that looked like money. The headline was, "The Tailored Loan. It'll fit you like it was made for you."

Citibank introduced the concept in seven states and, finding immediate success, quickly expanded it into seventeen states. Now, the FED stepped in and halted the expansion on the basis of interstate banking laws. But Citibank challenged the FED on the issue and won. Person-to-Person Financial Centers then expanded into more than thirty-five states and employed over 18,000 people.

In time, I understand, Citibank realized that the people who really want financial advice are not the ones they had created the institution for but wealthier people. What to do? Person-to-Person, along with its employees, was transformed into the foundation of Citicorp Mortgage, which became a national institution.

Despite the eventual learning, the case is still an example of the creation of a new category.

New Product Keywords

I saved this lesson for last, because we're entering more usual territory. I'm referring to the use of words that are particularly germane to new products, such as "new" and "introducing."

There is what I sometimes refer to as a little jar of words that we reach into as we need them. Knowing them well lets us select the ones we think are just right for each occasion. In this imaginary jar we find the following:

- New
- Now
- Introducing
- Announcing
- Presenting
- At Last

- Finally
- Here
- Free
- Free Sample
- Coupon: Save!

In addition, there's one punctuation mark, best used with tasteful restraint. I'm referring, of course, to the exclamation point.

"New!" often works best. It's crisp, punchy, and in focus groups consumers usually remark, "If it says 'new,' I'll try it." They also repeat, "If there's a coupon, I'll try it."

The word "free" always attracts predictable attention. The three-syllable choices – "introducing," "announcing," and "presenting" – seem to carry a bit more prestige or, at least, add a weightier cadence. Both "at last" and "finally" imply that the new product is overdue and it's about time someone thought of it. This intimation of overdue moment implies an immediate need for it.

The other words in the list offer slightly different feelings, some subjective, and are best decided on as the occasion arises.

Name Development

Creative name development especially invites, along with slogan writing, the craft of the verbal miniaturist. We work with syllable-size variables. As we sit, thinking and tinkering, it's as if we're in a dark room, trying to thread a needle. We poke and poke as best we can. When we get exactly the right, bright name, it's as if the room has lit up, and we can thread the needle with ease. We seem to experience an inspired oneness between the product or service and what it offers people, and the word or words come with the identification. But how enticingly and maddeningly close we can get without getting to exactly the right name.

Over the years, I've developed what I think is the most acute approach to name development. It's linguistically based, so it enables us to create names that have a human feel, as opposed to names that can feel computer-generated – and often are. The latter names, while they may be unique, often look and sound odd, and I think that, at least initially, they strike consumers as what I've come to call intellectual and emotional strangers. Consumers need time to wrap their minds around them and warm up to them, and helping the processes along can be costly. They work best for major companies, which have the funds to keep the product or service in front of consumers until they get used to the strange appellation. But most new products have a short window to prove themselves or be banished from the shelves forever, so names that seem immediately understandable and likable usually give them a better chance to succeed.

Here is my approach. It's based on, as you might guess by now, a version of The Creative Exploratory.

Phase One: Input

By now, you're familiar with The Creative Exploratory and the need to have as much relevant marketing information as you can get before you ideate. So we need not tarry here, except to note that store visits with careful label reading in the category can be an especially helpful preparatory step.

Phase Two: Creative Development

Once you're up to speed in terms of information, it's time to begin to ideate. You're looking for names that express the principal benefit in bright, consumer-friendly ways. They're succinct, inviting and memorable. Concentrating on the primary benefit provides the single-minded focus for the message a name can adroitly express.

In The Creative Exploratory, we can establish the areas in which to generate names based on ways to express the primary benefit or on the various forms names can take. Since the content is tightly focused, the first grouping is usually small, such as names inspired by thinking in areas like "Product" or "Lifestyle." I usually find the second way to group ideas better. We know there will be a group of core words that the name is most likely to contain or grow out of. For instance, in a new main-meal preparation, we know that some of the core words will be "taste," "delicious," and probably "quick" and "easy."

Our job is to discover the core words that apply to the assignment and create with them. The names we derive group under these headings:

- Single Core Words
- Core Word Combinations
- Core Words/Joined
- Core Words/Altered

Since we understand that we work primarily only with core words, we can leave the word "core" out if we wish. Then the groups are simply labeled this way:

- Single Words (Tide)
- Word Combinations (Good Season's)
- Joined Words (Payless)
- Altered Words (Altima)

To give unencumbered wings to our inspiration, it's usually good to ideate freely before we begin to group the names, until we feel we've plumbed our immediate ideas.

As we ideate, we think over the attributes and benefits of the product, particularly the primary benefit, see the product in the lives of consumers, consider it in terms of the competition, and cast a glance at evolving trends, along with latest bits of colloquial language consumers are using to indicate they're hip.

When our list of names becomes extensive, we begin to group them and create subgroups. For example, under each type of core-word, we can develop names that subgroup under product benefits, product or company heritage (real or implied, as in Mama Celeste), lifestyle of the consumer, use-occasions, or any of the other areas that The Creative Exploratory may lead us to.

Names made up of combinations may include phrases, as in "I Love My Carpet."

Altered words might include mnemonics or abbreviations (Sunoco for Sun Oil Company, FedEx for Federal Express, or "T" for turbo charged.

When we've gathered the low-hanging fruit and reached as high and far as we can with our current information, we can turn to the tools that will help us explore more of the likely possibilities. My basic guideline is never burn up your imagination trying to think of something you can look up.

The first tool I recommend is a comprehensive thesaurus. I suggest Rodale's *The Synonym Finder.* It's big enough to list, not only the more obvious synonyms of a word, but also, in every entry, the words and phrases closely and somewhat remotely associated with it. So you won't have to keep flipping to other entries. This one tool alone, used imaginatively, can help you get a pretty good handle on the applicable resources of the language. Each time a core word comes to you that relates to the assignment, go to the thesaurus, look over the words and phrases associated with it, and write down the ones that apply. You can get by with an online thesaurus, particularly when you're doing a simple naming assignment.

I also recommend a different kind of, if you will, thesaurus, which I find helpful: *Word Menu.* This relatively recent addition to the wordsmith's craft groups words under different categories; for instance, if you're working on a new fragrance and want to know the names of different flowers, you'll find them under the heading "Flowers."

Now, it's time for the greatest naming resource – a small dictionary. Once you've thought enough so that you know what you're looking for, leaf through it. The seemingly onerous task will repay your diligence by putting all of the words that are likely to work at our disposal, because you know that the kind of names you're looking for will almost always come from everyday English.

You don't have to read the definitions, although looking into one here and there to refine your understanding can add interest and benefits to the task. Nothing makes the job seem longer than trying to hurry. Go through it at peace with yourself, looking for interesting tidbits along the way. When I embark on yet another trip through the dictionary, I'm reminded of the advice that Albert Schweitzer – the theologian turned physician, as well as organist, who gave us the ethic of Reverence for Life – offered about how to do something we really don't want to do, that is, "to do it with great devotion."

The dictionary I find the most helpful for this purpose is *The American Heritage Large Type Dictionary.* It's easy on our eyes, and the 330 or so pages contain pretty much all of the words that most people use in their daily lives. Online dictionaries generally don't permit page by page browsing.

As you go along, write down any words you think are relevant to the project and any creative naming responses you have to them.

I've gone through various small dictionaries so many times over the years that I find I can do many naming assignments confidently without demanding the labor of myself, unless, of course, I find the assignment surprisingly demanding. When I go to a dictionary these days, I often limit myself to looking over all the words that begin with letters that might especially apply to the assignment; for instance, all the words that begin with the same letter as the name of the company, or, if I'm developing a name for a line extension, all the ones that begin with the same letter as the mother brand. Why? I'm simply trying to see if I might find a wonderfully apt name by looking into that usual source of euphony, alliteration.

I also suggest a basic rhyming dictionary, so that, when you have a keyword, you can quickly plum the possibilities of the other most usual source of euphony, rhyme. Think how aptly the device works in, say, Lean Cuisine. Online rhyming dictionaries are adequate.

You'll also find it helpful to have a dictionary of prefixes and suffixes, especially when you develop names that should have a more technical feel. Although I think I'm very familiar with these syllables, I employed a dictionary of them when I developed the name for Chesebrough-Pond's science-emphasizing skin cream, Dermasil.

If you're naming over-the-counter drugs, you might also acquire a medical dictionary. The standard one is Stedman's.

I also suggest you acquire a collection of foreign-language dictionaries, particularly French-English, Italian-English, and Spanish-English, along with other ones. Once I was naming a tropical drink and looked into a Hawaiian-English dictionary. Foreign-language phrase books are also helpful. These resources are particularly valuable when you're creating a name for an ethnic food or an image-driven product that may benefit from a little foreign enchantment. How far do you have to look into a handbook about getting along in Italian to find the name "Prego?"

Finally, a selection of cookbooks and books about beverages will be helpful when you're naming new food or beverage products.

Does the approach work? Compare it with what usually goes on in an ad agency when the time comes to think up names for a new product.

As often as not, a memo goes out, asking everyone who has a bit of time, including the secretaries, to think up whatever names they can. The individual lists are collected, edited, and assembled into a master list, which is then forwarded to the client.

While the method we suggest is extensive, it's equal to the task. Clients who've retained me are often astonished by the thoroughness of the approach. In the book on marketing creativity, "Jump Start Your Brain," I'm the only naming expert the author mentions.

One reason is that by the time I make my presentation, I can do so with a knowledge of the resources of the English language as they apply to the project.

Presenting Names

A great deal of subjectivity comes to bear on the selection of names. So we want to demonstrate the merits of the name we recommend.

Before you settle on a recommended name, click onto the U. S. Government Patent and Trademark site, select Trademarks, and do a preliminary search to make sure the name is available in the category.

I suggest that the presentation take the following form. Create a title page with the name of the project on it. At the bottom of the page, note the date on which it was completed, so that, if additional efforts are required, you and the client will be able to keep track of the versions.

On page one, make the first heading "Recommended Name" and put what you've decided is just the right name there.

Now, to magnify what you believe is the rightness of the choice, demonstrate how our selection can work in the marketplace. Mint a slogan or introductory headline that uses the name to good advantage and include it just below your recommendation. I've gone so far as to write an introductory TV script.

What about the anxiety that the entire presentation is hanging by a single name? Or your own knowledge that more than one of the names you've devised, while not as exact and stylish as your first choice, also strike you as excellent candidates?

Label the next section of the presentation "Other Favorites." I suggest that you include from two to ten of the best possibilities.

What about the rest of the presentation?

I recommend that you add the simple title "More Names." Under this heading, group all of your remaining ideas under the headings offered earlier, that is, "Core Words," "Core Word Combinations," "Core Words/ Joined," and "Core Words/Altered."

You may also want to arrange the names in each group in alphabetical order. It enhances the impression of orderliness and makes locating names the client wants to discuss easier. It also helps you spot and delete repetitions. All you need to do is click "sort" on the word-processing program and choose "alphabetical." (Block a section at a time before you sort it, or you'll find yourself with a jumble of names.)

To improve the look of your presentation, I suggest you choose a simple font like New Times Roman or Arial, increase its size from the usual 12-points to 14-points, and center everything. Number the pages and bind the presentation as you choose. I prefer binders with a clear front cover.

Now, for the artwork. It helps if the client can see your favorite name suggestions as new logos. So I suggest that the art director make preliminary designs of some of the recommended names, even if all he or she does is select appropriate typefaces and backgrounds, blow them up to various degrees, print them out in color, and mount them on small squares of foamboard or put them in PowerPoint.

In the actual presentation, proceed as you do with advertising. Set up the problem so that the recommended name appears to be exactly the right, bright answer to it. Present the recommendation done up as a preliminary logo design. Then reveal the slogan or introductory headline that features it and indicates its marketing potential and, if you have it, a script or storyboard that shows the name in action.

If the client buys the recommendation, count your blessings and stop. But more than likely the client, whether or not your recommendation is received favorably, will be waiting to see what else you have.

Next, present your other favorites, preferably done up as rough logos, too. If you make the sale by now, you can stop.

If the client still awaits the appearance of other candidates, the time has come to pass out The Creative Exploratory. You can introduce it by saying something like, "I'd like to share the names we created on the way to our recommendation. The list is extensive and revealing, because we examined all the relevant possibilities of the language to arrive at our recommendation."

Then go through it, reading the names out loud and stopping for comments as they occur. Some clients prefer to read The Exploratory quietly. Hopefully, members of the client team will check names as you proceed.

While the task may be one you hoped to get away without, you'll find it's reassuring to come prepared to cover the creative terrain more thoroughly and exactly than the client has likely ever seen it covered.

If you get approval of a name or the decision to take a number of them to test with consumers, the client's legal department will usually take a look before a final selection is made.

If fortune is on your side, one day you'll have the pleasant intellectual and emotional reward of seeing the name on the product, as a bright little gem of your creative imagination, like a diamond that's been cut just right.

How to Create Trademarkable Names

It's dispiriting to think up what we believe is exactly the right name and then discover that it's not trademarkable. How do we deal with this issue?

Although the legal staff at the agency or the client oversee the matter, it helps to know certain things. Many simple word choices are tied up in existing trademarks. But, on the outside chance that the ones we like may still be available, we should include them in our exploratory.

But it's usually better to lean toward names that are more highly evolved. Once again, being very exact about the unique values that apply to the assignment will help inspire unique names.

One route to the goal is take a word that says exactly what you have in mind and then add other words to it or alter it in a variety of ways. When we alter the word itself, the change cannot, for legal reasons, apply only to the spelling; it has to affect the sound, too. We can also join two likely words and alter them into a unique single word.

Obtaining final legal approval from the client's legal team can sometimes become a challenge. As one candidate after another is rejected, you'll have to call on your ingenuity. At more fortuitous times, the legal department may come to the rescue. For instance, when I developed the name Dermasil, I arrived at the initial presentation with my usual ten or so pages of suggestions. The marketing people especially liked two of them: "Dermacel" and "Dermacin." But the legal department at the company had trademark issues with both of them. Knowing, as they did, the variations that would be available, they suggested the last syllable "-il," which completed the name.

There is another useful lesson here. Naming is such an exact craft that when you find a word that everybody likes but that runs into a legal snare, don't abandon it. Experiment with it. Add a word before it or a word after it. Alter it. Tinker until you arrive at an acceptable version of the word.

If you find yourself working without legal input, you can make, as mentioned above, at least a preliminary check of the availability of a name online. The computer setup for ascertaining trademark availability is also quite extensive at the business and science branch of the New York Public Library at 34th Street and Madison Avenue. You'll find yourself in the company of lawyers, inventors, and a variety of other people peering into the possibilities of owning a trademark. Other mercantile libraries offer helpful resources, too.

Naming Websites

When the Internet began, proclivity was acceptable and some non-sense names have remained leading sites, such as Google and Yahoo. But now there are so many dot.com companies struggling for identity and Web traffic that the usual values have become important. The goal is to provide a name that communicates the main benefit, or at least main use-occasion, but in a way that captures the assumed hipness of the internet. Examples are facebook.com and youtube.com. The names contain or imply the claim. Options can easily be checked by going to a registration site, such as the ones at Hostwinds.com, Verio.com, or Networksolutions.com and entering it. The preferred suffix is, of course, ".com" for commerce and ".org" for organizations. Only settle for ".net" if you can also register ".com" or ".org." Why? If you only own ".net," a lot of people will mistakenly enter the name as ".com," so a lot of the traffic you would normally get will go elsewhere.

It's important that the URL contain the core keyword in the category. It will go a long way to helping the site appear in organic search. The creative part is to take the keyword and then add a word or two or otherwise modify it so that you arrive at the most relevant and engaging name you can that's still available.

Naming Toll-Free Numbers

At times, we're called on to think up names that will serve as toll-free numbers. Once again, we aim to capture the main benefit, succinctly and winningly. One that is quite good for appropriateness and aided recall is the UPS toll-free number, 1-800-PICK-UPS. It's a compact, multifaceted creation. The primary meaning presents the claim, while the secondary meanings ask for the order and indicate ease, promptness, and competence.

Phase Three: The Consumer Interface

Occasionally, clients may elect to go with a name on judgment but, more often than not, they will want consumer input, particularly major companies. A selection of names may be taken to focus groups, even if just as a disaster check. More usually, the client will want to submit a list of the most promising candidates for quantitative testing.

There are different ways to ferry the names through these processes. In focus groups, you might just type them up on white cards for the moderator to pass around. He can ask the respondents to sort them in terms of preference. He might also ask them to pick their three or so favorites and then sort them. A discussion will follow.

Other moderators prefer to hold the names up and solicit ratings, often on a scale from one to five, and then to ask for comments. If the names are going to be held up, the art director can enlarge each name and mount it. Notice that we're not using the designs we may have done up for the presentation. The variability will get in the way of a judgment of the appeal of the names themselves.

When the time arrives for quantitative testing, there's not much to do except wait to hear which name consumers choose as their favorite. If you've explored the possibilities imaginatively and thoroughly and narrowed your choices based on appropriateness and likability, you can be pretty sure that a name or a number of them will do well.

The best result is obviously when the winner is the name you recommended.

If by some chance, none of the names are sufficiently liked, retain your confidence. The results of the research will indicate any shortcomings consumers found with your offerings, and you should be able to make just the right adjustments easily. Part of the reason you'll be able to react deftly is that you've developed a thoroughgoing knowledge of the linguistic possibilities. Now, all you have to do is source your knowledge with the refinement in focus that the research has provided. Go ahead and thread the needle.

CONCLUSION

I trust you've found the explanation of intelligently creative copywriting I've presented helpful. My goal in writing The Creative Copywriter's Companion was to include everything you need to optimize the potential of your creative talent.

You now have the knowledge to explore and be daring in knowing ways, not random ones. While simple-minded cockiness is OK, inspired competence usually outperforms it.

Be patient with your ability to absorb and implement all the lessons. I suggest you use the book, not only to learn now, but as a reference over the years.

In time, you should be able to create the right, bright advertising in a way that makes it seem relatively easy. Here's an example.

I was retained, along with a great art director, to do a television assignment for a marketing-consulting firm. We went to the briefing, where the strategy was presented and the assignment was described as really tough.

Afterward, he and I went to a restaurant to have lunch and ideate a bit. During the meal, we came up with concepts for different campaigns and over twenty spots. We felt we had covered the most likely possibilities and had a few deft candidates for the title of exactly the right advertising. He would draw up key visuals, and I would mint the final slogans and write the scripts. As we left, we were talking about how well the work had gone. As he headed toward his car, he said with a smile, "And it's so easy." "Yeah," I replied, "Apparently it's either easy or impossible." In other words, if you have a creative imagination, learn the craft, and conduct your life with some wisdom, you can actually have a pretty easygoing and enjoyable career.

Finally, mass communication is one of the most powerful forces in the modern world, and someone who is a master of it is one of the most effective people. I encourage you to remember that you possess sufficient skill to be, not only unusually effective, but thoughtfully so. When you conduct yourself in this way, I believe you will find, to the degree that our modest profession can provide it, great contentment, sufficient financial rewards, and frequent instances of immoderate delight.

I wish you remarkable success as a great copywriter.

THE END

ABOUT THE AUTHOR

Tom Attea has held copywriting and creative director positions at some of New York's finest advertising agencies. Today, he is the president and creative director of Heavy Creative, Inc., which specials in digital advertising but still does traditional advertising and new product development when invited.

Tom's longest stay was at Young & Rubicam, where he wrote many humorous commercials for Dr Pepper, as well as long-running campaigns for such products as Jell-O and Gulf Oil. He was also a vice president and creative management supervisor at Rosenfeld, Sirowitz & Lawson, during the period it was voted Advertising Agency of the Year by *Advertising Age* magazine.

His creative work has won many awards, including four Clios in one year, Gold and Silver Lions from the Cannes commercial film festival, the Gold Telly, The Effie Award, as we well as awards from The Copy Club, The Art Directors Club, The One Show, the Andy Awards, International Broadcast Awards, and the Gold Mobius Award for writing what was judged "Best B2B Internet Services Advertisement." Four of the 12 landmark commercials he wrote for Dr Pepper are in the permanent collection of Paley Museum of Media in New York.

APPENDIX –
EXAMPLE OF A CREATIVE BRIEF

This example is based on the Creative Brief at a number of New York agencies, along with my own thoughts. I've also added short explanations to each section, not just for my readers, but for clients who may not be marketing people. I think you'll find it gives clients an organized way to tell you about their businesses.

Creative Brief

Client:
Date:

Background/Situation Analysis
(Your overview of the business. Where you are currently and where you want to go?)

Product, Service, or Website Url
(Company name/website address)

Marketing Objective
(What you want to achieve; the call to action)

Primary Brand Promise/Primary Benefit
(What is the single most inviting and persuasive thing we can say about your business to the target market?)

Secondary Business Promise/Secondary Benefit(S)
(What are other benefits we can say that will persuade people to convert?)

Primary Support Point/Reason to Believe
(What can we say to prove or backup the primary business promise?)

Secondary Support Point(S)/Reasons to Believe
(What else can we say to prove or back up the promise or promises?)

Primary Target Audience
(Who are the people we want to reach?)

Target Audience – Primary Need
(What is the most important need that we can meet?)

Target Audience – Current Behavior
(How are they adjusting to the need now?)

Target Audience – Desired Behavior
(How do we want them to meet their need?)

Target Audience – Primary Barrier to Change
(What's standing in the way of the target market to do what we'd like them to?)

Target Audience – Secondary Barrier(S) to Change
(Anything else standing in the way?)

Secondary Target Audience(S)
(Is there any other group or other groups of people we'd like to reach?)

Obstacles To Success
(What's standing in the way of our success? Competition? Being new?)

Competitive Framework – Include Websites
(Who is our competition, what are they promising, and what are their website URLs?)

Deliverables/Tactics
(What do you need? Website copy, a landing page, Adwords campaign, Internet video, print ads, TV spot?)

Copy/Art Mandatory Elements
(What must I include? The logo, a copyright notice, a legal disclaimer?)

Tone & Manner
(B2B professional, light and inviting consumer language, hard sell, serious, sympathetic)

Offers/Incentives
(Do we have any bonuses or discounts to incentivize the conversion?)

Keywords, if Known
(Basic keywords in the category; if you don't know them, I'll be looking into the Google keyword tool before I write the copy)

Contact Information
(Client phone number, email, and address)

Bio(S) if Applicable
(Who are the most senior people in the company; nice to include a photo)

Testimonials if Applicable
(What have customers said about your product or service that might persuade others to do business with you? Focus groups show that most people trust other everyday people even more than they trust experts)

CPSIA information can be obtained
at www.ICGtesting.com
Printed in the USA
FFHW011313250219
50705312-56091FF